TOMO-CHAN IS A GIRL!

3

Fumita
Yanagida
Presents

CHARACTERS

Aizawa Tomo

First-year high schooler.
In love with her childhood friend, Junichiro.
Her family runs a karate dojo.

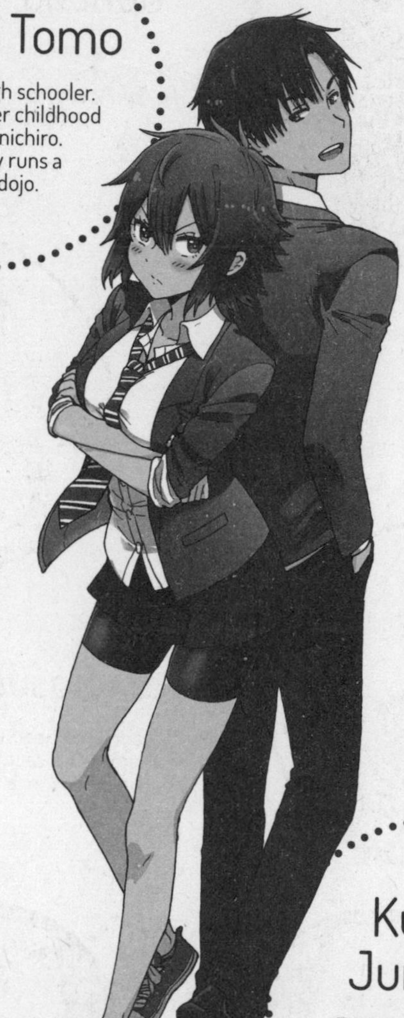

Kubota Junichiro

First-year high schooler.
Thinks of Tomo as a friend.
Treats her like a guy.

Gundou Misuzu

First-year high schooler.
Tomo's classmate and best friend.
Childhood friend of Junichiro.
Sharp-tongued.

Carol Olston

First-year high schooler.
British. The school idol.
Kosuke's childhood friend
and fiancée.

Misaki Kosuke

Second-year high school student.
Men's karate club captain.
The school's prince.

Mifune

Tanabe

Ogawa

CONTENTS

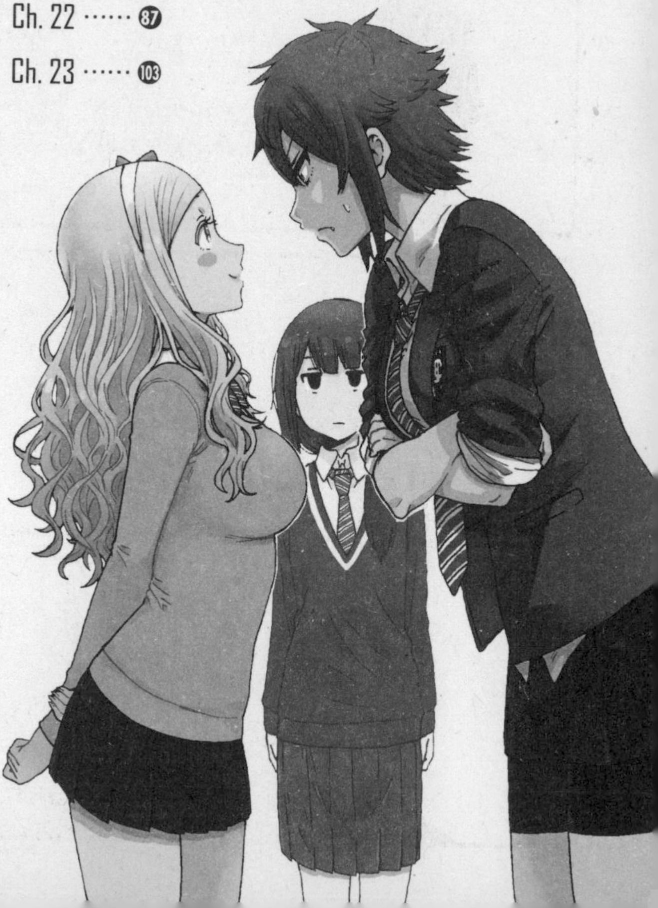

Ch. 18

I Thought You'd Just Go With It

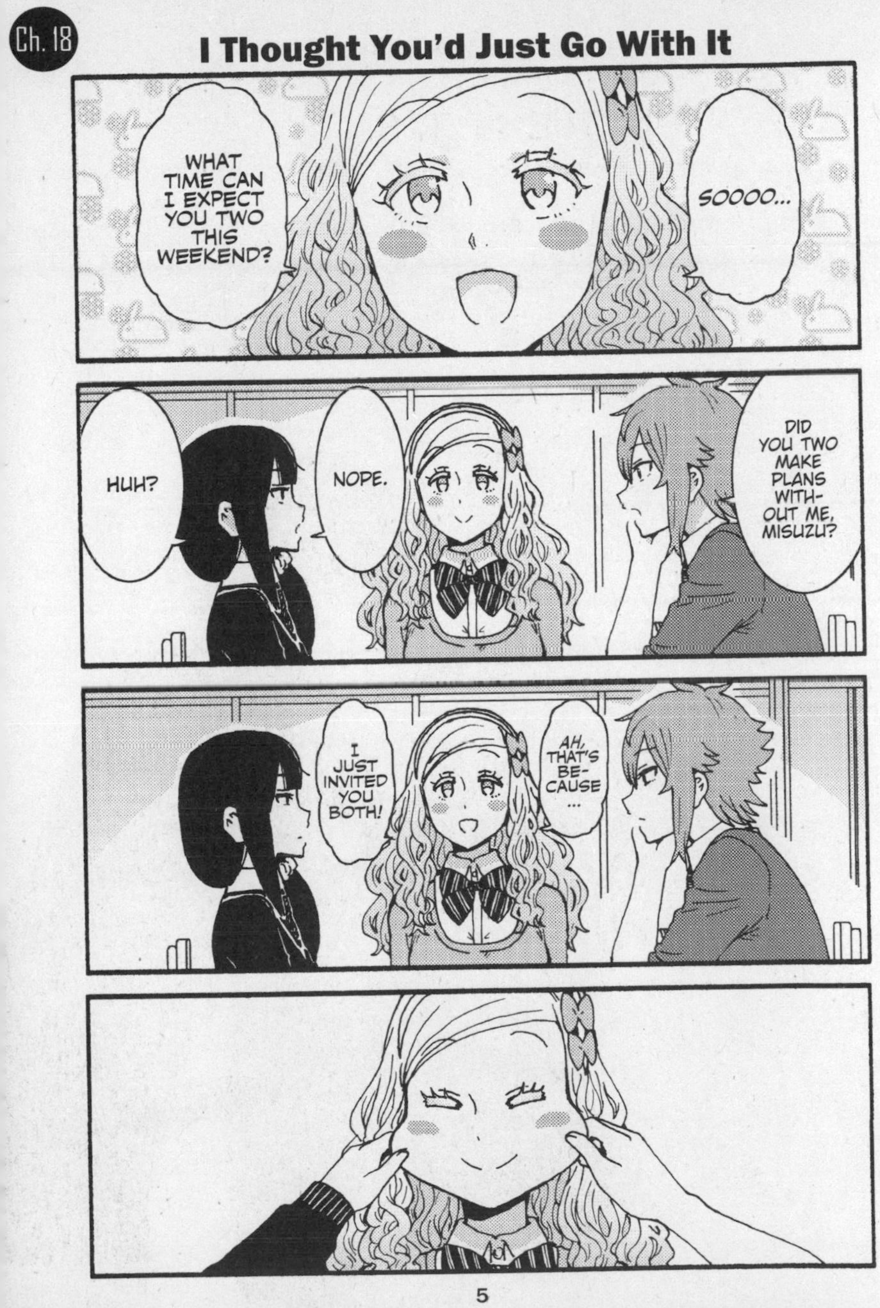
SOOOO...
WHAT TIME CAN I EXPECT YOU TWO THIS WEEKEND?
DID YOU TWO MAKE PLANS WITHOUT ME, MISUZU?
NOPE.
HUH?
AH, THAT'S BECAUSE...
I JUST INVITED YOU BOTH!

Répondez, S'il Vous Plaît!

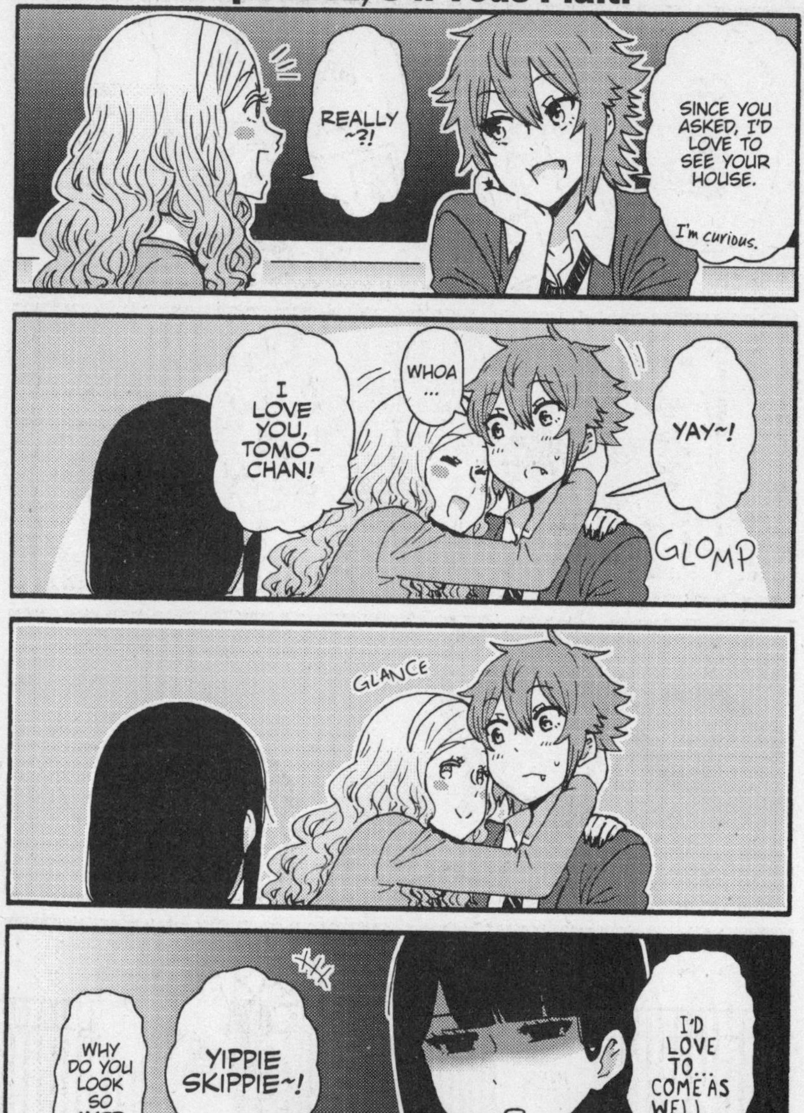
SINCE YOU ASKED, I'D LOVE TO SEE YOUR HOUSE.
I'm curious.
REALLY ~?!
YAY~!
WHOA ...
I LOVE YOU, TOMO-CHAN!
GLOMP
GLANCE
I'D LOVE TO... COME AS WELL...
YIPPIE SKIPPIE~!
Ugghaa
WHY DO YOU LOOK SO MAD?

Heavenly Gates

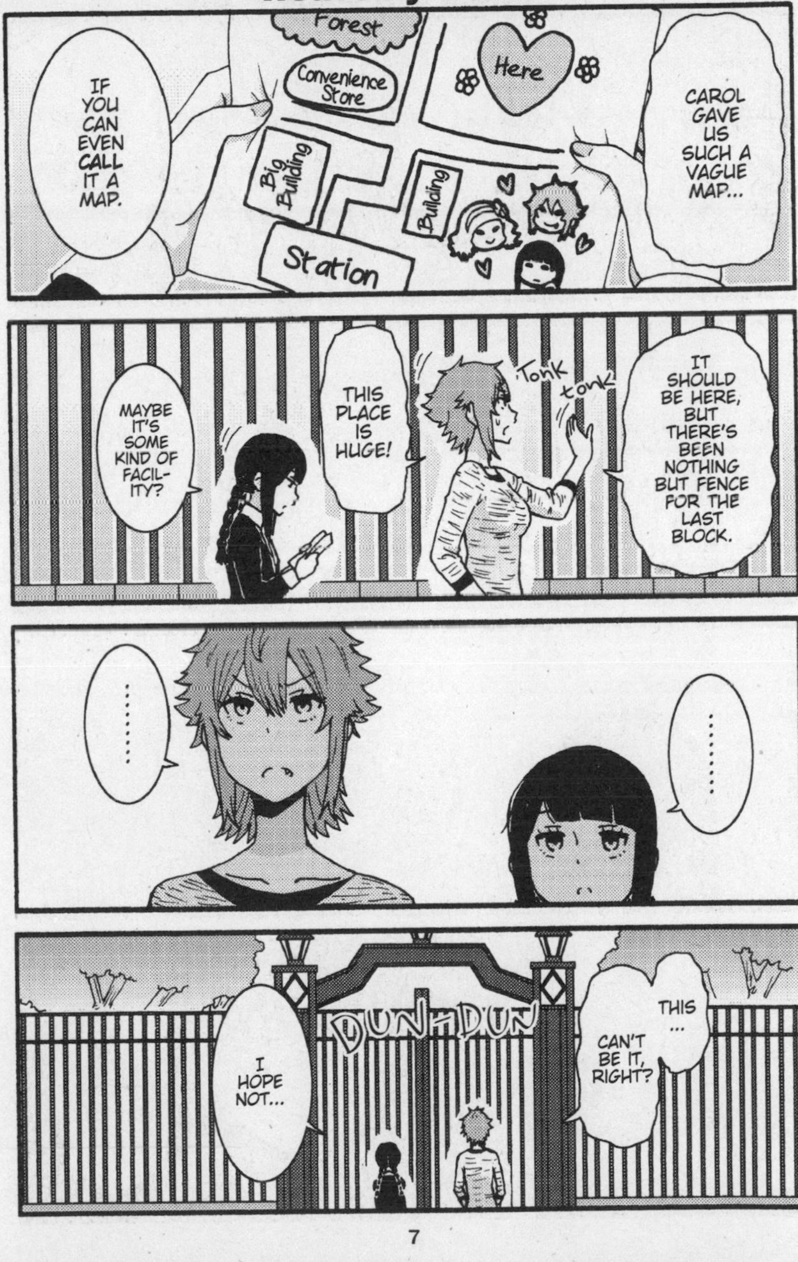

CAROL GAVE US SUCH A VAGUE MAP...
Here
Forest
Convenience Store
Building
Big Building
Station
IF YOU CAN EVEN CALL IT A MAP.
IT SHOULD BE HERE, BUT THERE'S BEEN NOTHING BUT FENCE FOR THE LAST BLOCK.
Tonk tonk
THIS PLACE IS HUGE!
MAYBE IT'S SOME KIND OF FACIL-ITY?
......
......
THIS... CAN'T BE IT, RIGHT?
DUN-DUN
I HOPE NOT...

Family Resemblance

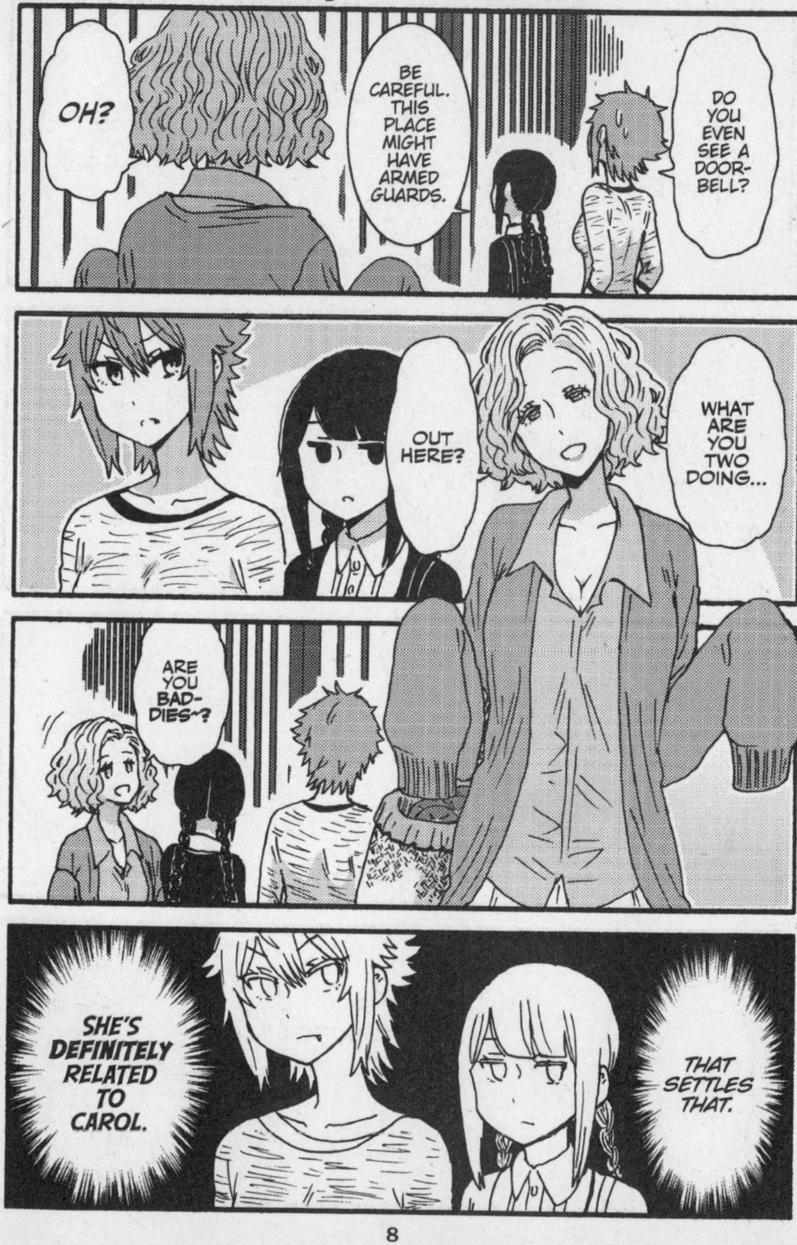
DO YOU EVEN SEE A DOORBELL?
BE CAREFUL. THIS PLACE MIGHT HAVE ARMED GUARDS.
OH?
WHAT ARE YOU TWO DOING...
OUT HERE?
ARE YOU BADDIES~?
THAT SETTLES THAT.
SHE'S DEFINITELY RELATED TO CAROL.

Suspicious "Minds"

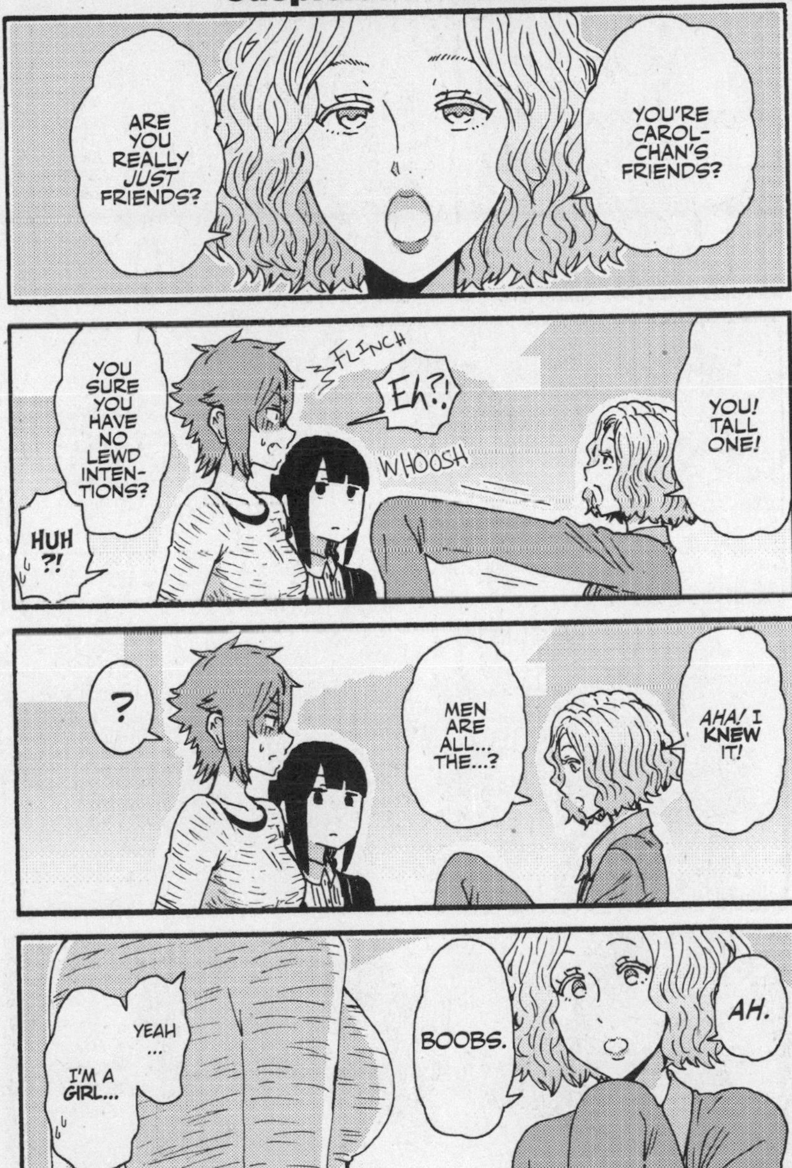

YOU'RE CAROL-CHAN'S FRIENDS?
ARE YOU REALLY JUST FRIENDS?
YOU! TALL ONE!
FLINCH
Eh?!
WHOOSH
YOU SURE YOU HAVE NO LEWD INTEN-TIONS?
HUH ?!
AHA! I KNEW IT!
MEN ARE ALL... THE...?
?
AH.
BOOBS.
YEAH ...
I'M A GIRL...

The Quest Begins

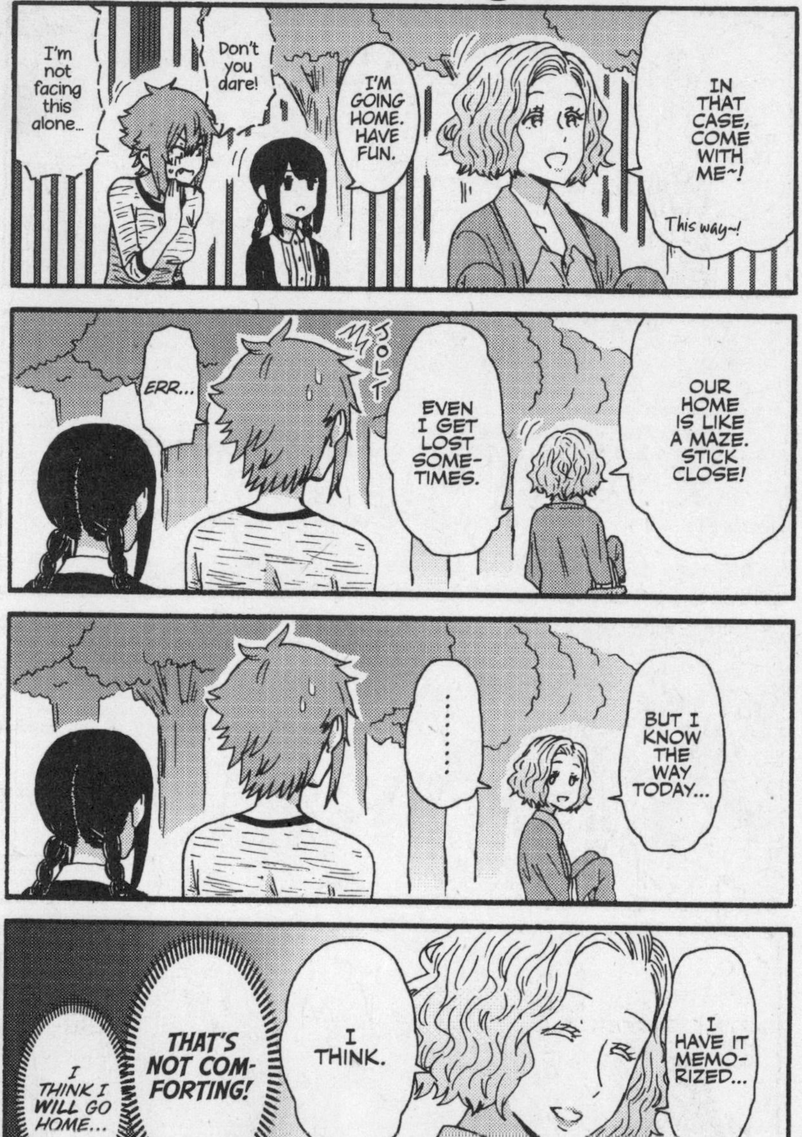
IN THAT CASE, COME WITH ME~!
This way~!
I'M GOING HOME. HAVE FUN.
Don't you dare!
I'm not facing this alone...
OUR HOME IS LIKE A MAZE. STICK CLOSE!
EVEN I GET LOST SOMETIMES.
JOLT
ERR...
BUT I KNOW THE WAY TODAY...
......
I HAVE IT MEMORIZED...
I THINK.
THAT'S NOT COMFORTING!
I THINK I WILL GO HOME...

Crazy Rich British

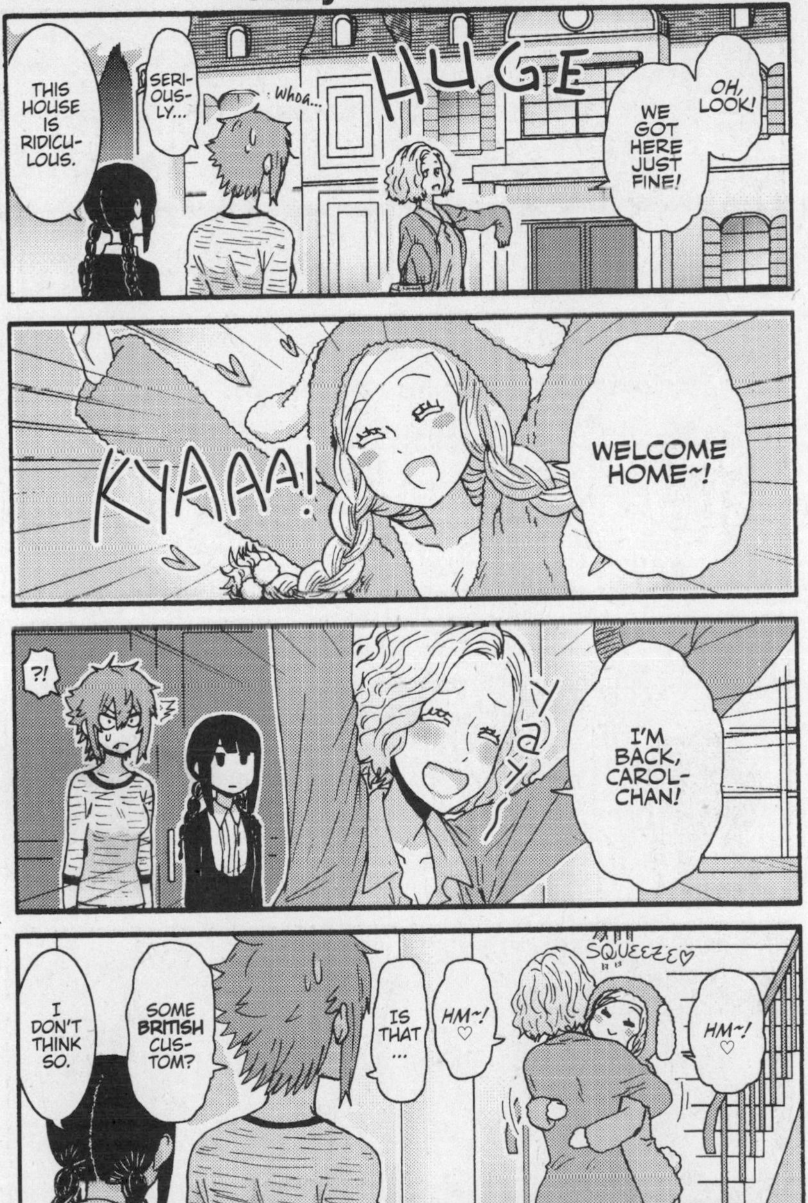
OH, LOOK!
WE GOT HERE JUST FINE!
HUGE
Whoa...
SERIOUSLY...
THIS HOUSE IS RIDICULOUS.
WELCOME HOME~!
KYAAA!
I'M BACK, CAROL-CHAN!
Yay~
?!
HM~! ♡
SQUEEZE♡
HM~! ♡
IS THAT...
SOME BRITISH CUSTOM?
I DON'T THINK SO.

Nonconformist

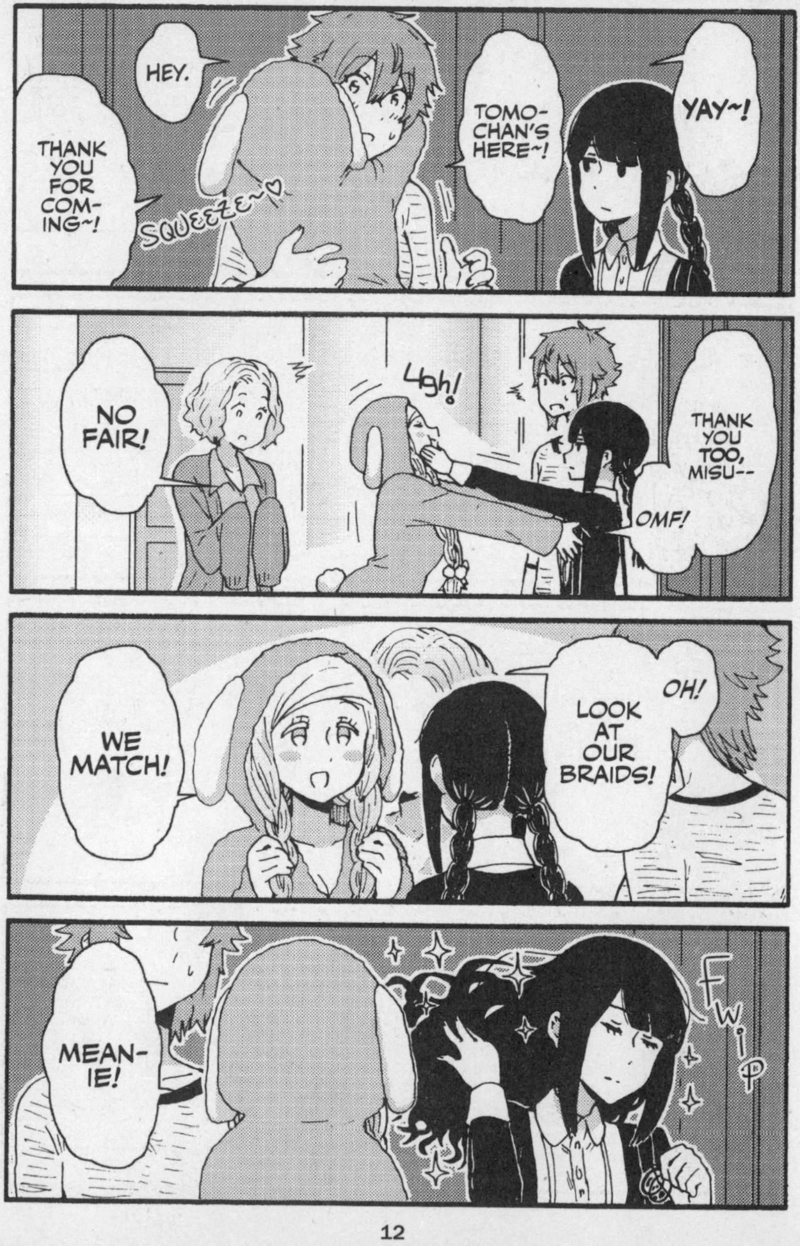
YAY~!
TOMO-CHAN'S HERE~!
HEY.
SQUEEZE~♡
THANK YOU FOR COMING~!
THANK YOU TOO, MISU--
OMF!
Ugh!
NO FAIR!
OH!
LOOK AT OUR BRAIDS!
WE MATCH!
Fwip
MEAN-IE!

The Young Family

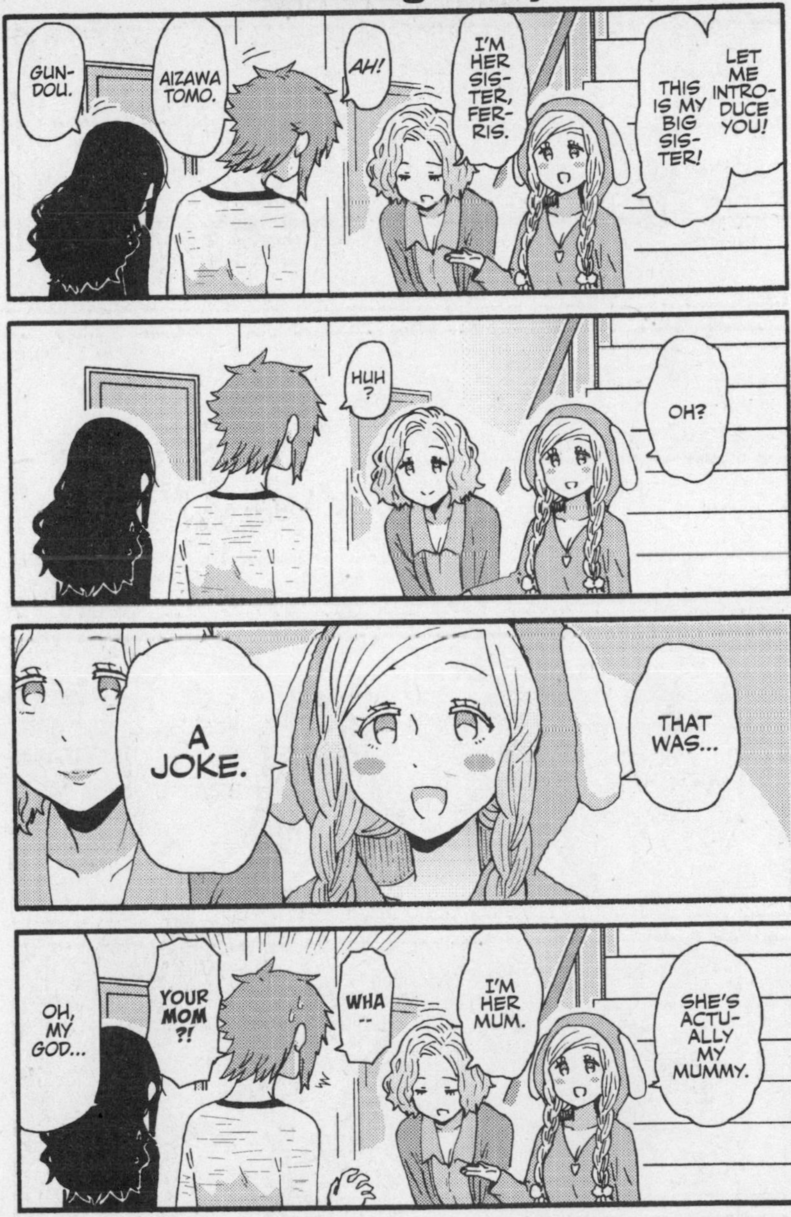

LET ME INTRODUCE YOU!
THIS IS MY BIG SISTER!
I'M HER SISTER, FERRIS.
AH!
AIZAWA TOMO.
GUNDOU.
OH?
HUH?
THAT WAS...
A JOKE.
SHE'S ACTUALLY MY MUMMY.
I'M HER MUM.
WHA--
YOUR MOM?!
OH, MY GOD...

Disturbing Math

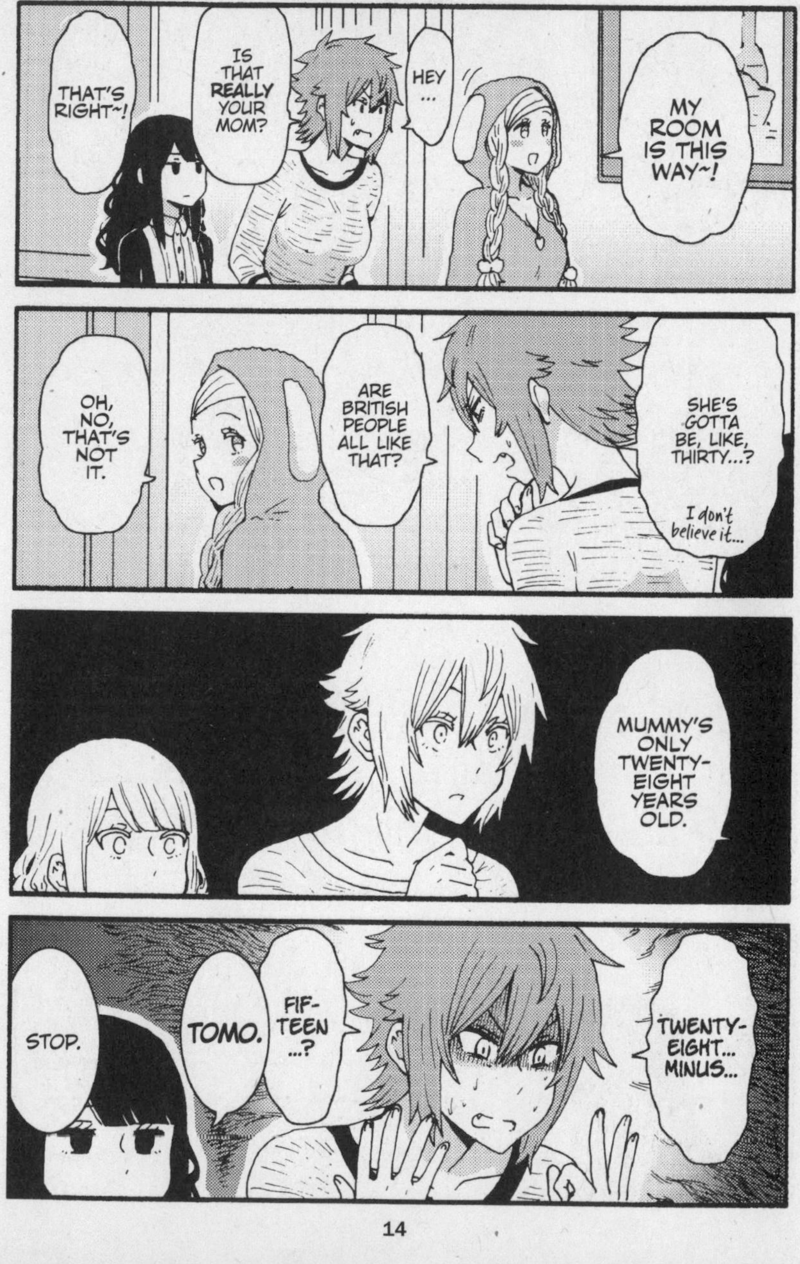
MY ROOM IS THIS WAY~!
HEY ...
IS THAT REALLY YOUR MOM?
THAT'S RIGHT~!
SHE'S GOTTA BE, LIKE, THIRTY...?
I don't believe it...
ARE BRITISH PEOPLE ALL LIKE THAT?
OH, NO, THAT'S NOT IT.
MUMMY'S ONLY TWENTY-EIGHT YEARS OLD.
TWENTY-EIGHT... MINUS...
FIF-TEEN ...?
TOMO.
STOP.

Princess Carol

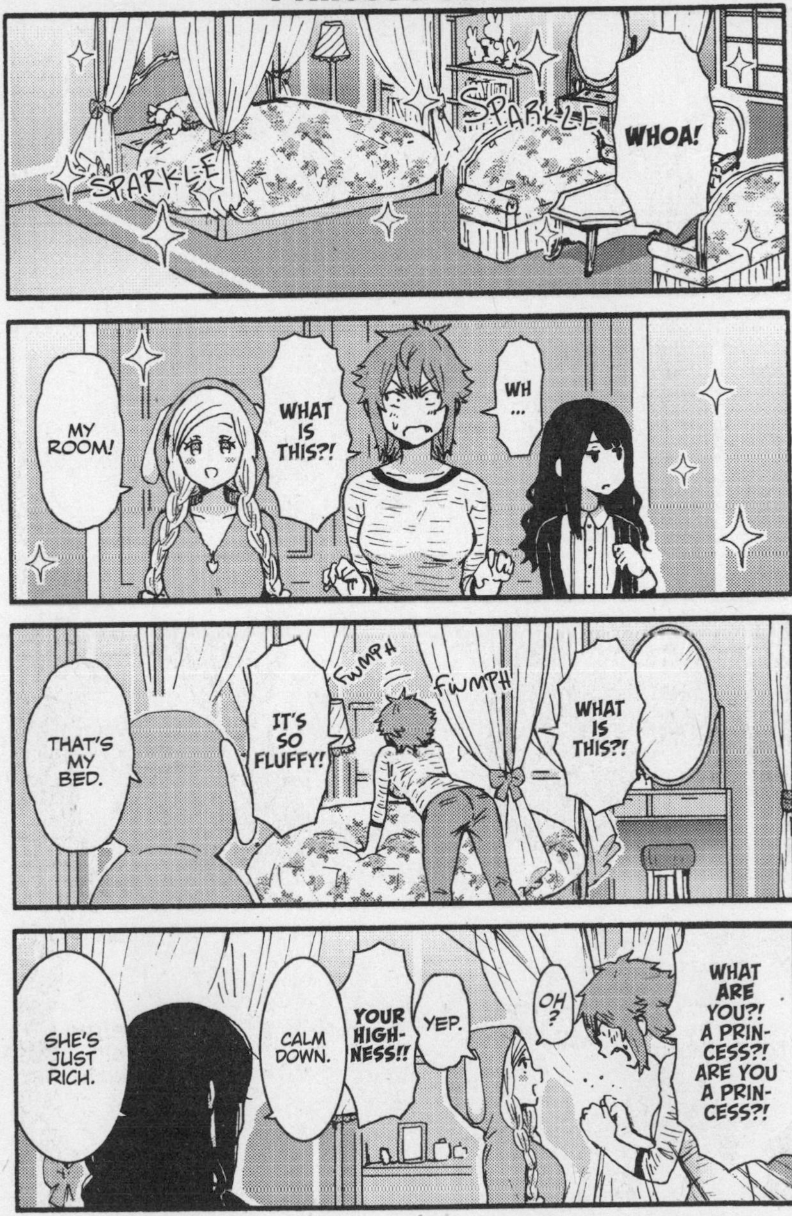
WHOA!
SPARKLE
SPARKLE
WH ...
WHAT IS THIS?!
MY ROOM!
WHAT IS THIS?!
FWUMPH
FWUMPH
IT'S SO FLUFFY!
THAT'S MY BED.
WHAT ARE YOU?! A PRIN-CESS?! ARE YOU A PRIN-CESS?!
OH?
YEP.
YOUR HIGH-NESS!!
CALM DOWN.
SHE'S JUST RICH.

Light Touch

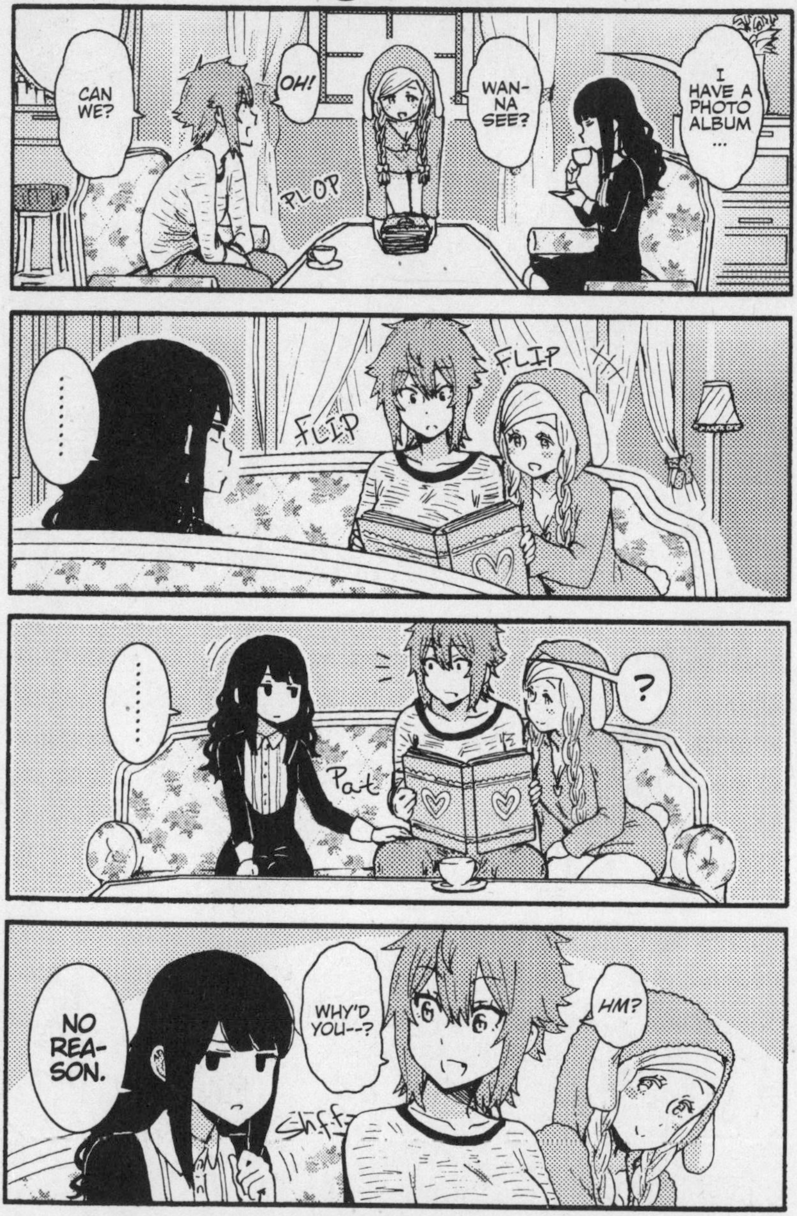
I HAVE A PHOTO ALBUM ...
WAN-NA SEE?
OH!
CAN WE?
PLOP
FLIP
FLIP
......
?
Pat
......
HM?
WHY'D YOU--?
NO REA-SON.

Not for Anyone Else

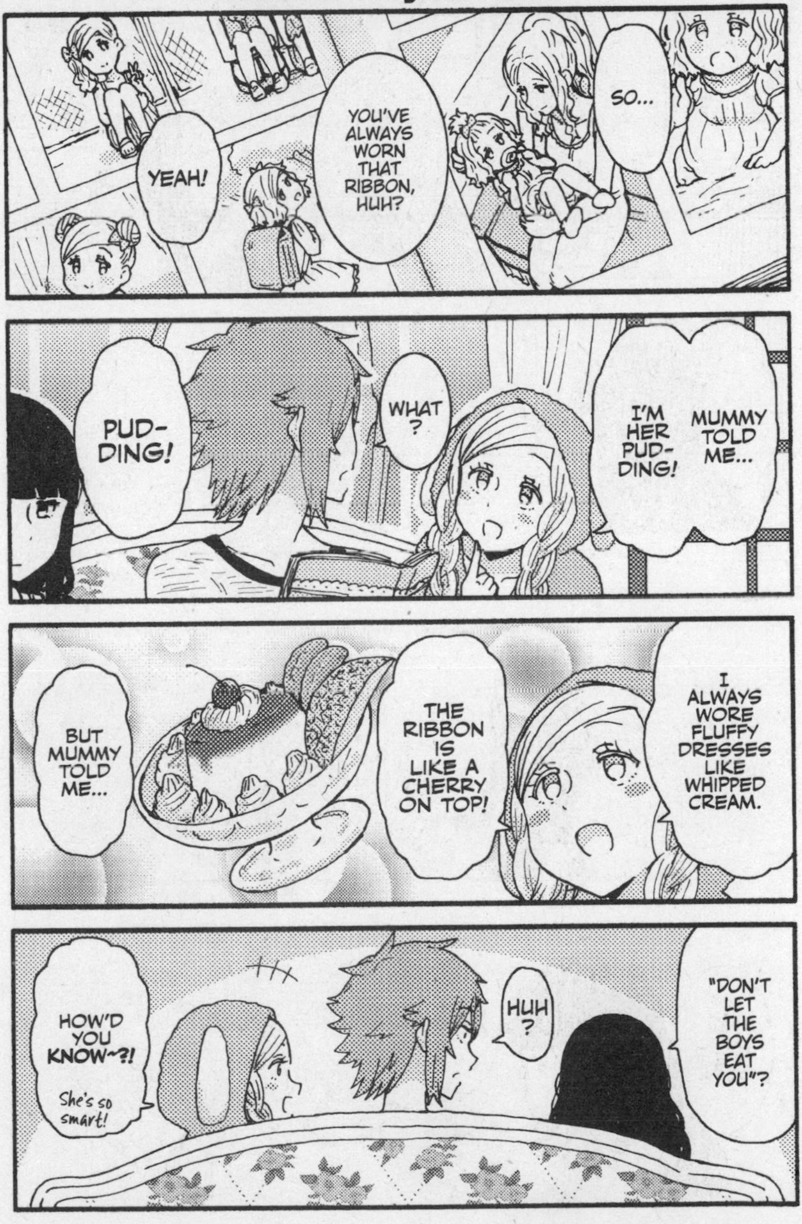
SO...
YOU'VE ALWAYS WORN THAT RIBBON, HUH?
YEAH!
MUMMY TOLD ME...
I'M HER PUD-DING!
WHAT?
PUD-DING!
I ALWAYS WORE FLUFFY DRESSES LIKE WHIPPED CREAM.
THE RIBBON IS LIKE A CHERRY ON TOP!
BUT MUMMY TOLD ME...
"DON'T LET THE BOYS EAT YOU"?
HUH?
HOW'D YOU KNOW~?!
She's so smart!

Helicopter Parent

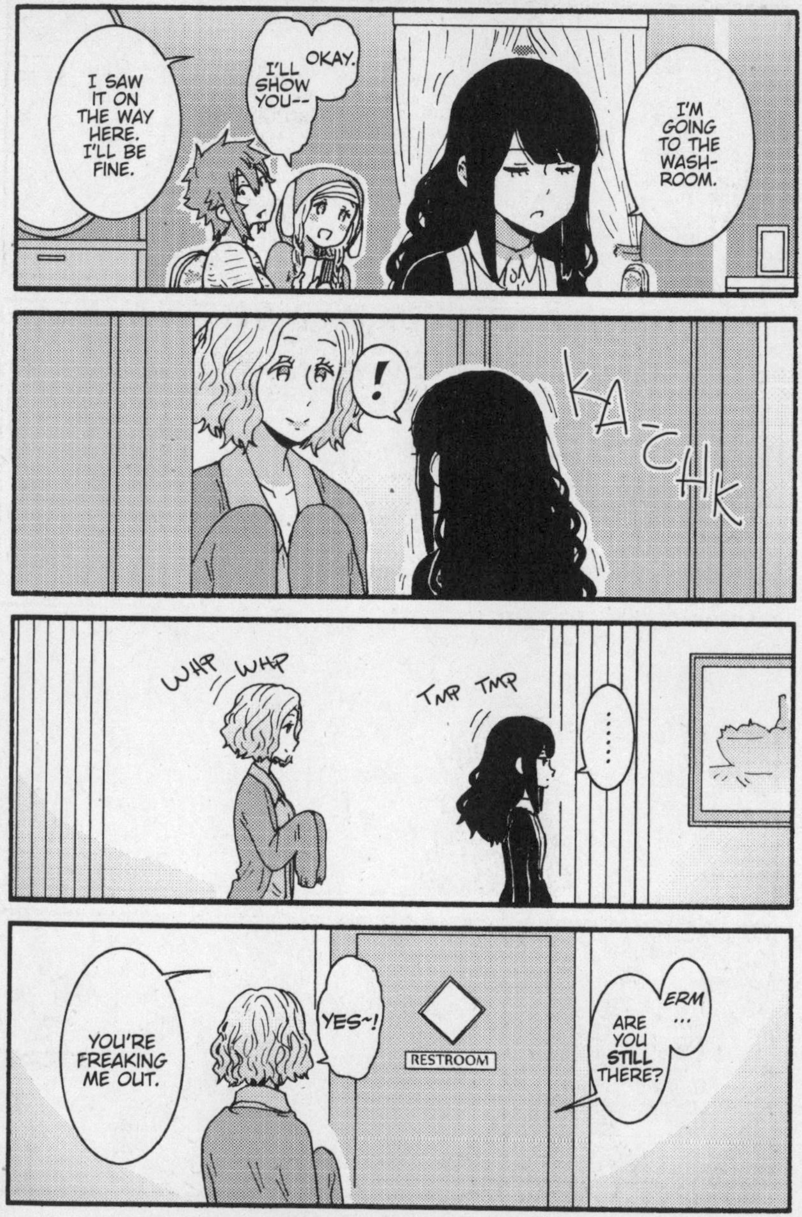
I'M GOING TO THE WASH-ROOM.
OKAY. I'LL SHOW YOU--
I SAW IT ON THE WAY HERE. I'LL BE FINE.
KA-CHK
!
......
TMP TMP
WHP WHP
ERM... ARE YOU STILL THERE?
RESTROOM
YES~!
YOU'RE FREAKING ME OUT.

Were We Playing?

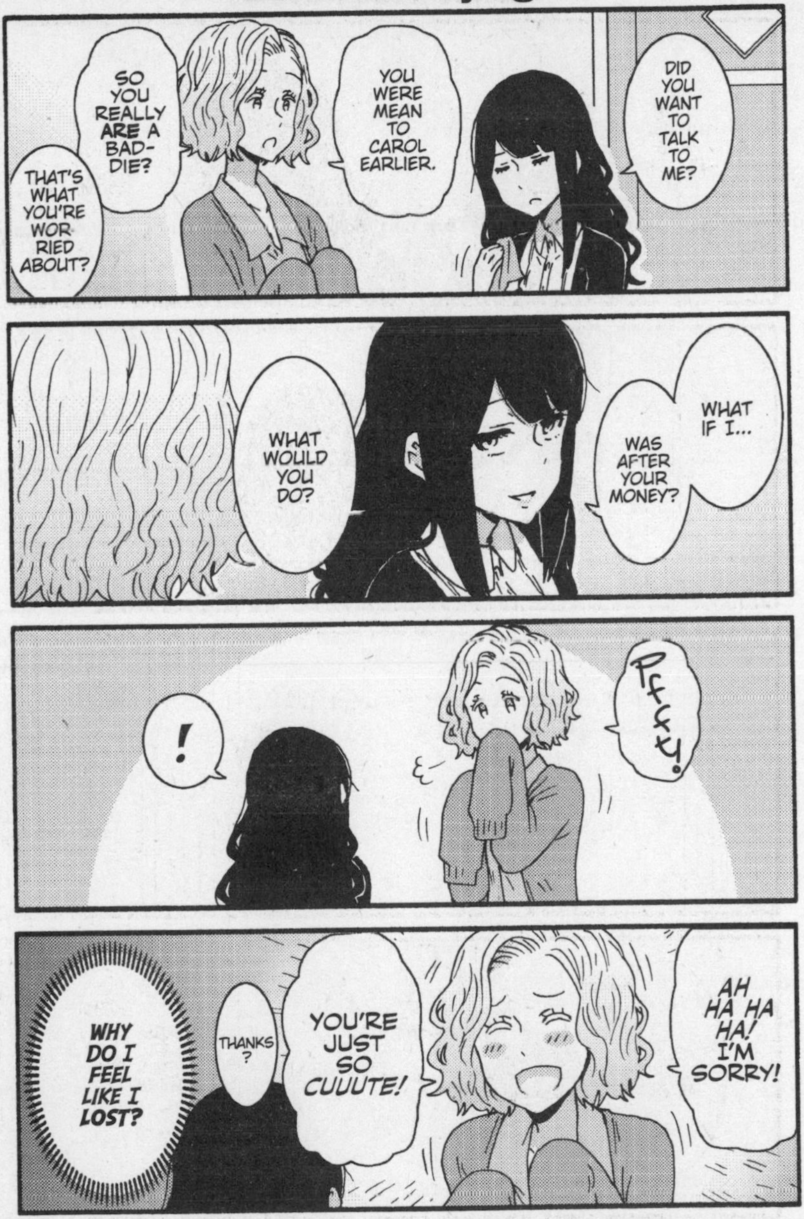
DID YOU WANT TO TALK TO ME?
YOU WERE MEAN TO CAROL EARLIER.
SO YOU REALLY **ARE** A BADDIE?
THAT'S WHAT YOU'RE WORRIED ABOUT?
WHAT IF I...
WAS AFTER YOUR MONEY?
WHAT WOULD YOU DO?
Pfft!
!
AH HA HA HA! I'M SORRY!
YOU'RE JUST SO CUUUTE!
THANKS?
WHY DO I FEEL LIKE I LOST?

As Manipulative As Me?

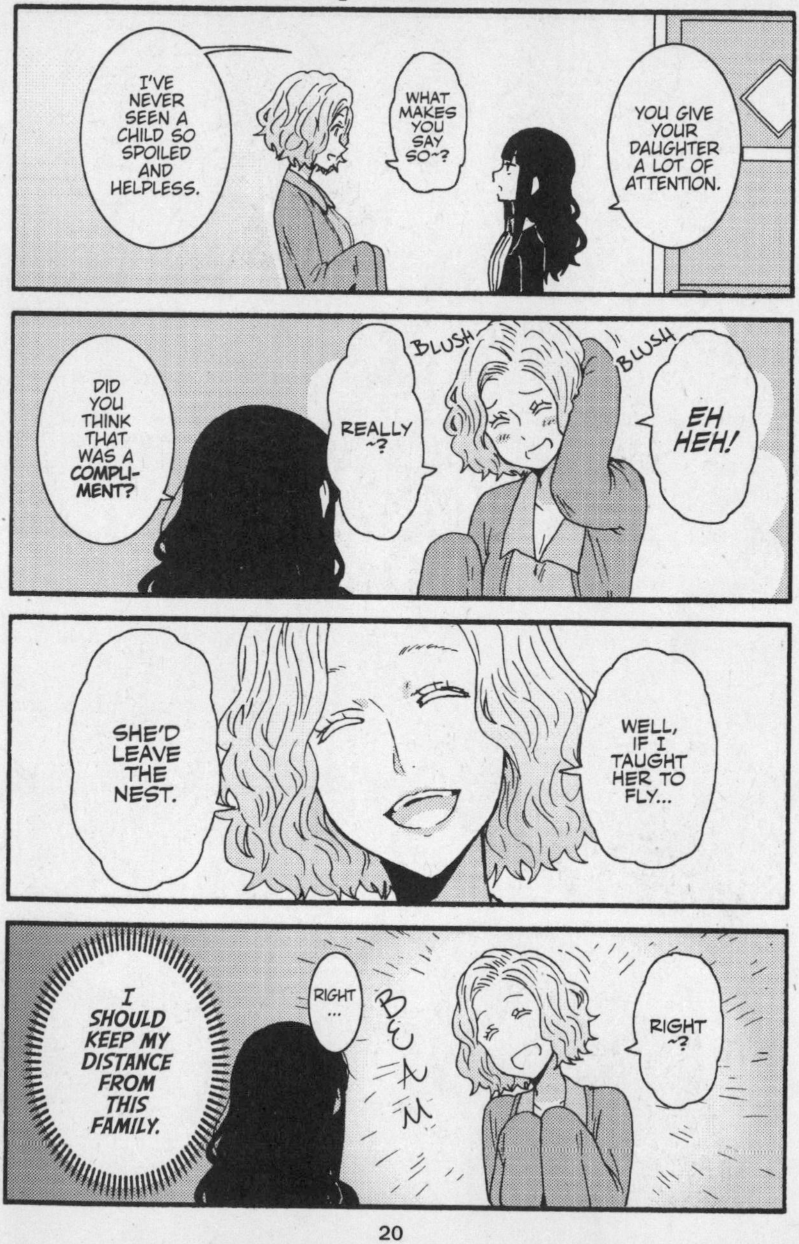
YOU GIVE YOUR DAUGHTER A LOT OF ATTENTION.
WHAT MAKES YOU SAY SO~?
I'VE NEVER SEEN A CHILD SO SPOILED AND HELPLESS.
EH HEH!
BLUSH
BLUSH
REALLY ~?
DID YOU THINK THAT WAS A COMPLIMENT?
WELL, IF I TAUGHT HER TO FLY...
SHE'D LEAVE THE NEST.
RIGHT ~?
BEAM
RIGHT...
I SHOULD KEEP MY DISTANCE FROM THIS FAMILY.

Savant

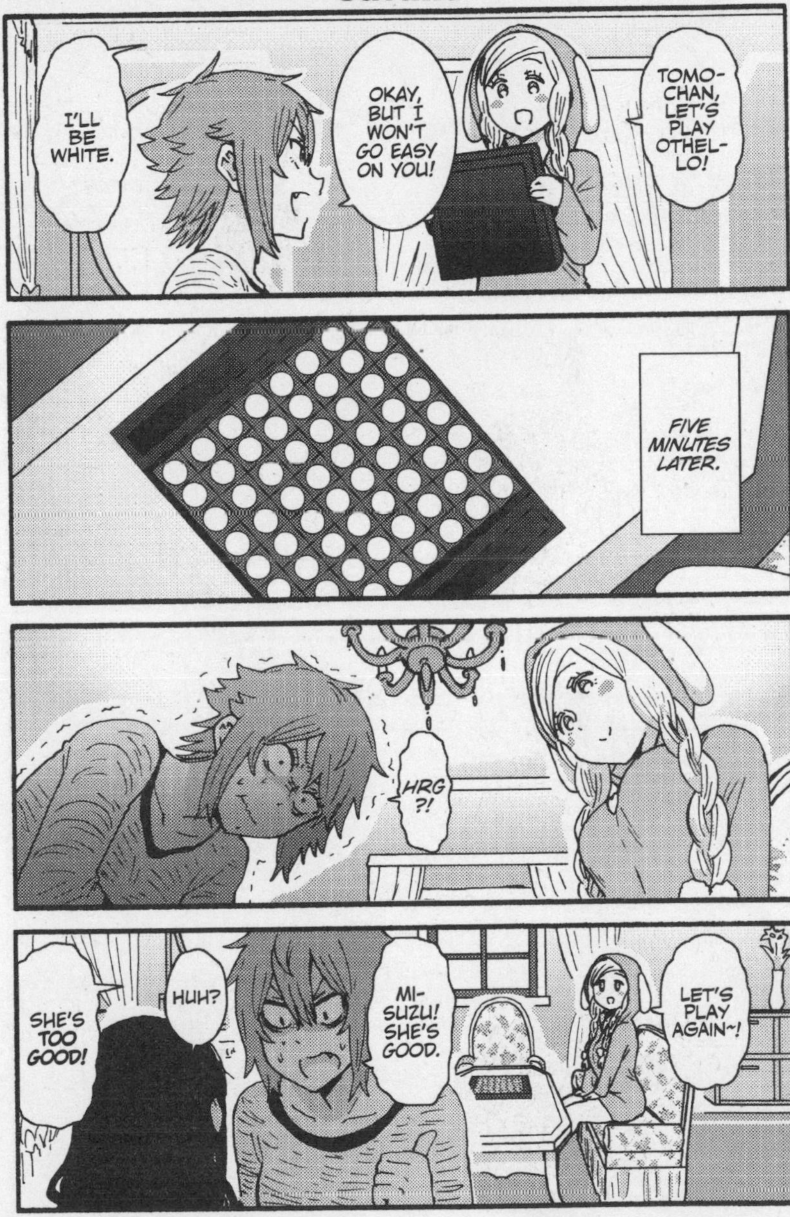
TOMO-CHAN, LET'S PLAY OTHEL-LO!
OKAY, BUT I WON'T GO EASY ON YOU!
I'LL BE WHITE.
FIVE MINUTES LATER.
HRG ?!
LET'S PLAY AGAIN~!
MI-SUZU! SHE'S GOOD.
HUH?
SHE'S TOO GOOD!

Utterly Destroyed

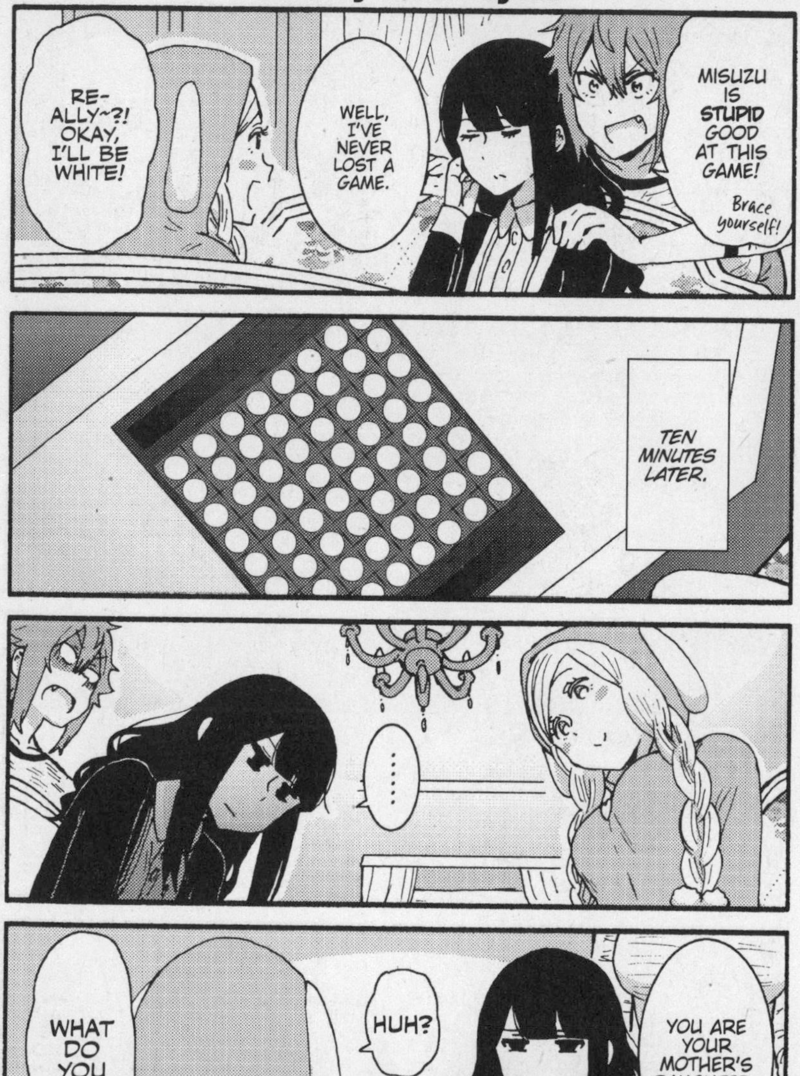
MISUZU IS **STUPID** GOOD AT THIS GAME!
Brace yourself!
WELL, I'VE NEVER LOST A GAME.
RE-ALLY~?! OKAY, I'LL BE WHITE!
TEN MINUTES LATER.
......
YOU ARE YOUR MOTHER'S DAUGHTER.
HUH?
WHAT DO YOU MEAN?

Goodbye Hugs

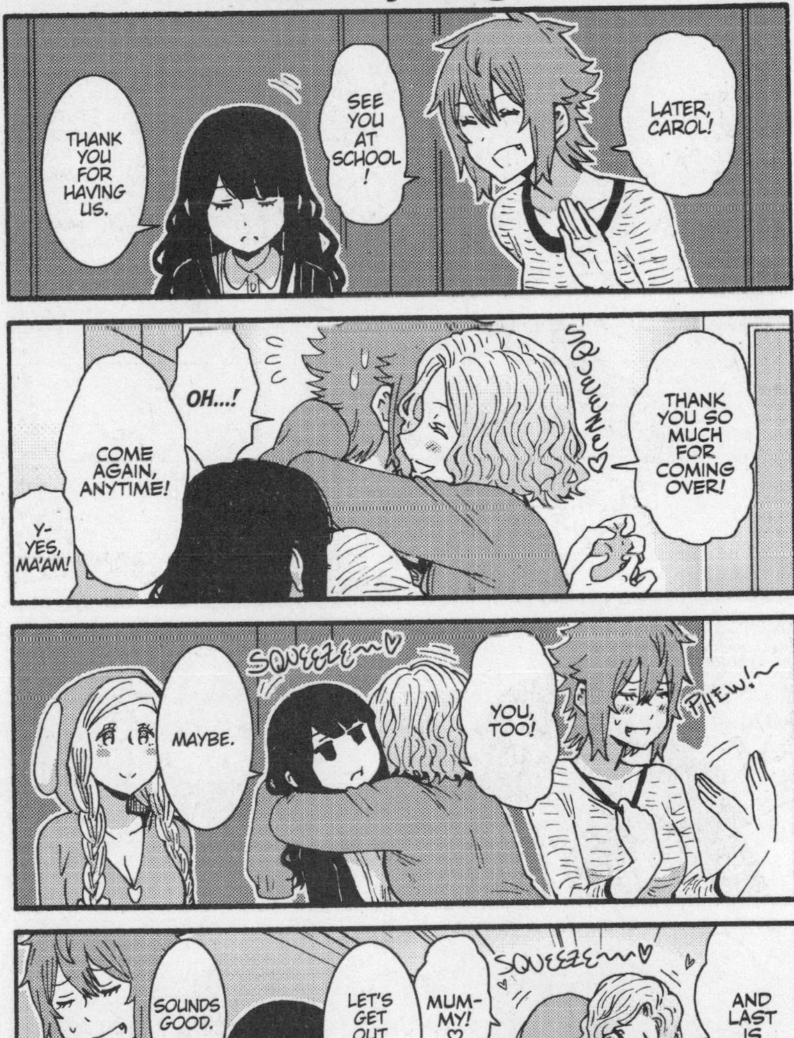
LATER, CAROL!
SEE YOU AT SCHOOL!
THANK YOU FOR HAVING US.
THANK YOU SO MUCH FOR COMING OVER!
SQUEEZE♡
OH...!
COME AGAIN, ANYTIME!
Y- YES, MA'AM!
PHEW!~
YOU, TOO!
SQUEEZE~~♡
MAYBE.
AND LAST IS CAROL-CHAN~! ♡
SQUEEZE~~♡
MUMMY! ♡
LET'S GET OUT OF HERE.
SOUNDS GOOD.

OMAKE

Are Your Ears Burning, Too?

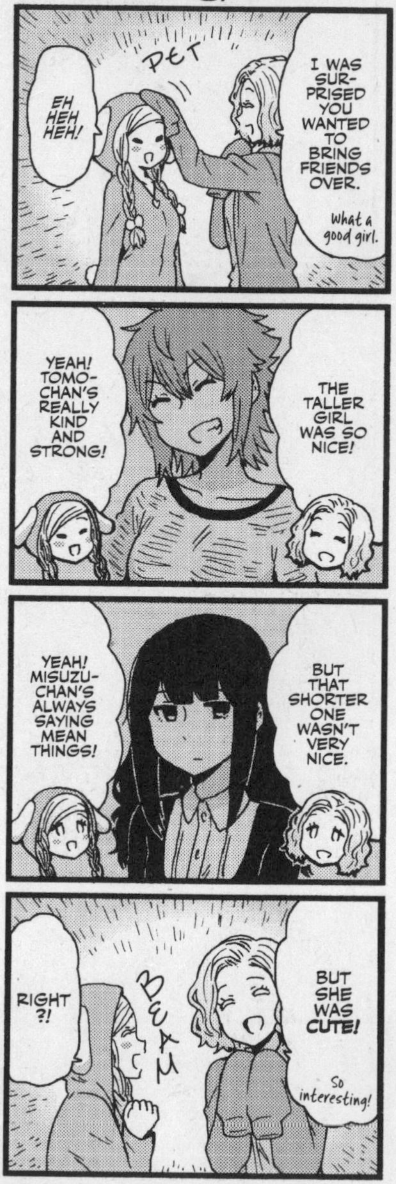
I WAS SURPRISED YOU WANTED TO BRING FRIENDS OVER.
What a good girl.
PET
EH HEH HEH!
THE TALLER GIRL WAS SO NICE!
YEAH! TOMO-CHAN'S REALLY KIND AND STRONG!
BUT THAT SHORTER ONE WASN'T VERY NICE.
YEAH! MISUZU-CHAN'S ALWAYS SAYING MEAN THINGS!
BUT SHE WAS CUTE!
So interesting!
BEAM
RIGHT?!

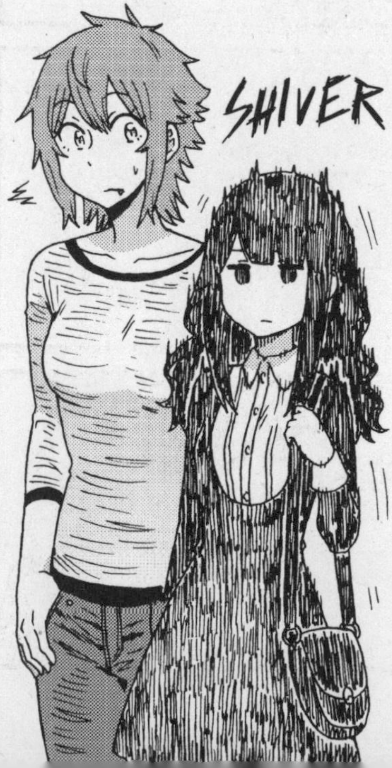
SHIVER

Ch. 19

It's Relative

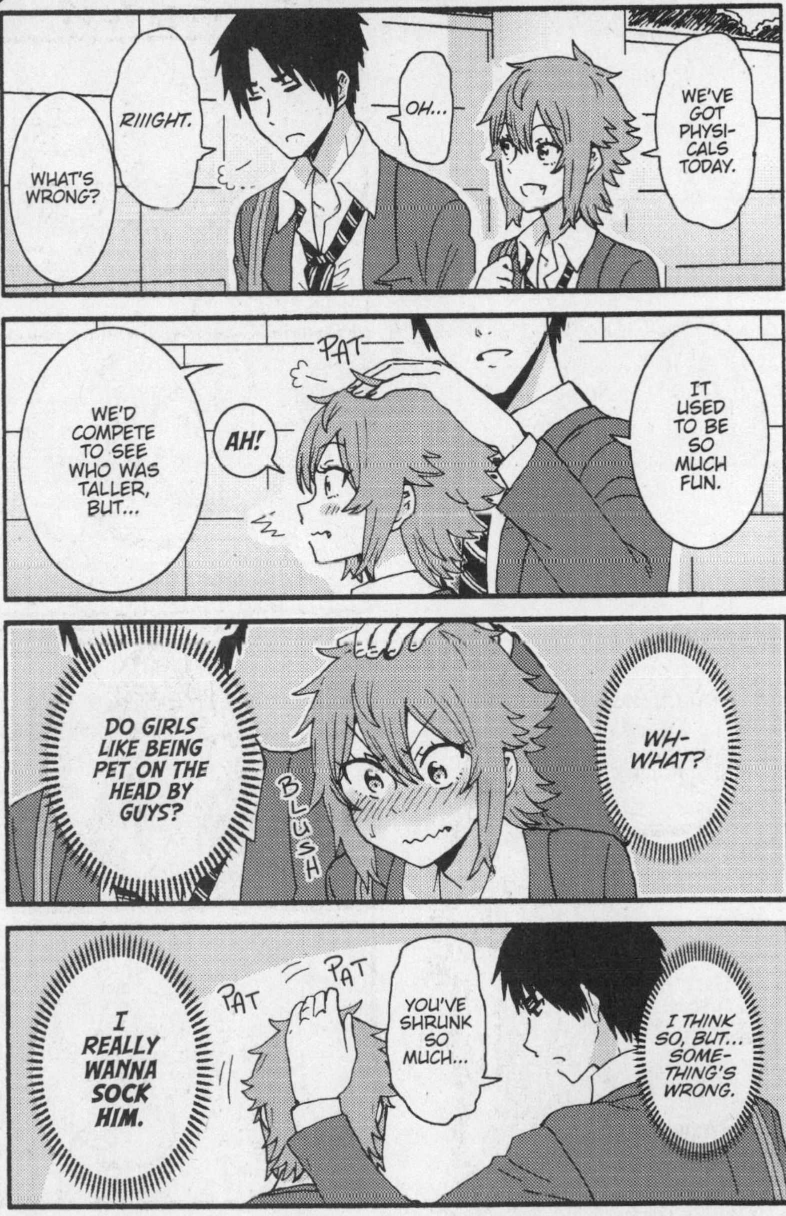
WE'VE GOT PHYSICALS TODAY.
OH...
RIIIGHT.
WHAT'S WRONG?
IT USED TO BE SO MUCH FUN.
PAT
AH!
WE'D COMPETE TO SEE WHO WAS TALLER, BUT...
WH-WHAT?
BLUSH
DO GIRLS LIKE BEING PET ON THE HEAD BY GUYS?
I THINK SO, BUT... SOMETHING'S WRONG.
YOU'VE SHRUNK SO MUCH...
PAT
PAT
I REALLY WANNA SOCK HIM.

WWTD?

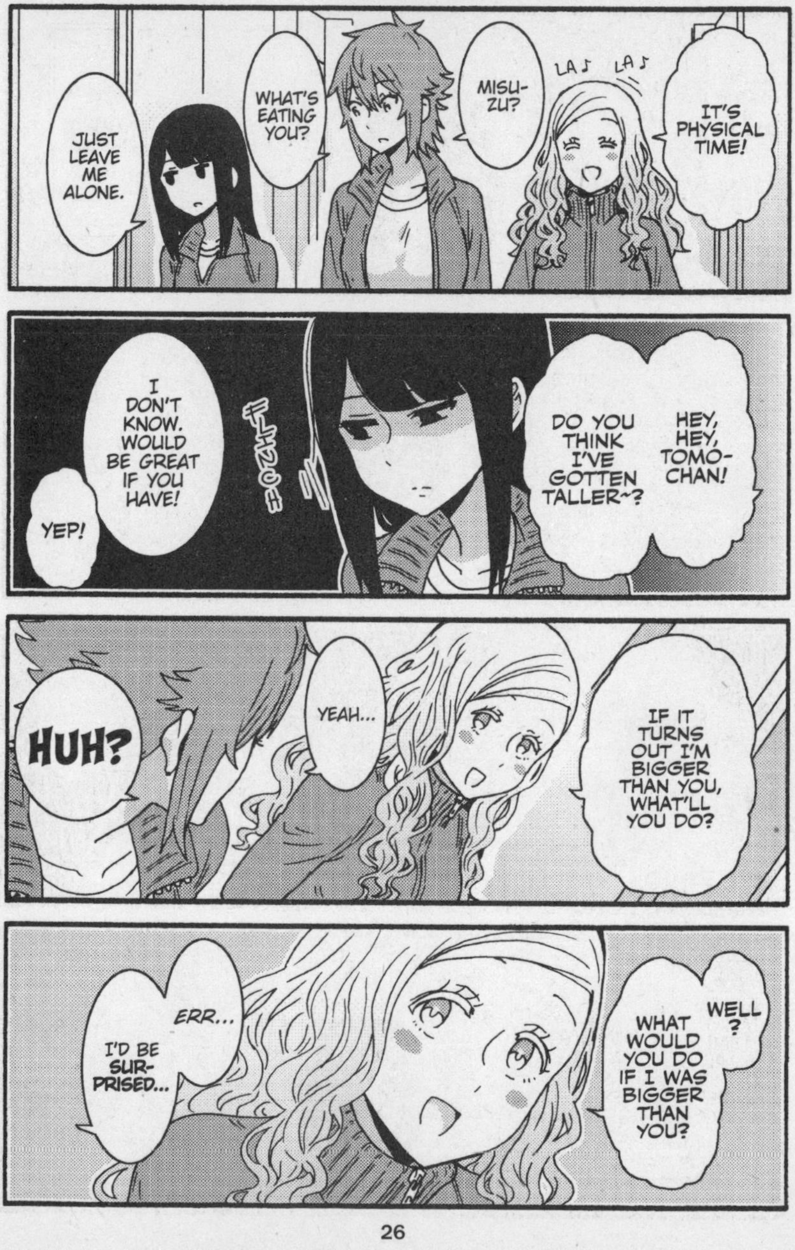
IT'S PHYSICAL TIME!
LA♪ LA♪
MISU-ZU?
WHAT'S EATING YOU?
JUST LEAVE ME ALONE.
HEY, HEY, TOMO-CHAN!
DO YOU THINK I'VE GOTTEN TALLER~?
I DON'T KNOW. WOULD BE GREAT IF YOU HAVE!
YEP!
IF IT TURNS OUT I'M BIGGER THAN YOU, WHAT'LL YOU DO?
YEAH...
HUH?
WELL?
WHAT WOULD YOU DO IF I WAS BIGGER THAN YOU?
ERR...
I'D BE SUR-PRISED...

Misuzu's Anxieties

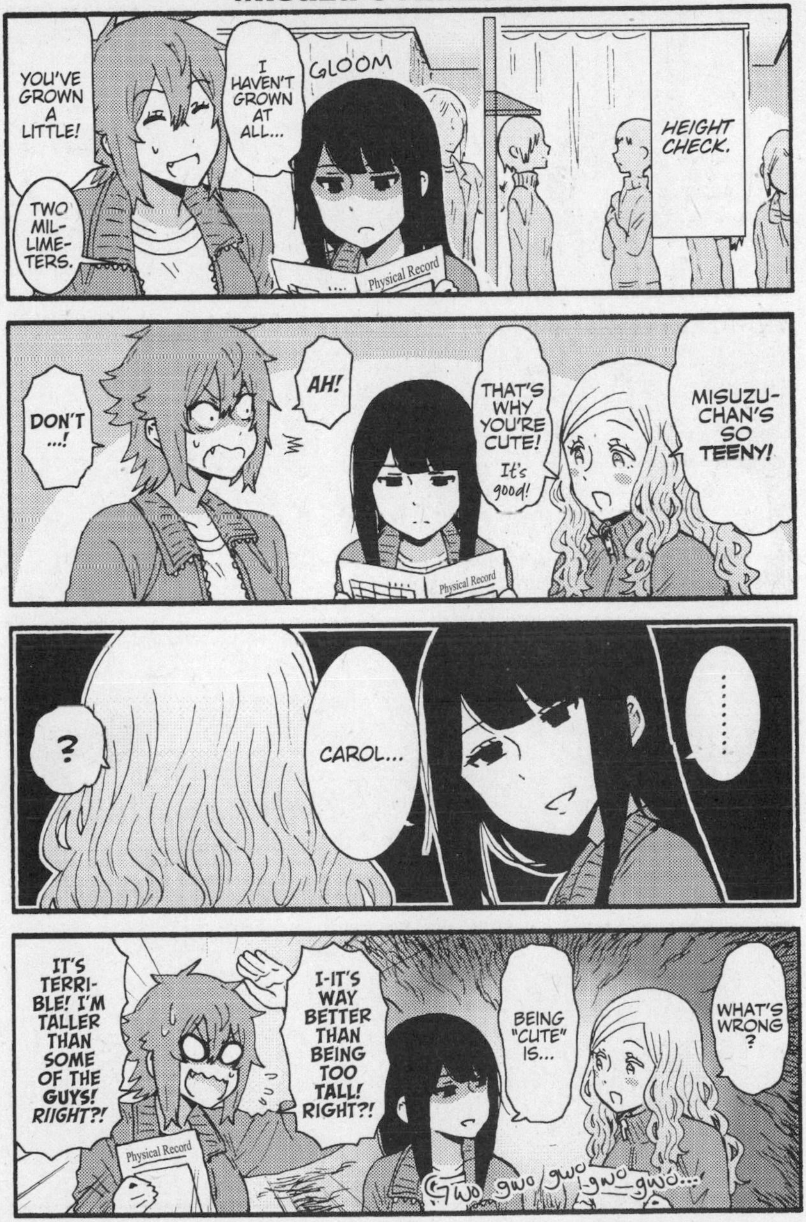

HEIGHT CHECK.
GLOOM
I HAVEN'T GROWN AT ALL...
YOU'VE GROWN A LITTLE!
TWO MIL-LIME-TERS.
....
Physical Record
MISUZU-CHAN'S SO TEENY!
THAT'S WHY YOU'RE CUTE!
It's good!
AH!
DON'T ...!
Physical Record
......
CAROL...
?
WHAT'S WRONG?
BEING "CUTE" IS...
I-IT'S WAY BETTER THAN BEING TOO TALL! RIGHT?!
IT'S TERRIBLE! I'M TALLER THAN SOME OF THE GUYS! RIIGHT?!
Physical Record
Gwo gwo gwo gwo gwo...

Carol's Anxieties

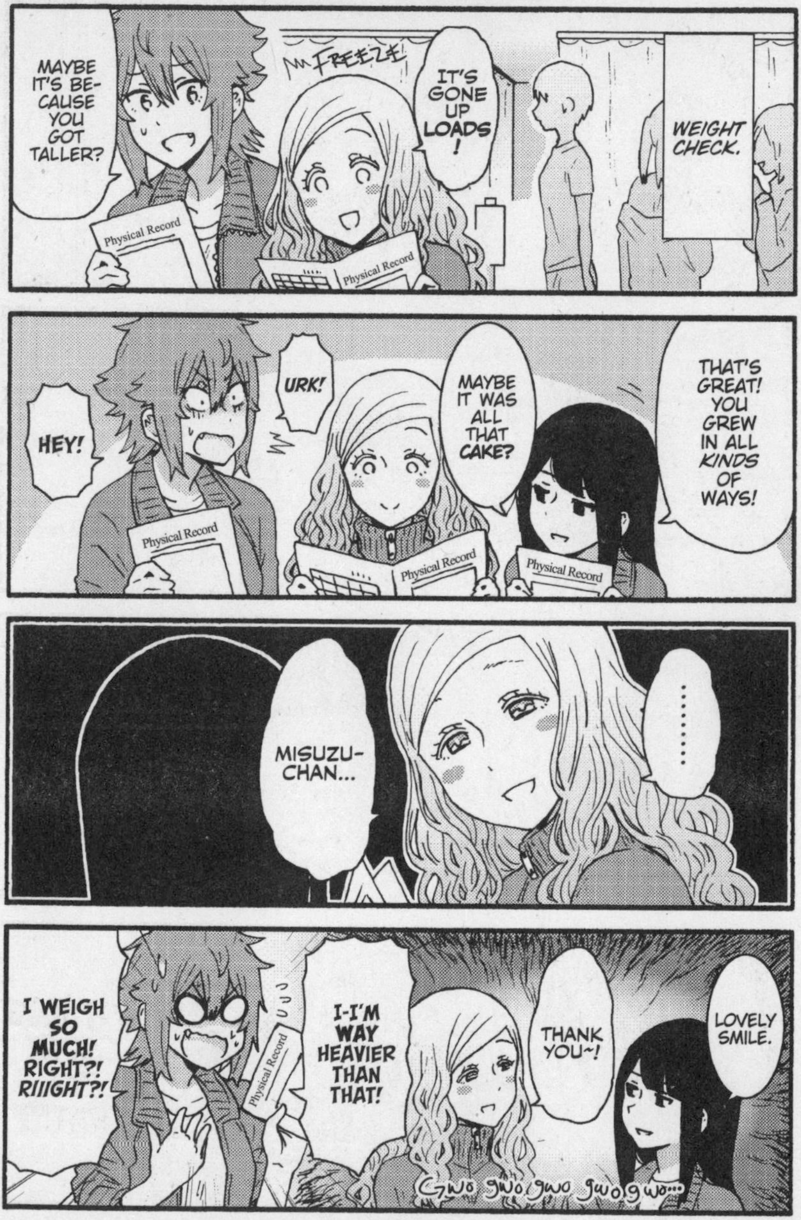
WEIGHT CHECK.
IT'S GONE UP LOADS!
FREEZE
MAYBE IT'S BE-CAUSE YOU GOT TALLER?
Physical Record
Physical Record
THAT'S GREAT! YOU GREW IN ALL KINDS OF WAYS!
MAYBE IT WAS ALL THAT CAKE?
URK!
HEY!
Physical Record
Physical Record
Physical Record
......
MISUZU-CHAN...
LOVELY SMILE.
THANK YOU~!
I-I'M WAY HEAVIER THAN THAT!
I WEIGH SO MUCH! RIGHT?! RIIIGHT?!
Physical Record
Gwo gwo gwo gwo gwo...

Muscle Talk

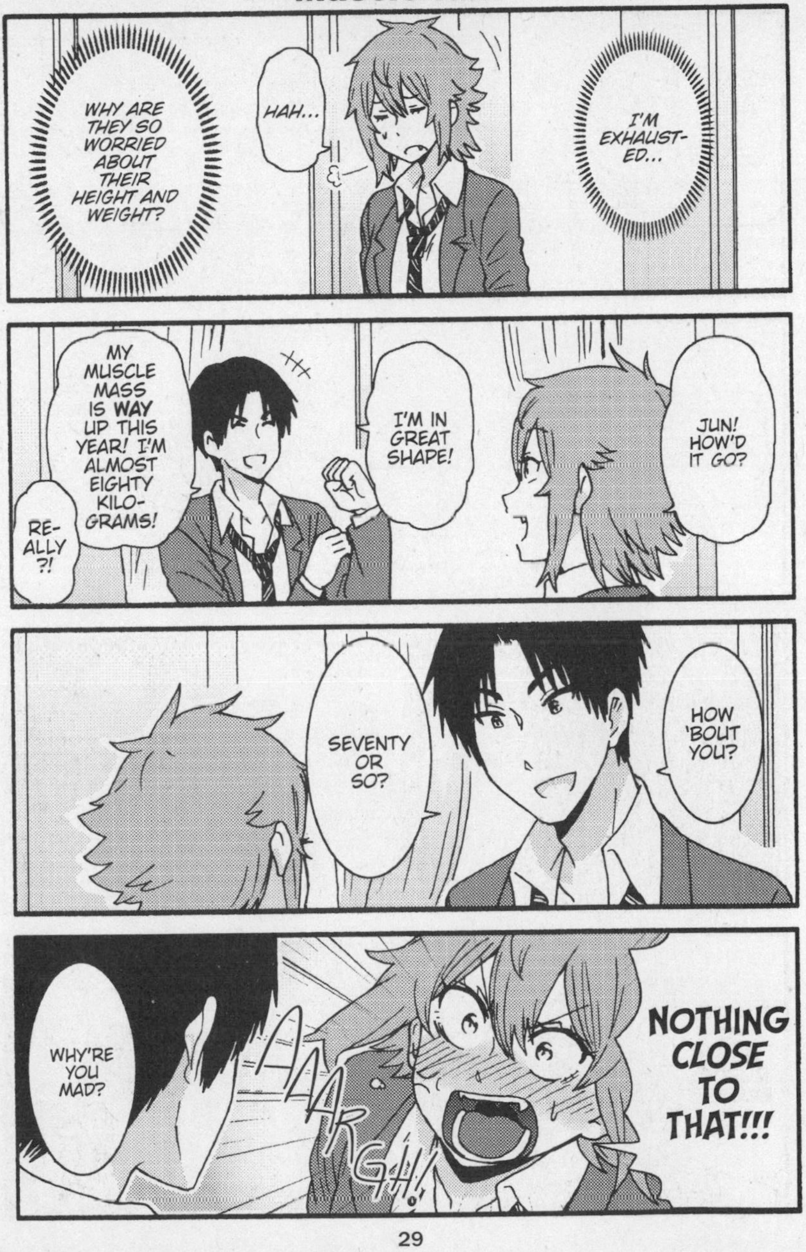
I'M EXHAUST-ED...
HAH...
WHY ARE THEY SO WORRIED ABOUT THEIR HEIGHT AND WEIGHT?
JUN! HOW'D IT GO?
I'M IN GREAT SHAPE!
MY MUSCLE MASS IS WAY UP THIS YEAR! I'M ALMOST EIGHTY KILO-GRAMS!
RE-ALLY ?!
HOW 'BOUT YOU?
SEVENTY OR SO?
NOTHING CLOSE TO THAT!!!
AAARGH!
WHY'RE YOU MAD?

TOMO-CHAN
IS A GIRL!

Ch. 20

I Was a Typical Kid!

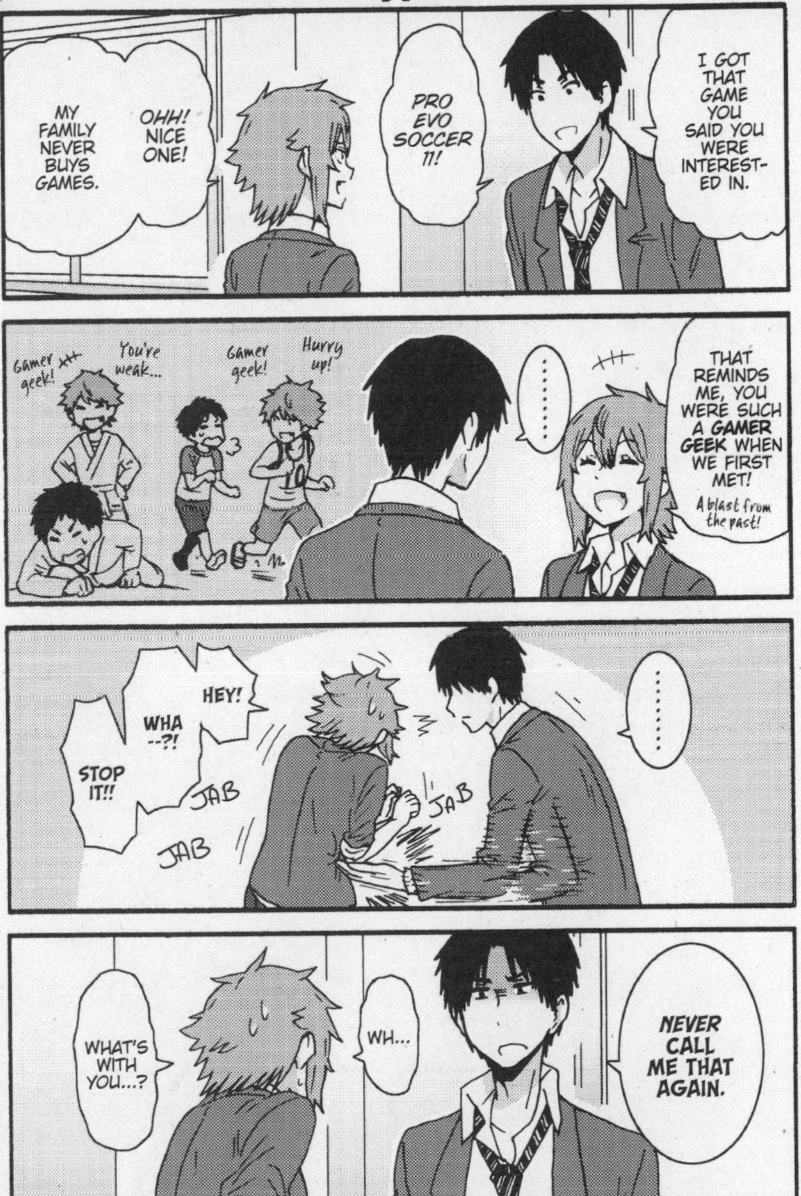

I GOT THAT GAME YOU SAID YOU WERE INTEREST-ED IN.
PRO EVO SOCCER 11!
OHH! NICE ONE!
MY FAMILY NEVER BUYS GAMES.
THAT REMINDS ME, YOU WERE SUCH A **GAMER GEEK** WHEN WE FIRST MET!
A blast from the past!
......
Hurry up!
Gamer geek!
You're weak...
Gamer geek!
......
JAB
HEY!
WHA--?!
STOP IT!!
JAB
JAB
NEVER CALL ME THAT AGAIN.
WH...
WHAT'S WITH YOU...?

Gaming and Cognition

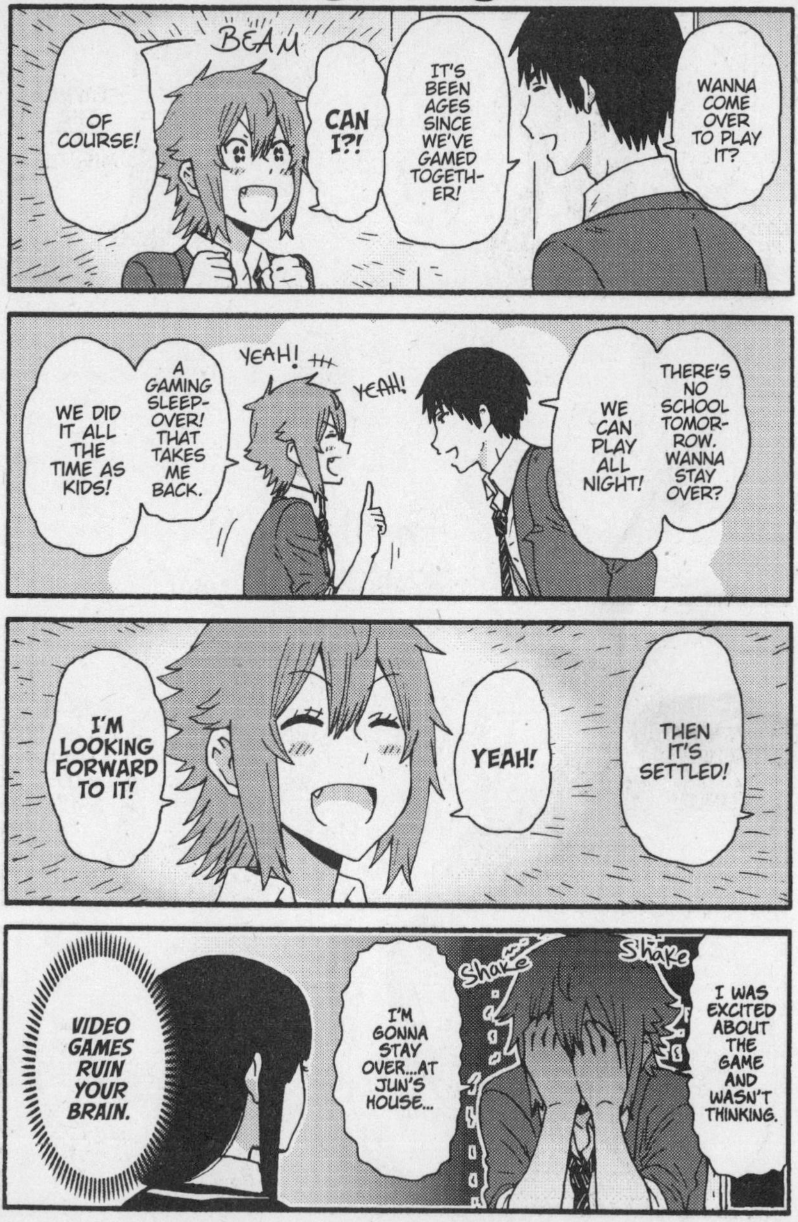
WANNA COME OVER TO PLAY IT?
IT'S BEEN AGES SINCE WE'VE GAMED TOGETH-ER!
CAN I?!
BEAM
OF COURSE!
THERE'S NO SCHOOL TOMOR-ROW. WANNA STAY OVER?
WE CAN PLAY ALL NIGHT!
YEAH!
YEAH!
A GAMING SLEEP-OVER! THAT TAKES ME BACK.
WE DID IT ALL THE TIME AS KIDS!
THEN IT'S SETTLED!
YEAH!
I'M LOOKING FORWARD TO IT!
Shake
I WAS EXCITED ABOUT THE GAME AND WASN'T THINKING.
Shake
I'M GONNA STAY OVER...AT JUN'S HOUSE...
VIDEO GAMES RUIN YOUR BRAIN.

Carol the Lifeline

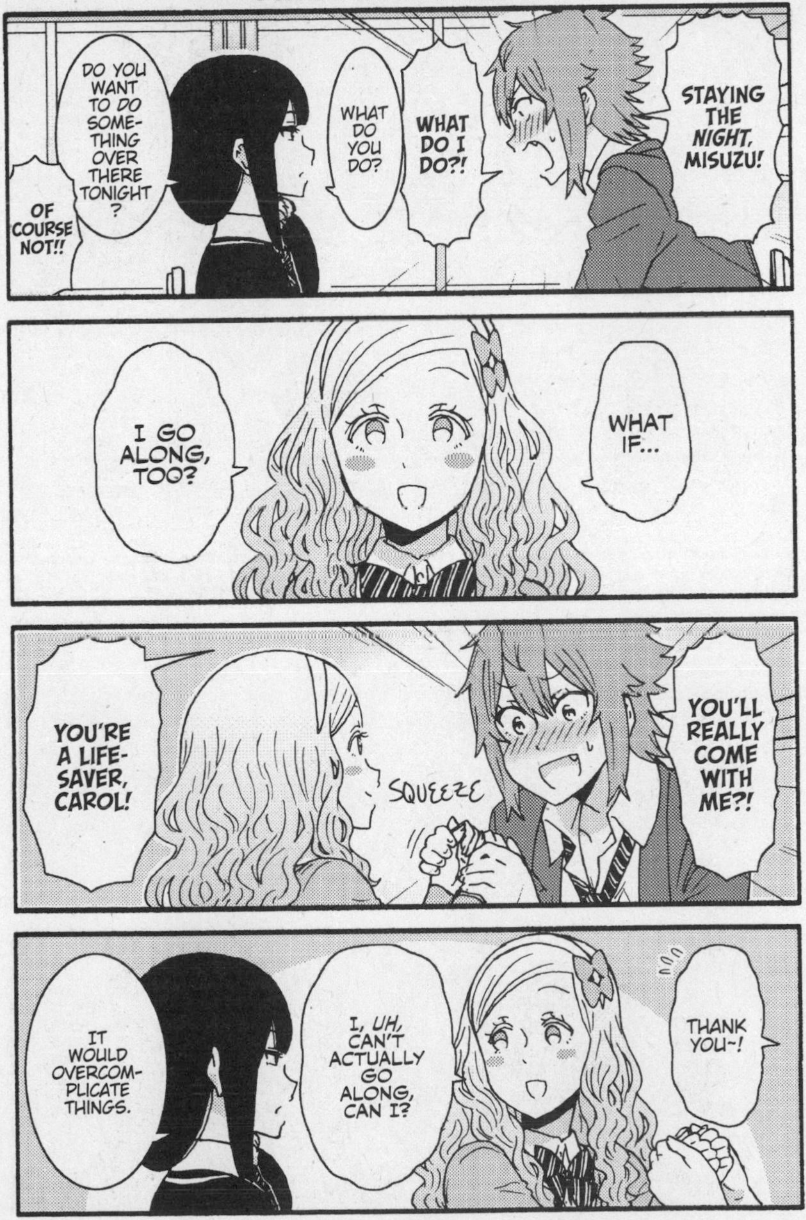
STAYING THE *NIGHT*, MISUZU!
WHAT DO I DO?!
WHAT DO YOU DO?
DO YOU WANT TO *DO* SOME-THING OVER THERE TONIGHT?
OF COURSE NOT!!
WHAT IF...
I GO ALONG, TOO?
YOU'LL REALLY COME WITH ME?!
SQUEEZE
YOU'RE A LIFE-SAVER, CAROL!
THANK YOU~!
I, *UH*, CAN'T ACTUALLY GO ALONG, CAN I?
IT WOULD OVERCOM-PLICATE THINGS.

A Common Cause

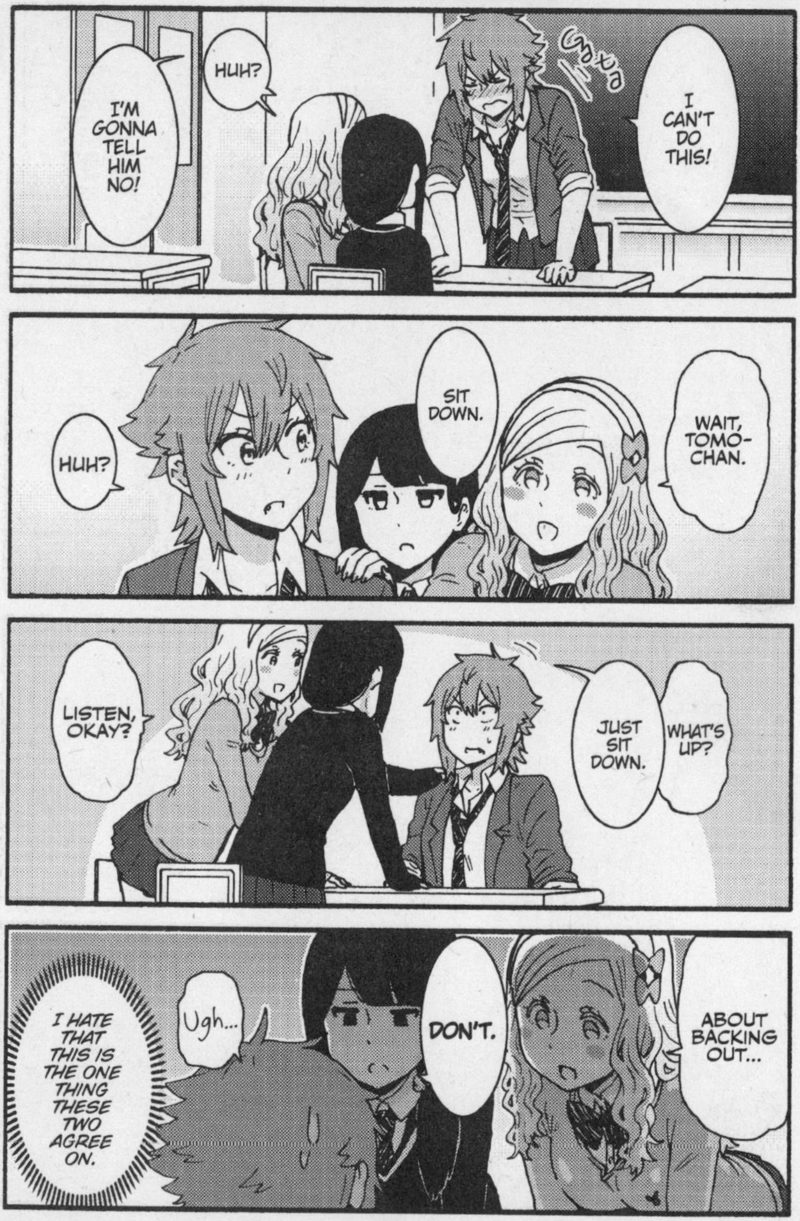
I CAN'T DO THIS!
HUH?
I'M GONNA TELL HIM NO!
WAIT, TOMO-CHAN.
SIT DOWN.
HUH?
WHAT'S UP?
JUST SIT DOWN.
LISTEN, OKAY?
ABOUT BACKING OUT...
DON'T.
Ugh...
I HATE THAT THIS IS THE ONE THING THESE TWO AGREE ON.

Technically Correct

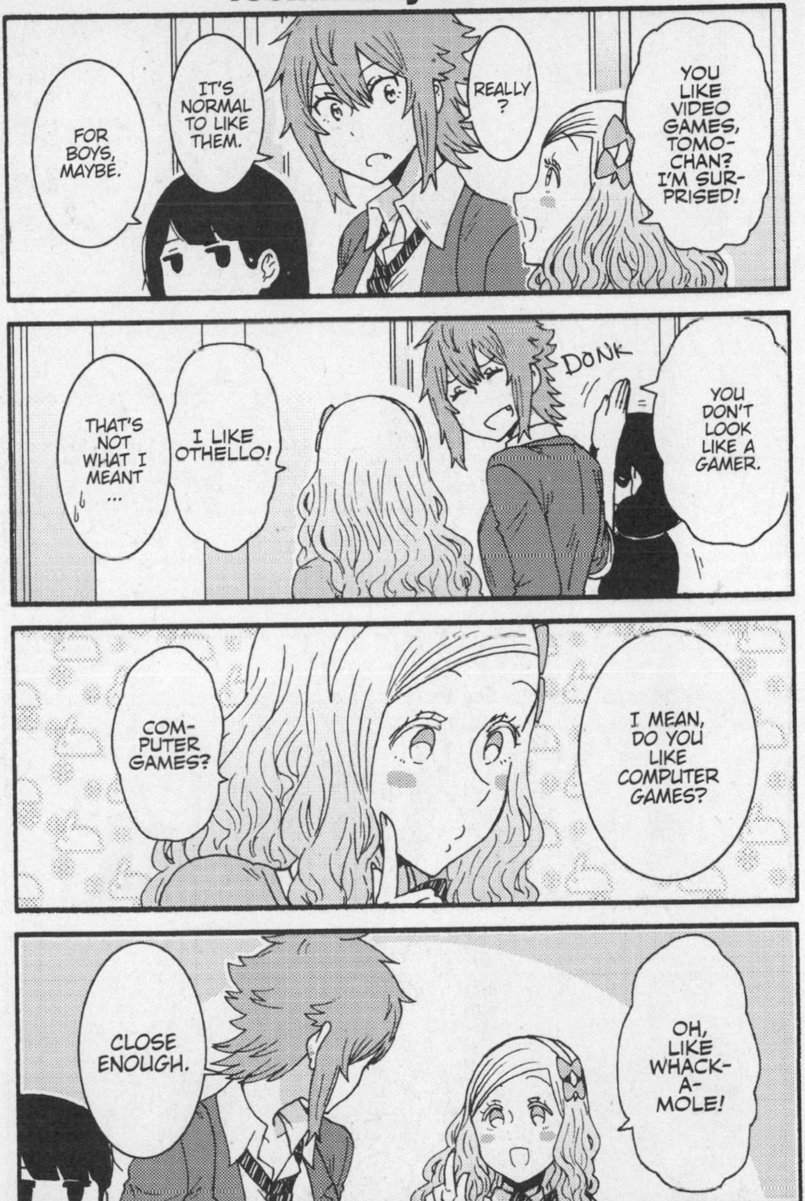
YOU LIKE VIDEO GAMES, TOMO-CHAN? I'M SURPRISED!
REALLY?
IT'S NORMAL TO LIKE THEM.
FOR BOYS, MAYBE.
YOU DON'T LOOK LIKE A GAMER.
DONK
I LIKE OTHELLO!
THAT'S NOT WHAT I MEANT...
I MEAN, DO YOU LIKE COMPUTER GAMES?
COMPUTER GAMES?
OH, LIKE WHACK-A-MOLE!
CLOSE ENOUGH.

Smooth, Very Smooth

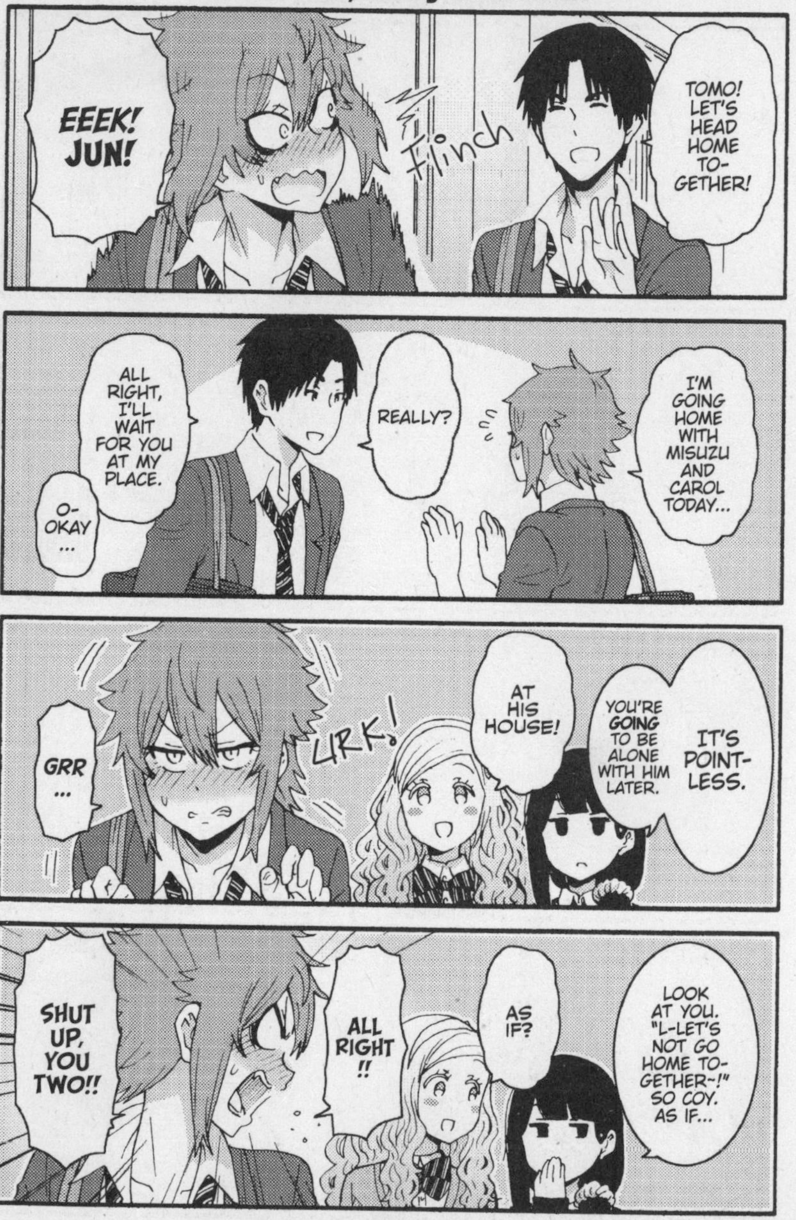
TOMO! LET'S HEAD HOME TO-GETHER!
Flinch
EEEK! JUN!
I'M GOING HOME WITH MISUZU AND CAROL TODAY...
REALLY?
ALL RIGHT, I'LL WAIT FOR YOU AT MY PLACE.
O-OKAY ...
IT'S POINT-LESS.
YOU'RE GOING TO BE ALONE WITH HIM LATER.
AT HIS HOUSE!
URK!
GRR ...
LOOK AT YOU. "L-LET'S NOT GO HOME TO-GETHER~!" SO COY. AS IF...
AS IF?
ALL RIGHT !!
SHUT UP, YOU TWO!!

Mach Speed

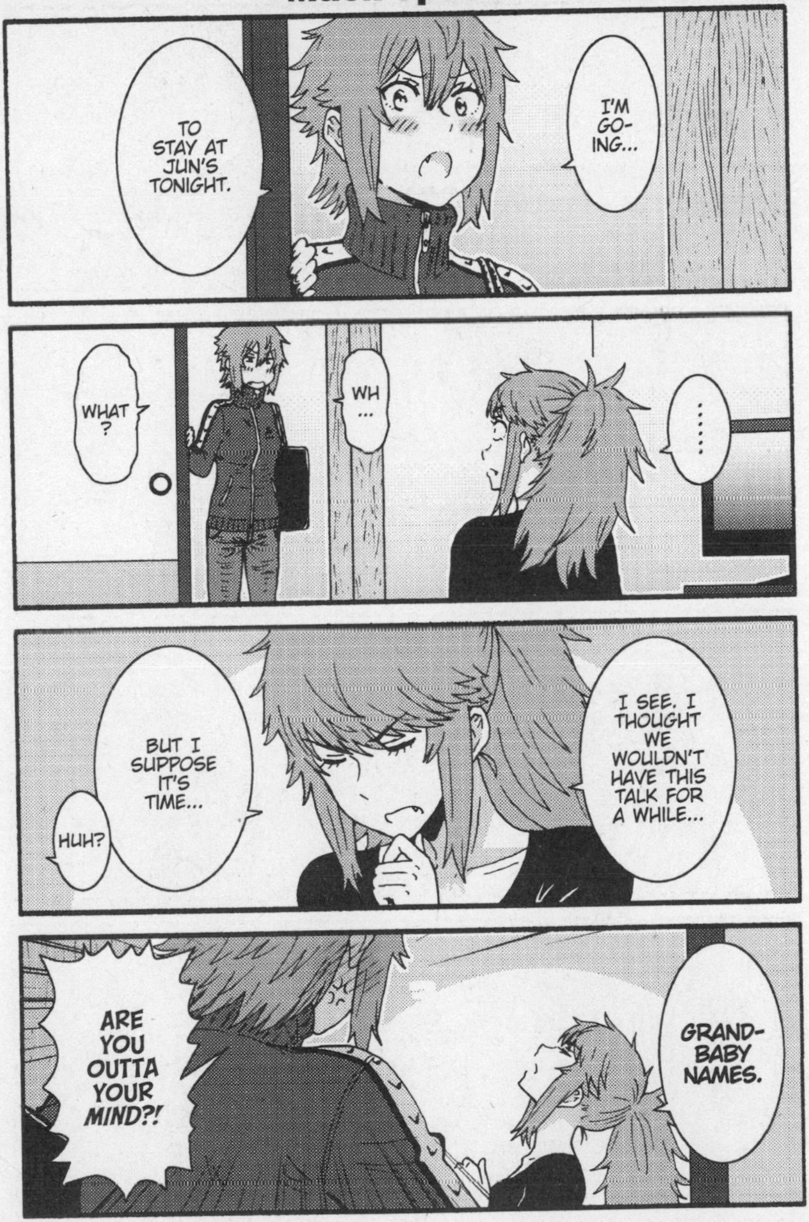
I'M GO-ING...
TO STAY AT JUN'S TONIGHT.
......
WH ...
WHAT ?
I SEE. I THOUGHT WE WOULDN'T HAVE THIS TALK FOR A WHILE...
BUT I SUPPOSE IT'S TIME...
HUH?
GRAND-BABY NAMES.
ARE YOU OUTTA YOUR *MIND?!*

No More Hand-Me-Downs

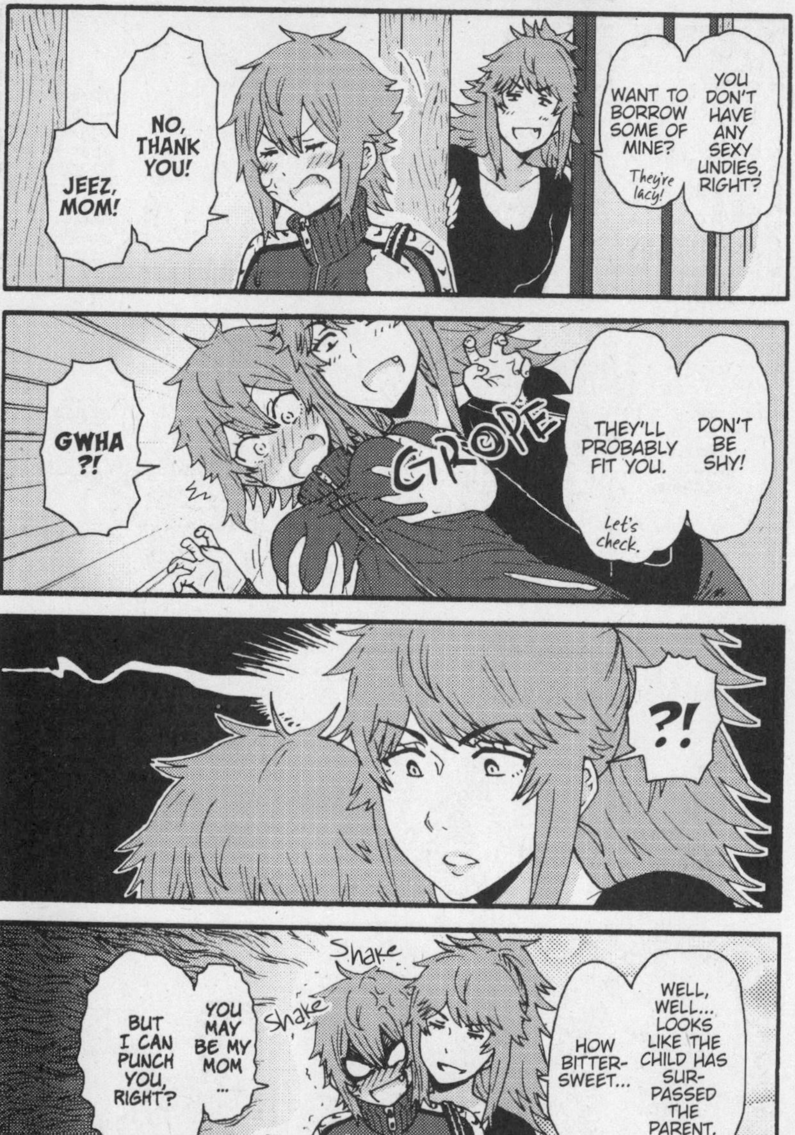
YOU DON'T HAVE ANY SEXY UNDIES, RIGHT?
WANT TO BORROW SOME OF MINE?
They're lacy!
NO, THANK YOU!
JEEZ, MOM!
DON'T BE SHY!
THEY'LL PROBABLY FIT YOU.
GROPE
Let's check.
GWHA ?!
?!
WELL, WELL... LOOKS LIKE THE CHILD HAS SUR-PASSED THE PARENT.
HOW BITTER-SWEET...
Shake
Shake
GROPE
GROPE
YOU MAY BE MY MOM ...
BUT I CAN PUNCH YOU, RIGHT?

Anticlimax

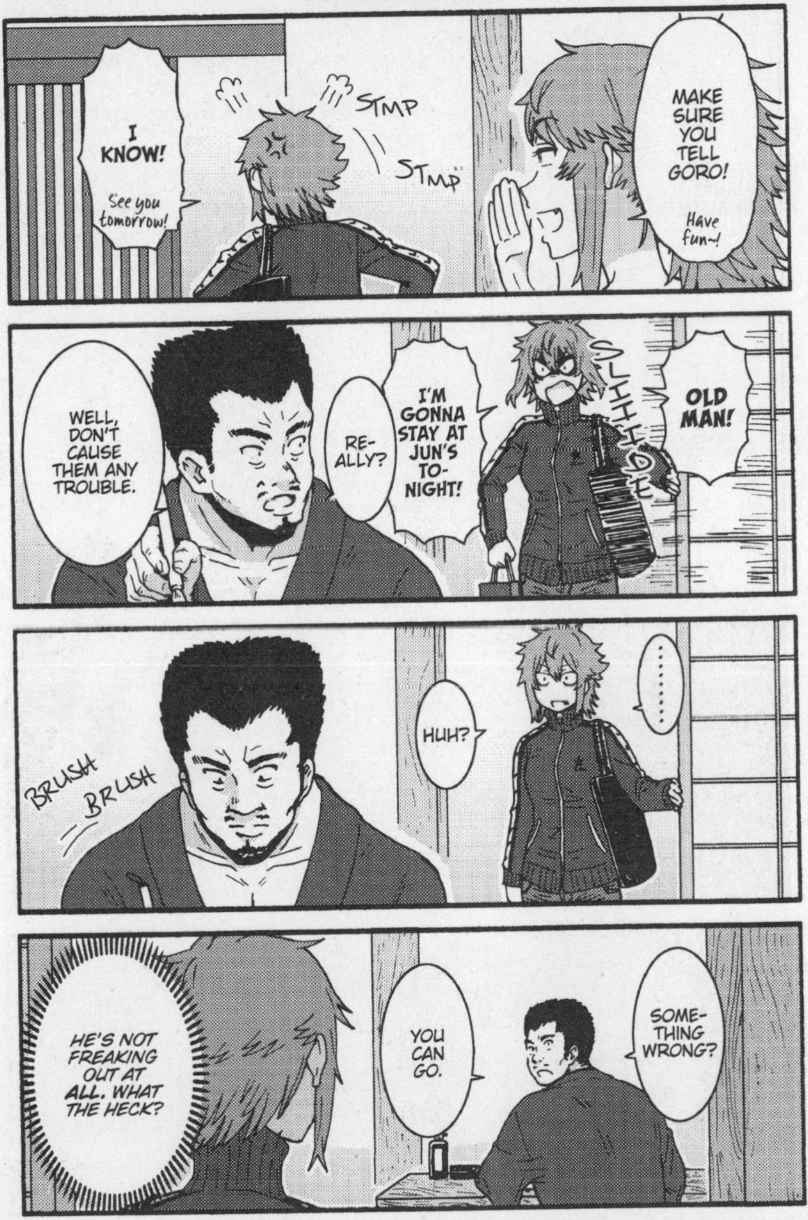
MAKE SURE YOU TELL GORO!
Have fun~!
STMP
STMP
I KNOW!
See you tomorrow!
OLD MAN!
SLIIIIDE
I'M GONNA STAY AT JUN'S TO-NIGHT!
RE-ALLY?
WELL, DON'T CAUSE THEM ANY TROUBLE.
......
HUH?
BRUSH
BRUSH
SOME-THING WRONG?
YOU CAN GO.
HE'S NOT FREAKING OUT AT ALL. WHAT THE HECK?

Four's Company, Two's a Crowd

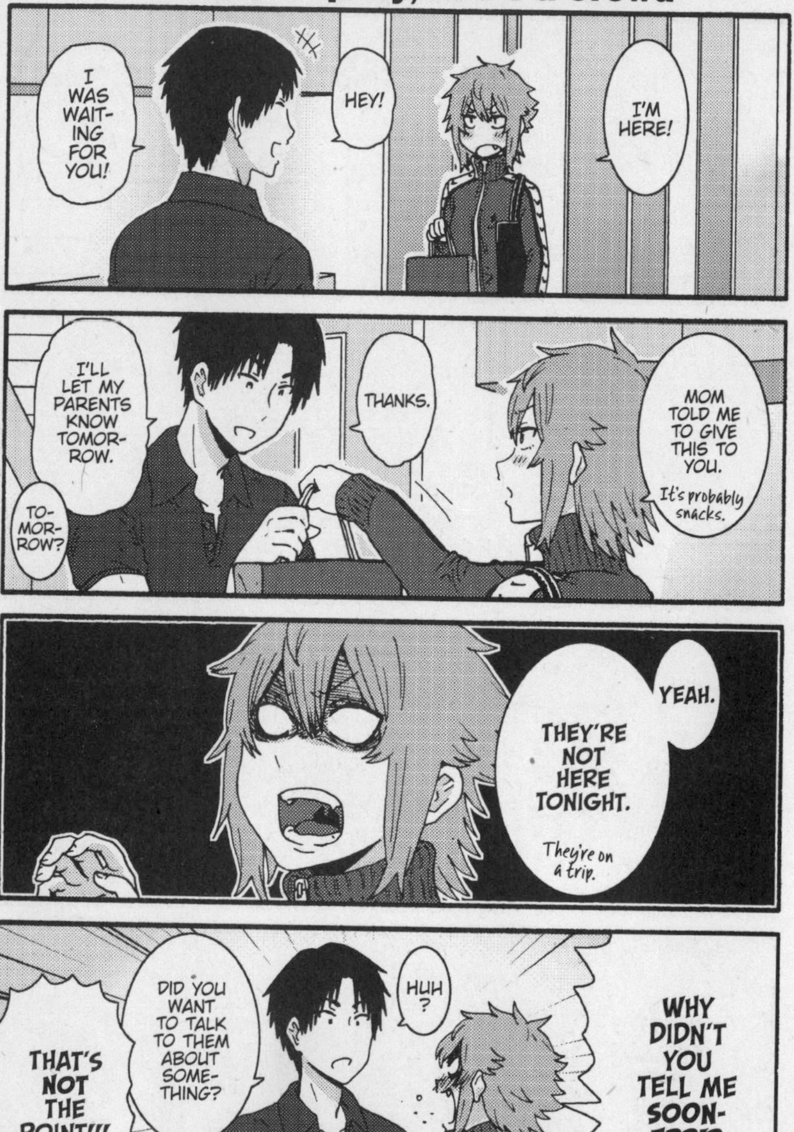

I'M HERE!
HEY!
I WAS WAITING FOR YOU!
MOM TOLD ME TO GIVE THIS TO YOU. It's probably snacks.
THANKS.
I'LL LET MY PARENTS KNOW TOMORROW.
TOMORROW?
YEAH.
THEY'RE NOT HERE TONIGHT.
They're on a trip.
WHY DIDN'T YOU TELL ME SOONER?!?
HUH?
DID YOU WANT TO TALK TO THEM ABOUT SOMETHING?
THAT'S NOT THE POINT!!!

Mach 2

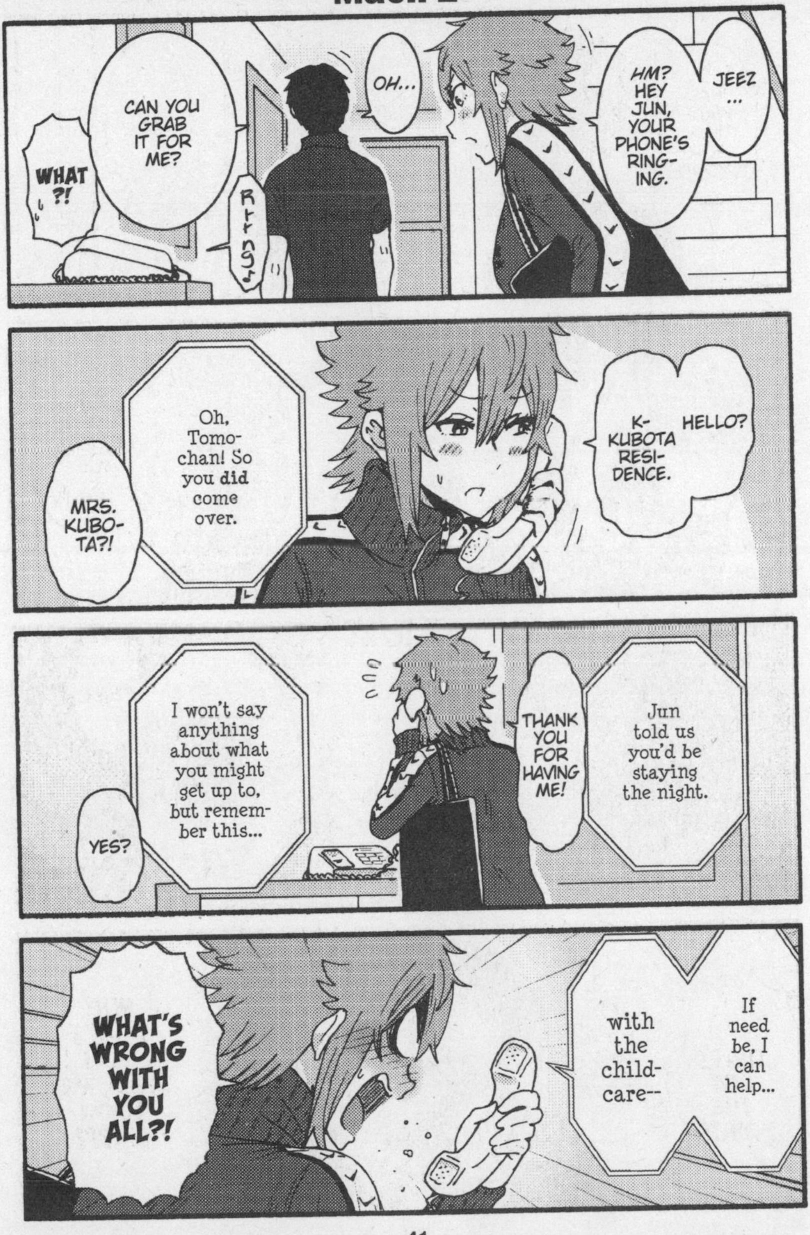
JEEZ ...
HM? HEY JUN, YOUR PHONE'S RING-ING.
OH...
Rrrng♪
CAN YOU GRAB IT FOR ME?
WHAT?!
HELLO?
K-KUBOTA RESI-DENCE.
Oh, Tomo-chan! So you **did** come over.
MRS. KUBOTA?!
Jun told us you'd be staying the night.
THANK YOU FOR HAVING ME!
I won't say anything about what you might get up to, but remem-ber this...
YES?
If need be, I can help...
with the child-care--
WHAT'S WRONG WITH YOU ALL?!

Like a Total Eclipse

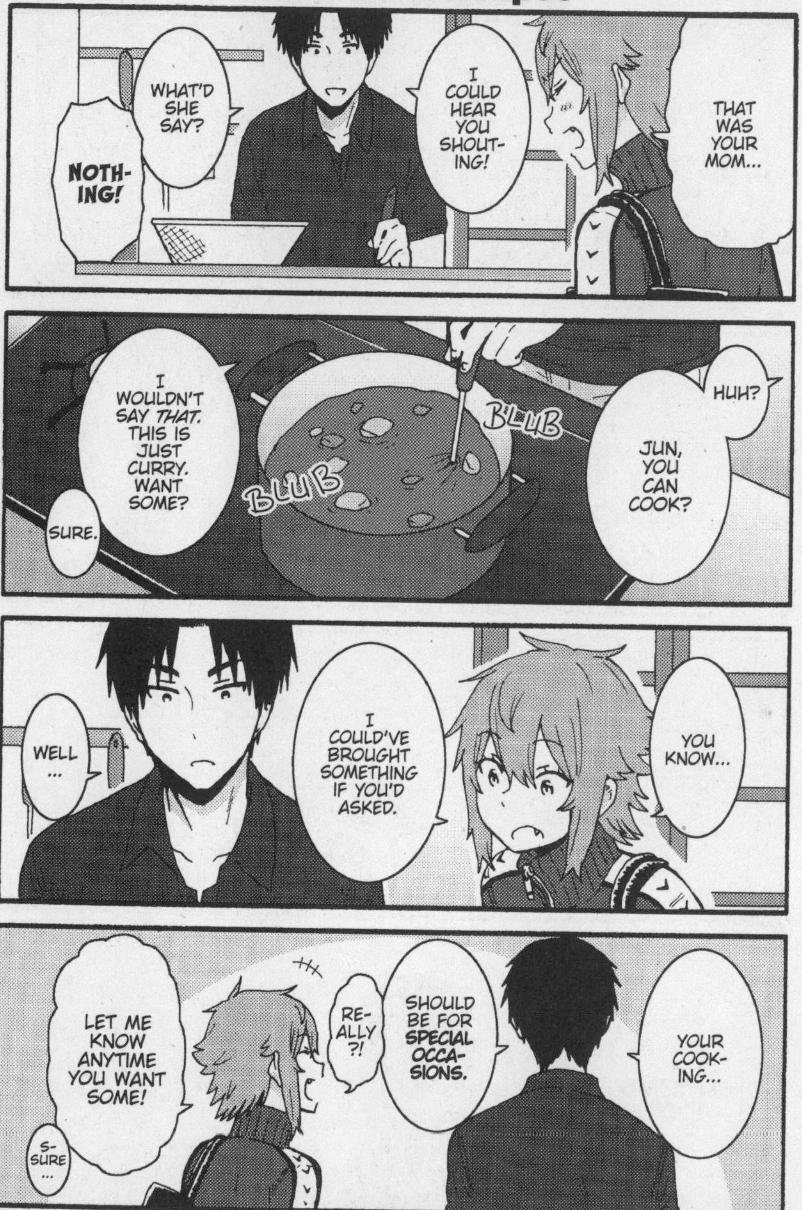
THAT WAS YOUR MOM...
I COULD HEAR YOU SHOUTING!
WHAT'D SHE SAY?
NOTHING!
HUH?
JUN, YOU CAN COOK?
BLUB
BLUB
I WOULDN'T SAY *THAT*. THIS IS JUST CURRY. WANT SOME?
SURE.
YOU KNOW...
I COULD'VE BROUGHT SOMETHING IF YOU'D ASKED.
WELL...
YOUR COOKING...
SHOULD BE FOR **SPECIAL OCCASIONS.**
REALLY?!
LET ME KNOW ANYTIME YOU WANT SOME!
S-SURE...

It Conserves Water

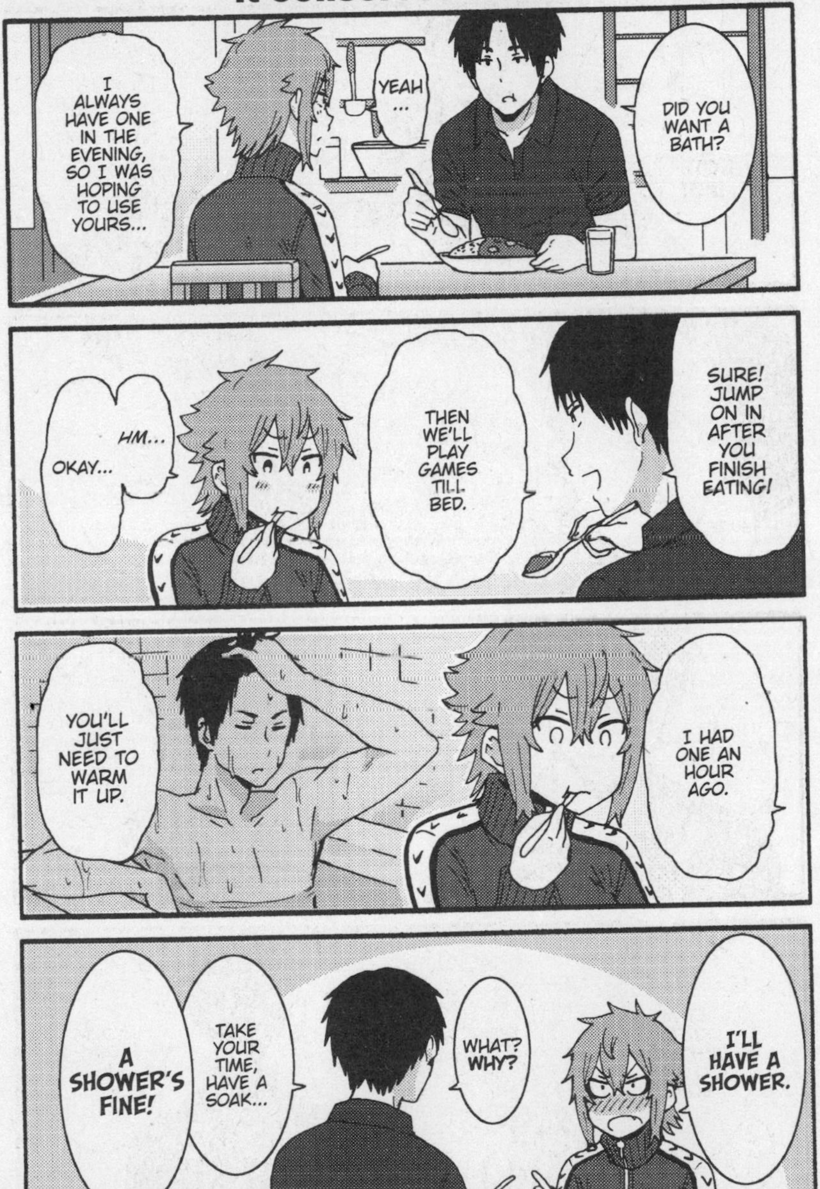
DID YOU WANT A BATH?
YEAH ...
I ALWAYS HAVE ONE IN THE EVENING, SO I WAS HOPING TO USE YOURS...
SURE! JUMP ON IN AFTER YOU FINISH EATING!
THEN WE'LL PLAY GAMES TILL BED.
HM... OKAY...
I HAD ONE AN HOUR AGO.
YOU'LL JUST NEED TO WARM IT UP.
I'LL HAVE A SHOWER.
WHAT? WHY?
TAKE YOUR TIME, HAVE A SOAK...
A SHOWER'S FINE!

A Moment...

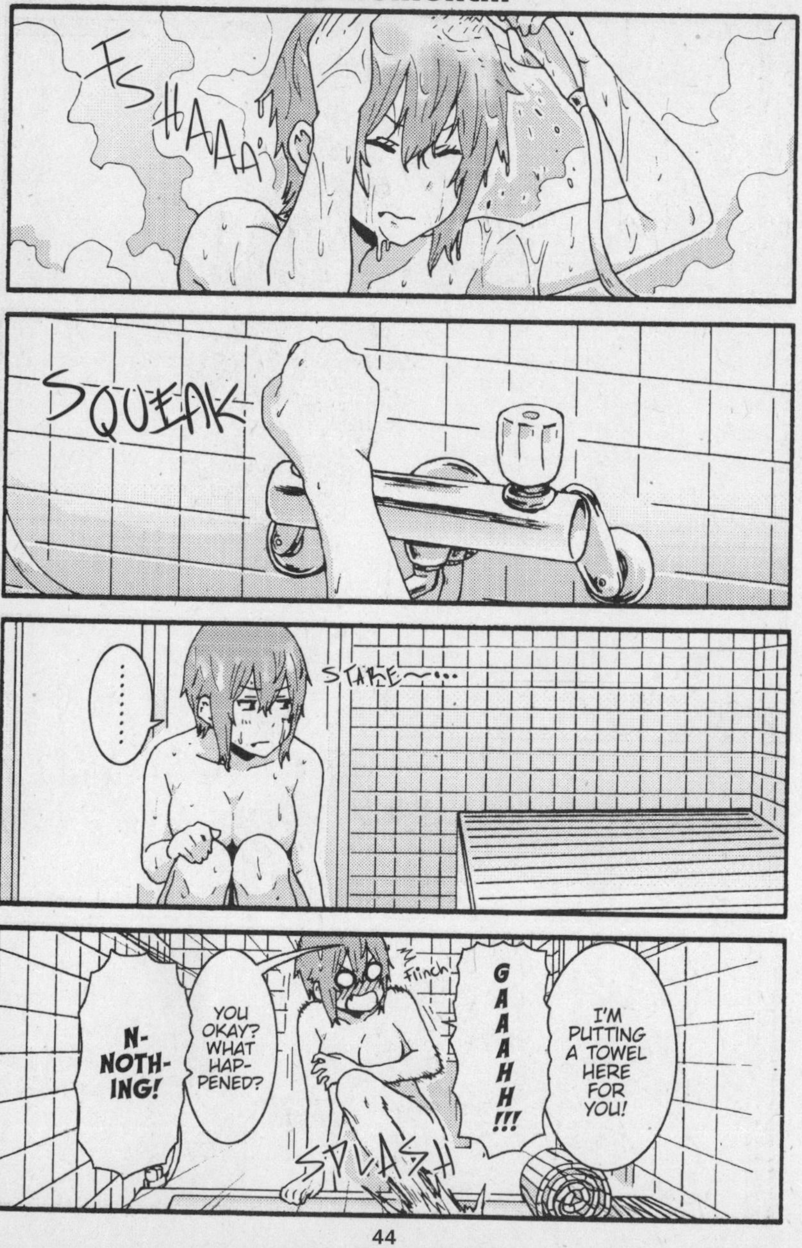
FSHAAAA
SQUEAK
STARE~...
......
I'M PUTTING A TOWEL HERE FOR YOU!
GAAAHH!!!
Flinch
YOU OKAY? WHAT HAP-PENED?
N-NOTH-ING!
SPLASH

Thinking of Her in My Bathroom

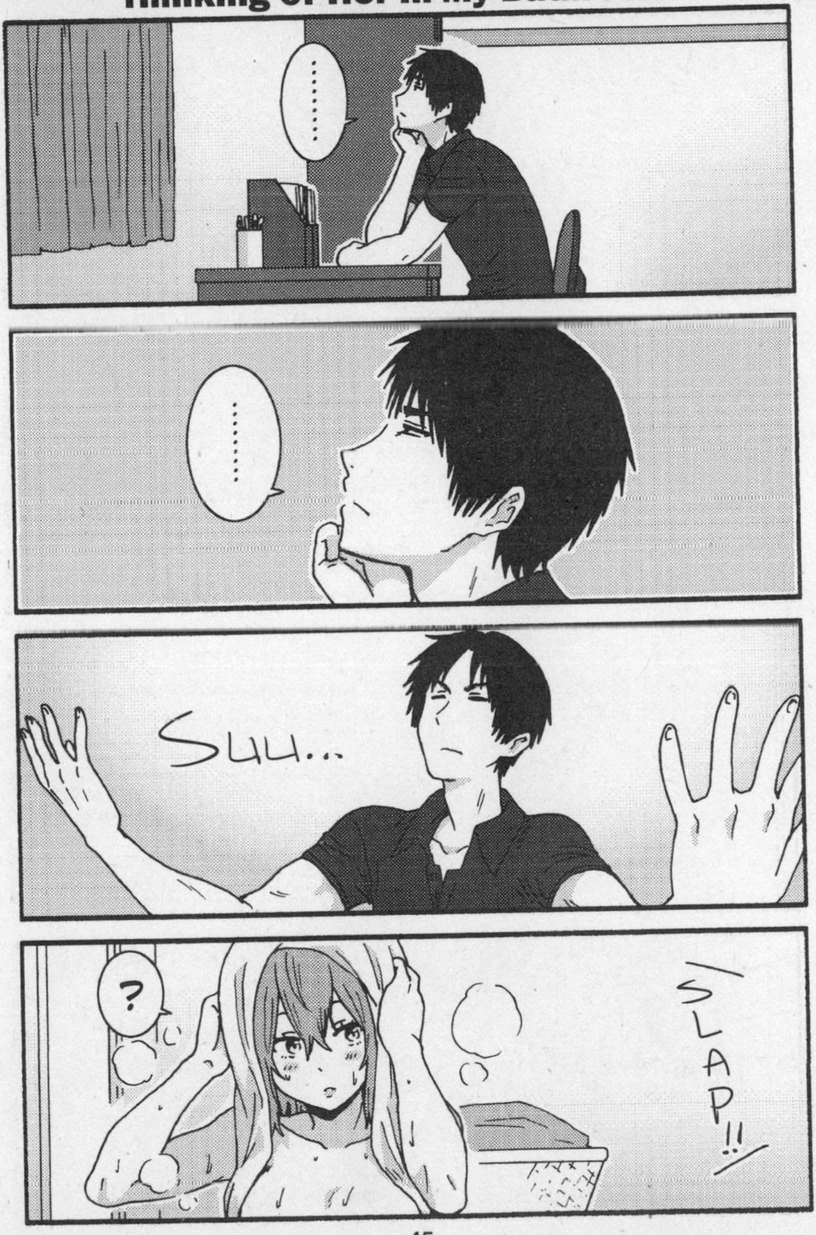
……
……
Suu...
?
SLAP!!

My Damp Friend

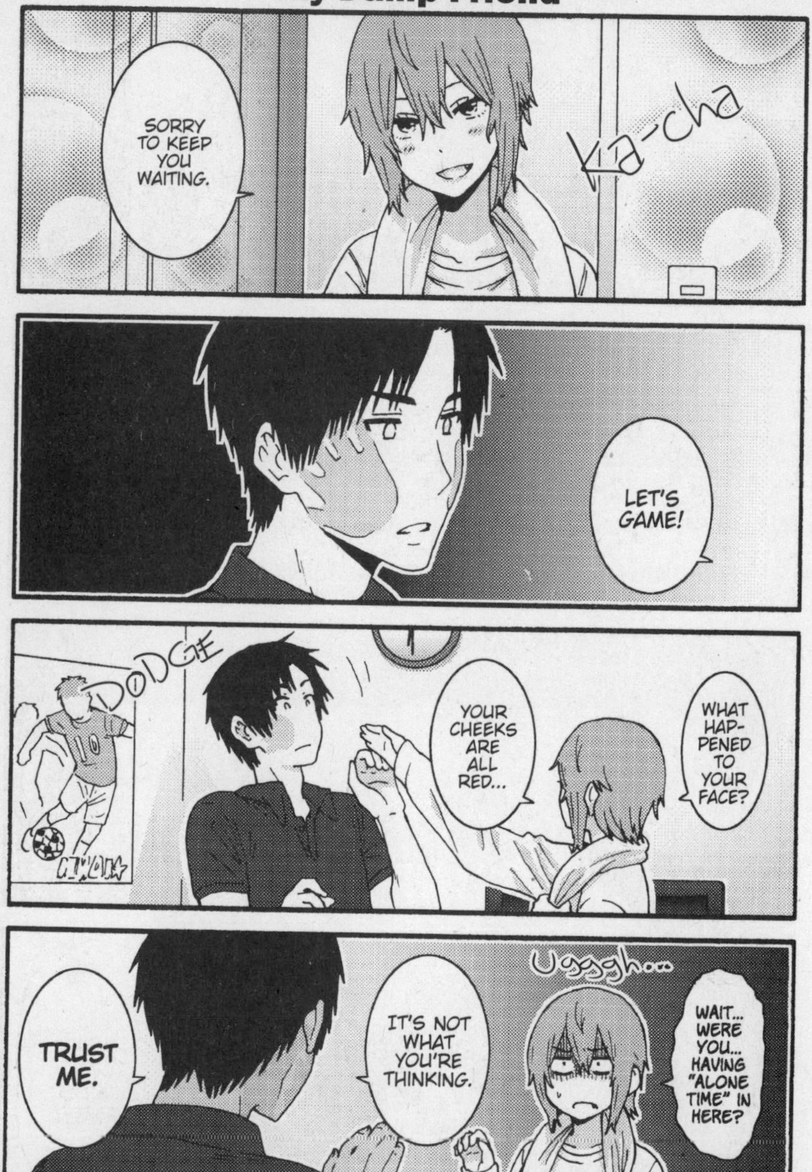
Ka-cha
SORRY TO KEEP YOU WAITING.
LET'S GAME!
WHAT HAP-PENED TO YOUR FACE?
YOUR CHEEKS ARE ALL RED...
DODGE
Ugggh...
WAIT... WERE YOU... HAVING "ALONE TIME" IN HERE?
IT'S NOT WHAT YOU'RE THINKING.
TRUST ME.

My Drying Friend

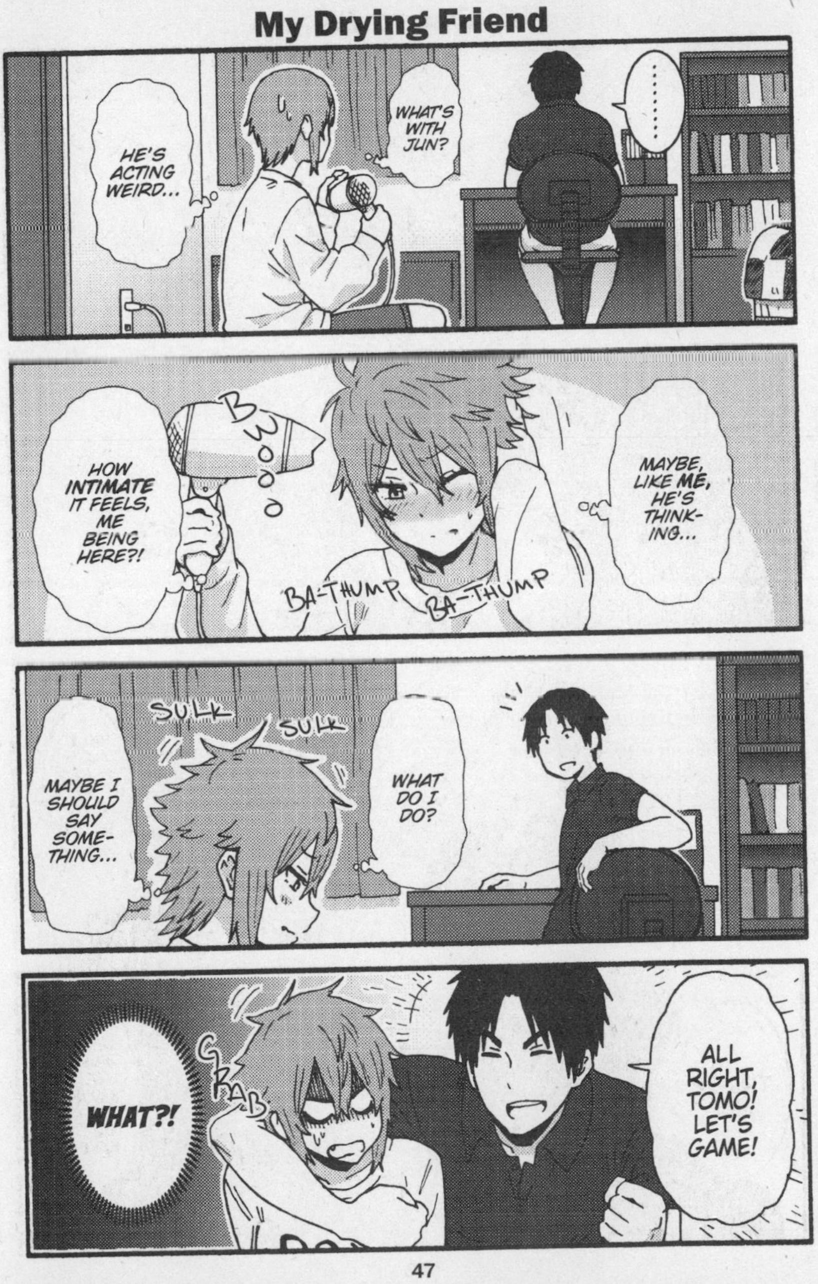

……
WHAT'S WITH JUN?
HE'S ACTING WEIRD...
MAYBE, LIKE ME, HE'S THINKING...
BWOOOO
HOW INTIMATE IT FEELS, ME BEING HERE?!
BA-THUMP BA-THUMP
WHAT DO I DO?
SULK SULK
MAYBE I SHOULD SAY SOMETHING...
ALL RIGHT, TOMO! LET'S GAME!
GRAB
WHAT?!

Glad You're Having Fun

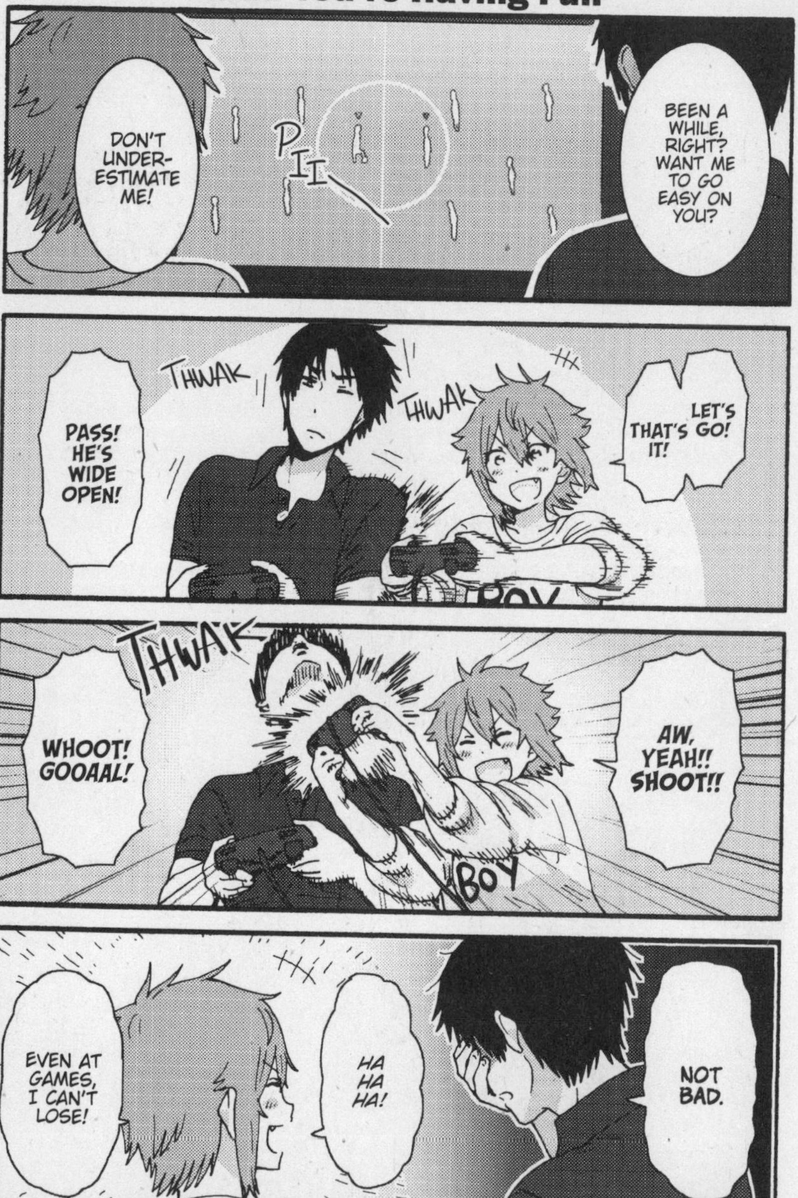

BEEN A WHILE, RIGHT? WANT ME TO GO EASY ON YOU?
PII
DON'T UNDER-ESTIMATE ME!
LET'S GO! THAT'S IT!
THWAK
THWAK
PASS! HE'S WIDE OPEN!
AW, YEAH!! SHOOT!!
THWAK
WHOOT! GOOAAL!
BOY
NOT BAD.
HA HA HA!
EVEN AT GAMES, I CAN'T LOSE!

Trust Your People

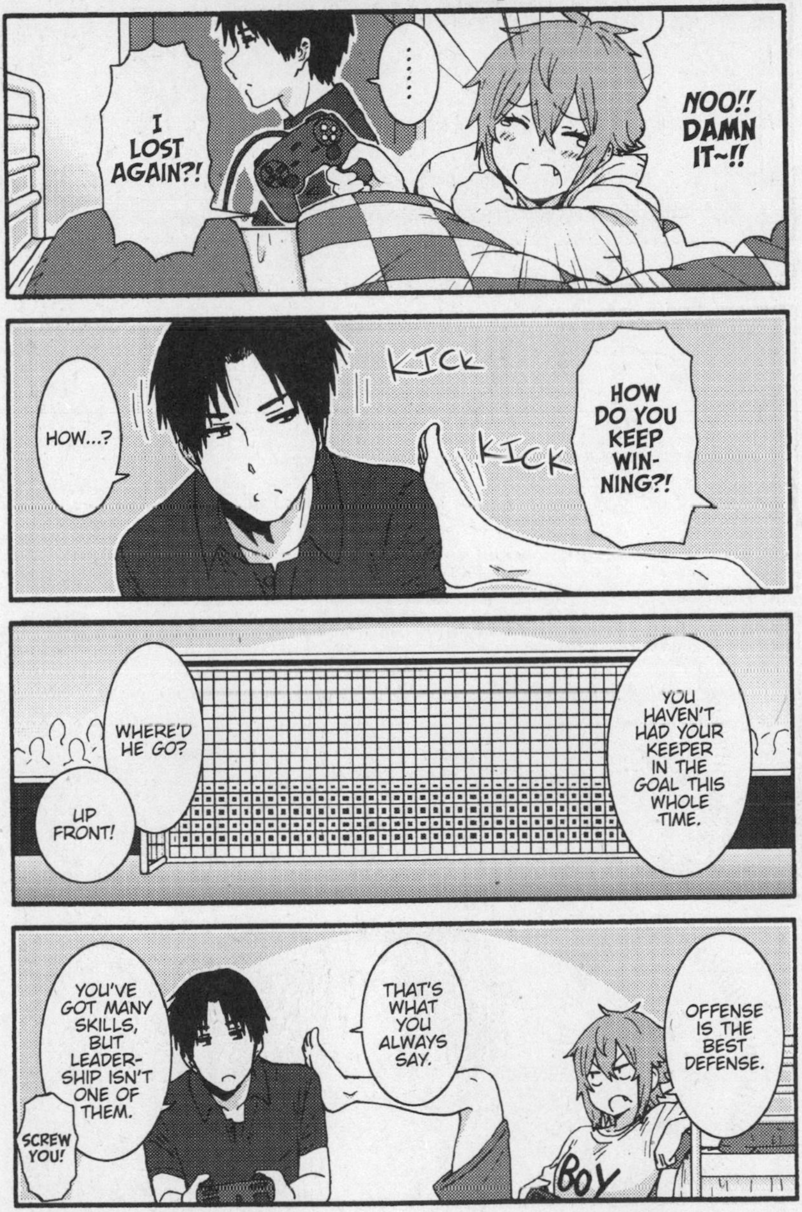

NOO!! DAMN IT~!!
......
I LOST AGAIN?!
HOW DO YOU KEEP WIN-NING?!
KICK
KICK
HOW...?
YOU HAVEN'T HAD YOUR KEEPER IN THE GOAL THIS WHOLE TIME.
WHERE'D HE GO?
UP FRONT!
OFFENSE IS THE BEST DEFENSE.
BOY
THAT'S WHAT YOU ALWAYS SAY.
YOU'VE GOT MANY SKILLS, BUT LEADER-SHIP ISN'T ONE OF THEM.
SCREW YOU!

Glimpse of the Past

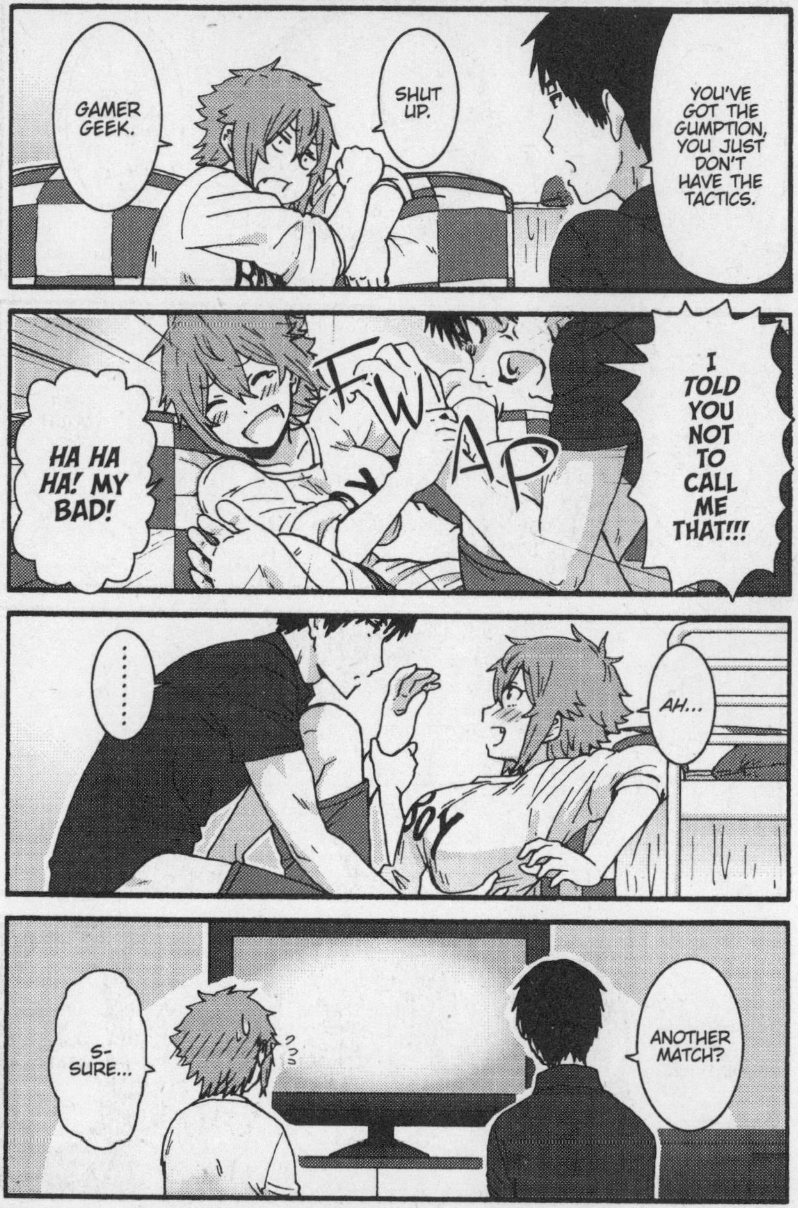

YOU'VE GOT THE GUMPTION, YOU JUST DON'T HAVE THE TACTICS.
SHUT UP.
GAMER GEEK.
I TOLD YOU NOT TO CALL ME THAT!!!
FWAP
HA HA HA! MY BAD!
AH...
......
ANOTHER MATCH?
S-SURE...

He's Such a Rebel

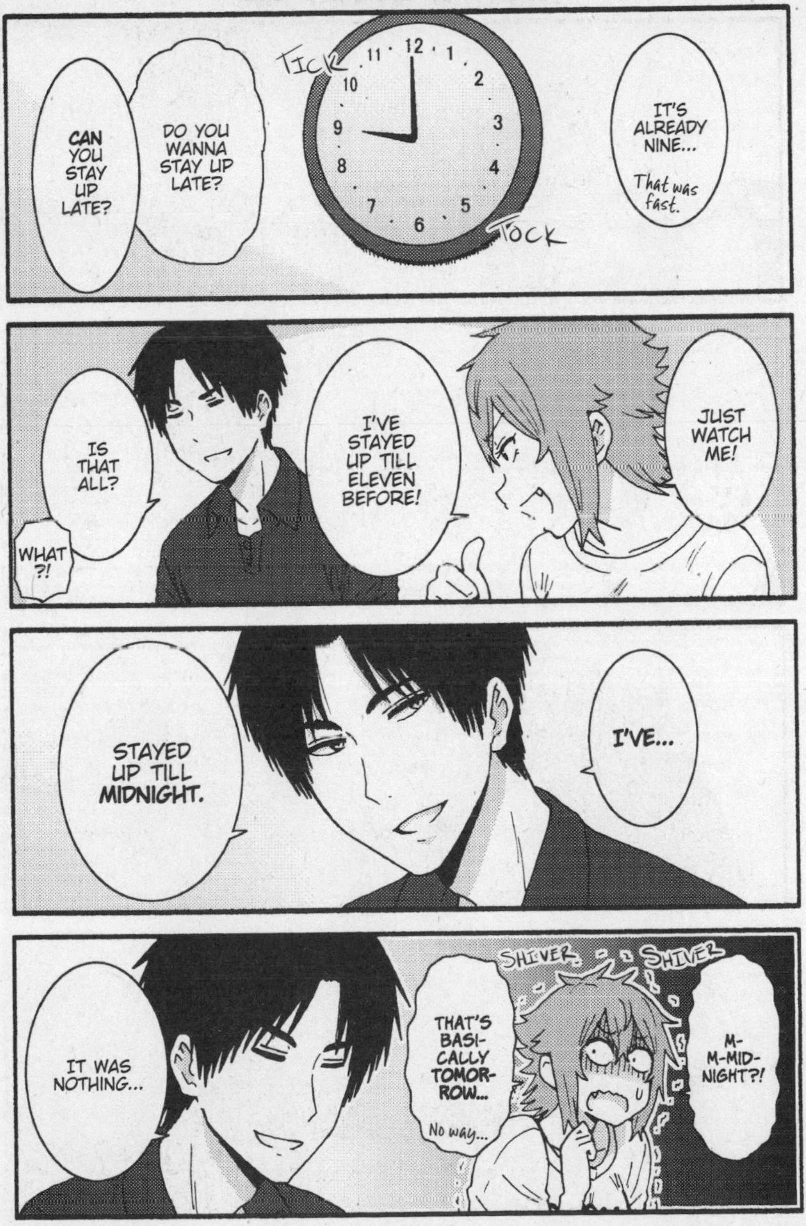
IT'S ALREADY NINE...
That was fast.
TICK
TOCK
DO YOU WANNA STAY UP LATE?
CAN YOU STAY UP LATE?
JUST WATCH ME!
I'VE STAYED UP TILL ELEVEN BEFORE!
IS THAT ALL?
WHAT?!
I'VE...
STAYED UP TILL MIDNIGHT.
SHIVER
SHIVER
M-M-MIDNIGHT?!
THAT'S BASICALLY TOMORROW...
No way...
IT WAS NOTHING...

Regrets?

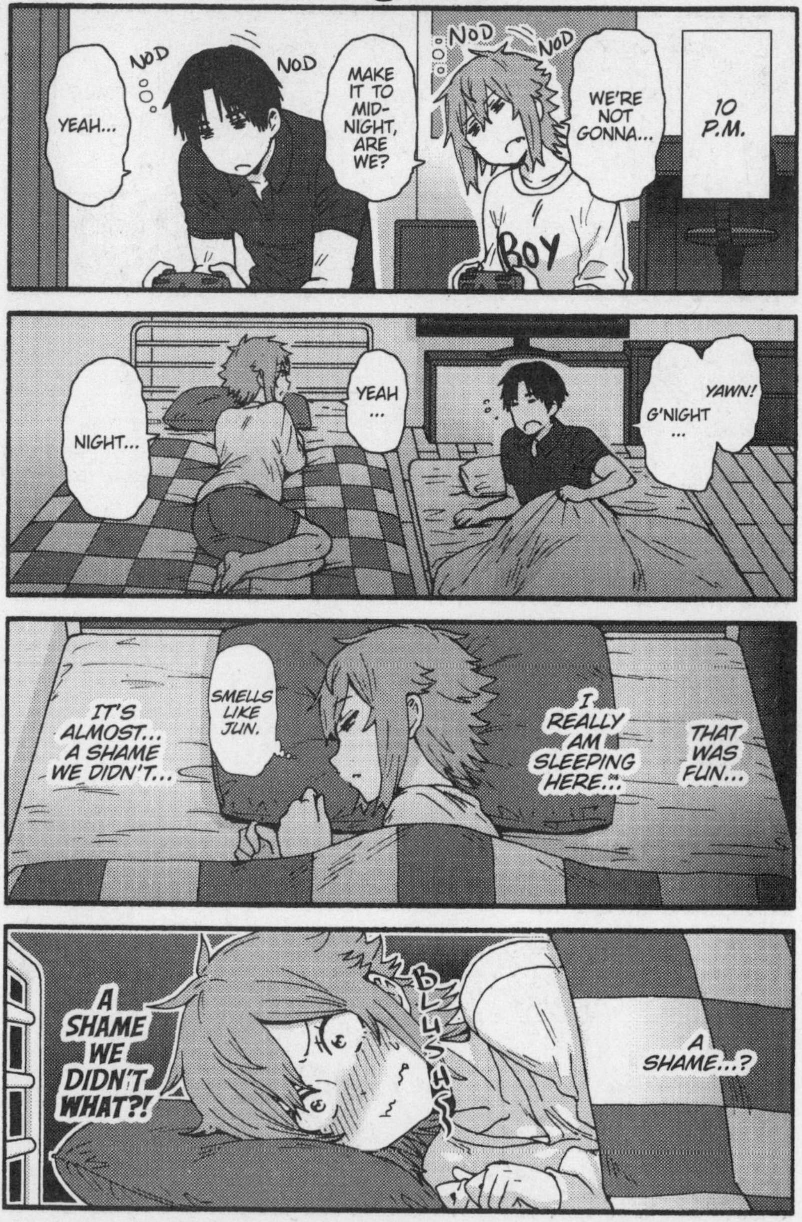

10 P.M.
WE'RE NOT GONNA...
NOD
NOD
MAKE IT TO MID-NIGHT, ARE WE?
NOD
NOD
YEAH...
YAWN! G'NIGHT...
YEAH...
NIGHT...
THAT WAS FUN...
I REALLY AM SLEEPING HERE...
SMELLS LIKE JUN.
IT'S ALMOST... A SHAME WE DIDN'T...
A SHAME...?
BLUSH
A SHAME WE DIDN'T WHAT?!

One-Sided Chat

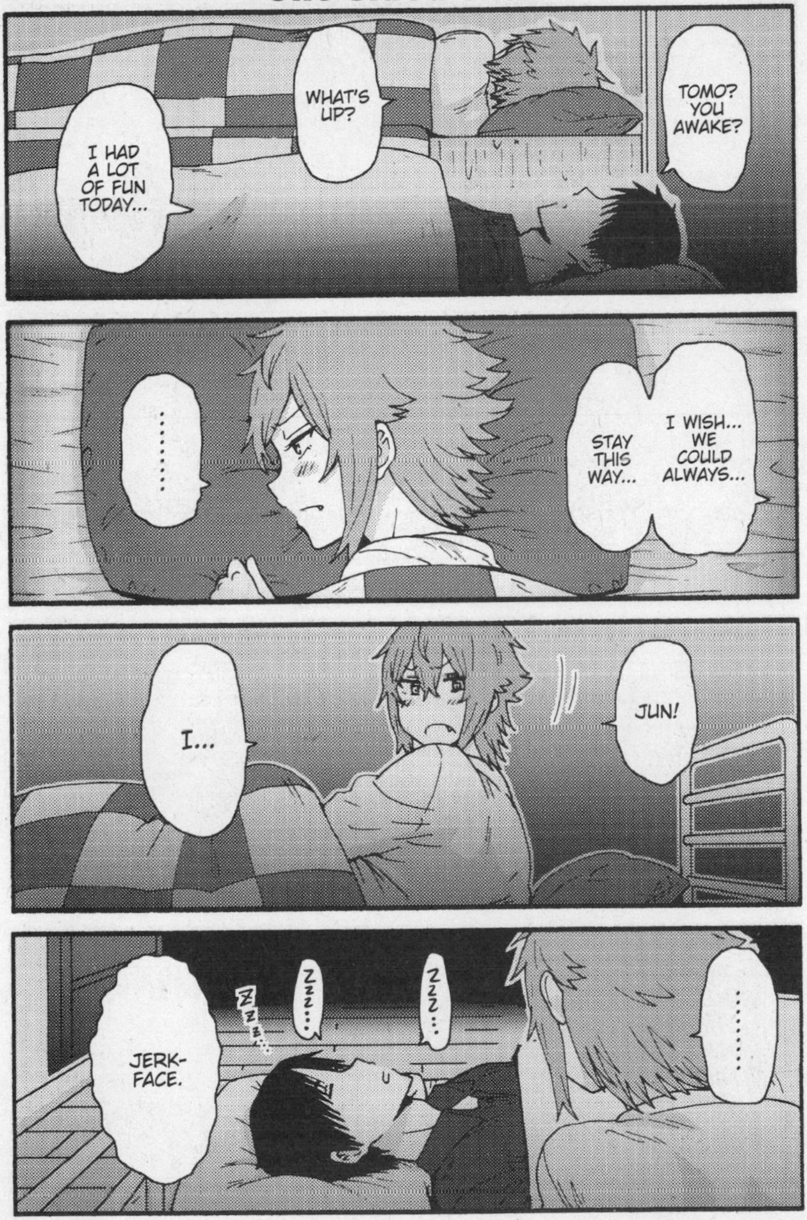
TOMO? YOU AWAKE?
WHAT'S UP?
I HAD A LOT OF FUN TODAY...
I WISH... WE COULD ALWAYS...
STAY THIS WAY...
......
JUN!
I...
......
ZZZ...
ZZZ...
ZZZ...
JERK-FACE.

Still Life

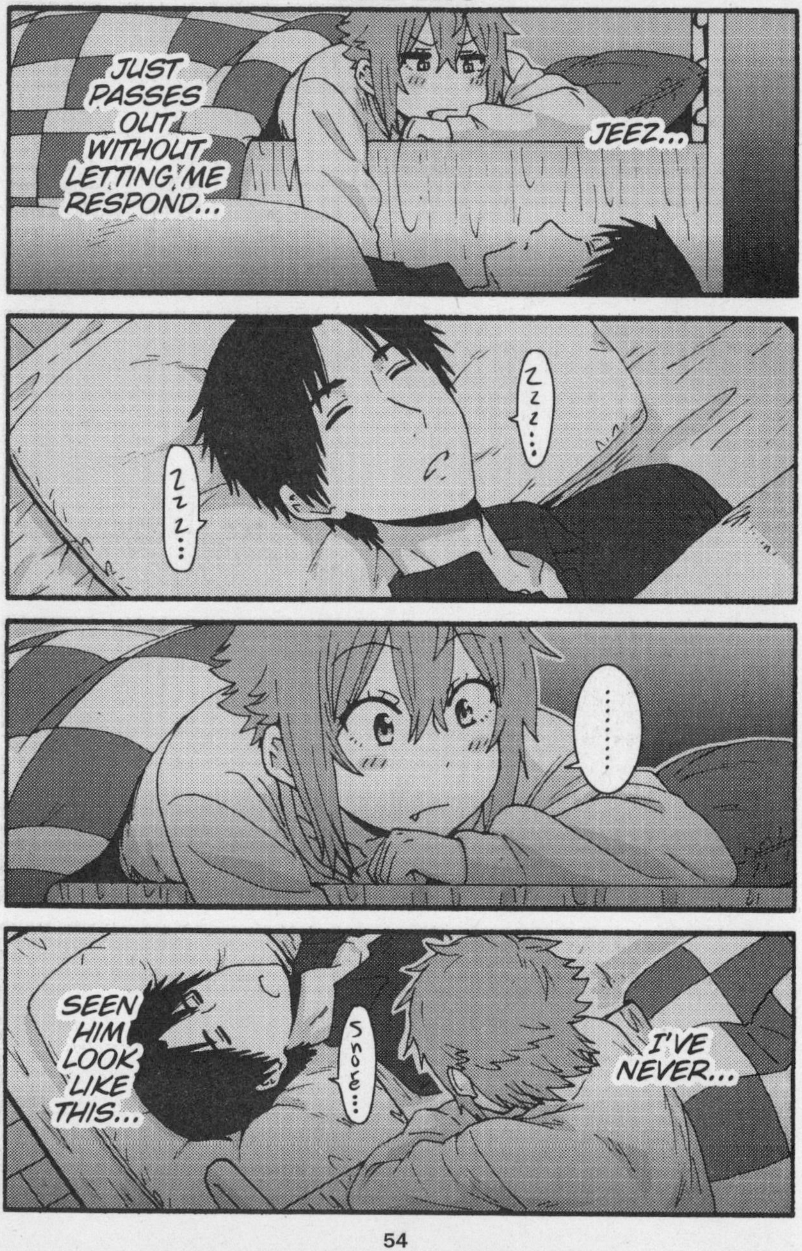
JEEZ...
JUST PASSES OUT WITHOUT LETTING ME RESPOND...
Zzz...
Zzz...
......
I'VE NEVER...
Snore...
SEEN HIM LOOK LIKE THIS...

Sleep and the Unjust

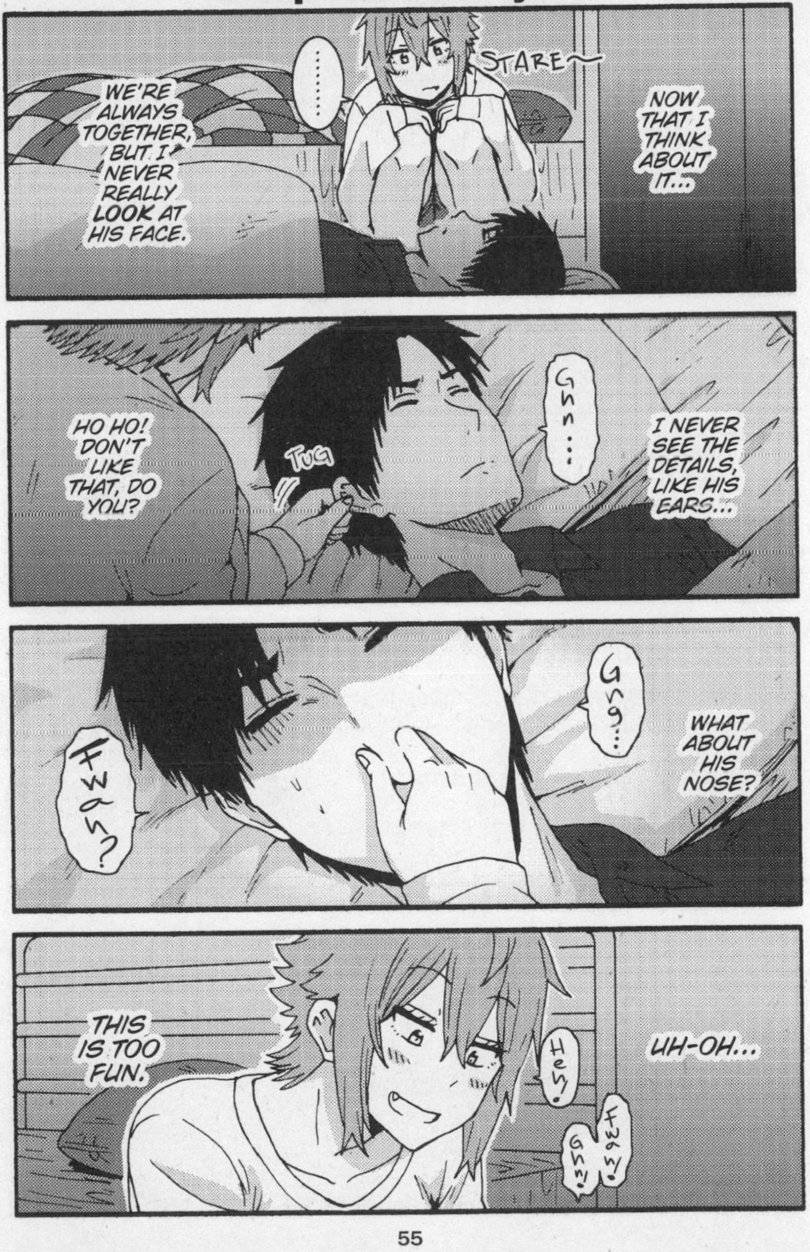
NOW THAT I THINK ABOUT IT...
STARE~
......
WE'RE ALWAYS TOGETHER, BUT I NEVER REALLY LOOK AT HIS FACE.
I NEVER SEE THE DETAILS, LIKE HIS EARS...
Gnn...
TUG
HO HO! DON'T LIKE THAT, DO YOU?
WHAT ABOUT HIS NOSE?
Gng...
Fwah?
UH-OH...
Fwah!
Gnn!
Heh!
THIS IS TOO FUN.

Sleep Wrestling

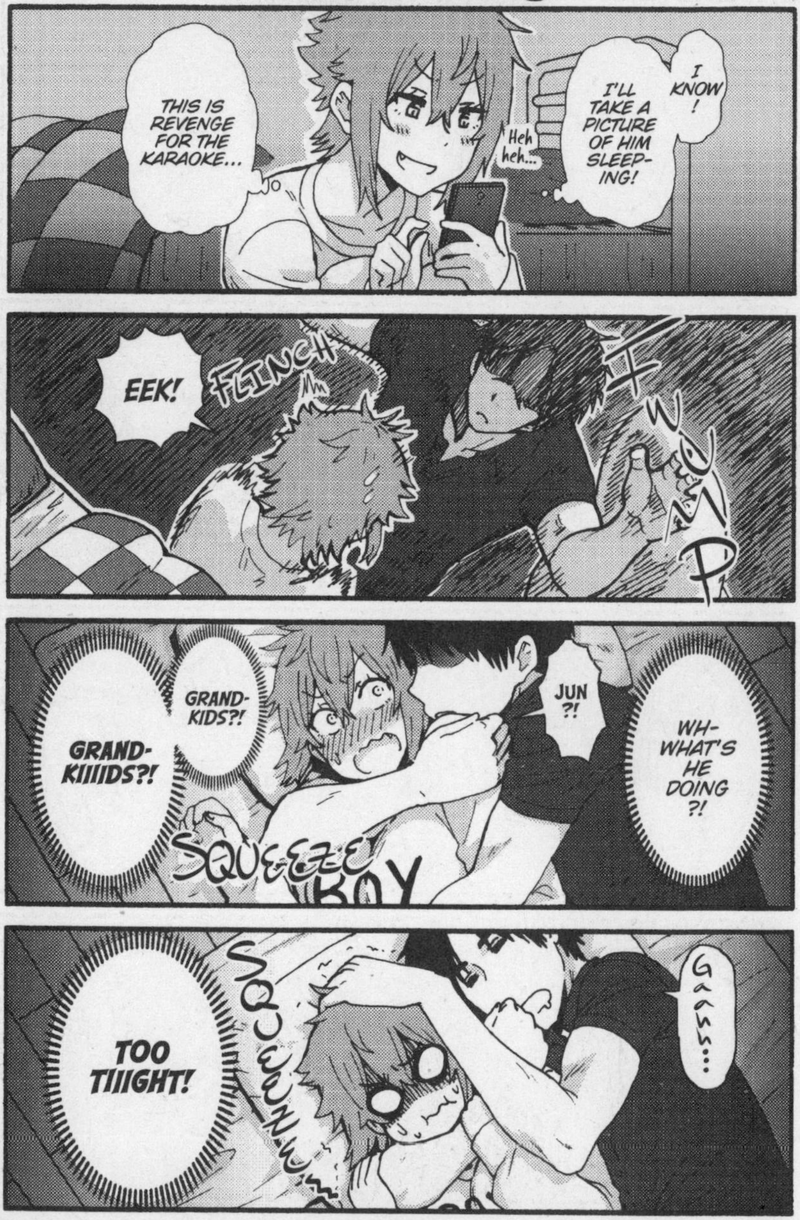
I KNOW!
I'LL TAKE A PICTURE OF HIM SLEEPING!
Heh heh...
THIS IS REVENGE FOR THE KARAOKE...
FLINCH
EEK!
WH-WHAT'S HE DOING?!
JUN?!
GRAND-KIDS?!
GRAND-KIIIIDS?!
SQUEEZE
Gauuh...
TOO TIIIGHT!

Morning

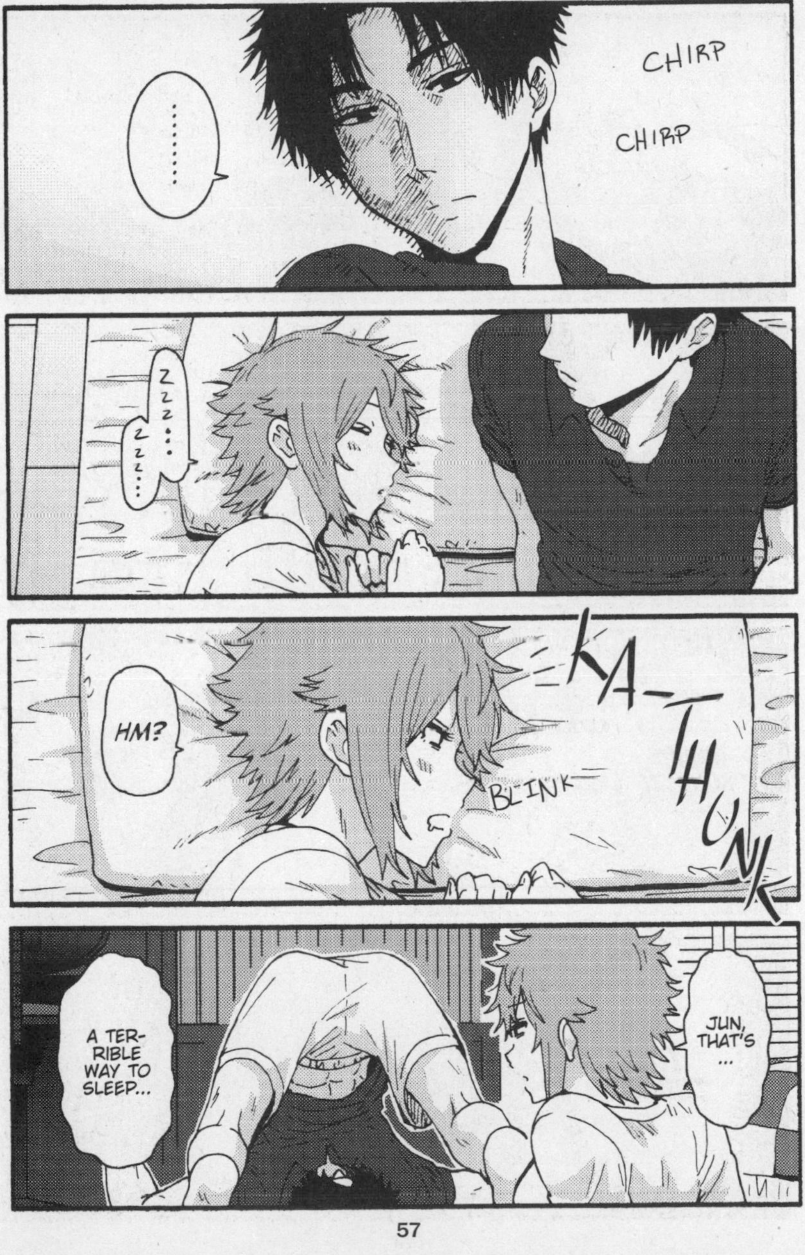
CHIRP
CHIRP
......
ZZZ...
ZZZ...
KA-THUNK
BLINK
HM?
JUN, THAT'S ...
A TER-RIBLE WAY TO SLEEP...

Lost Time

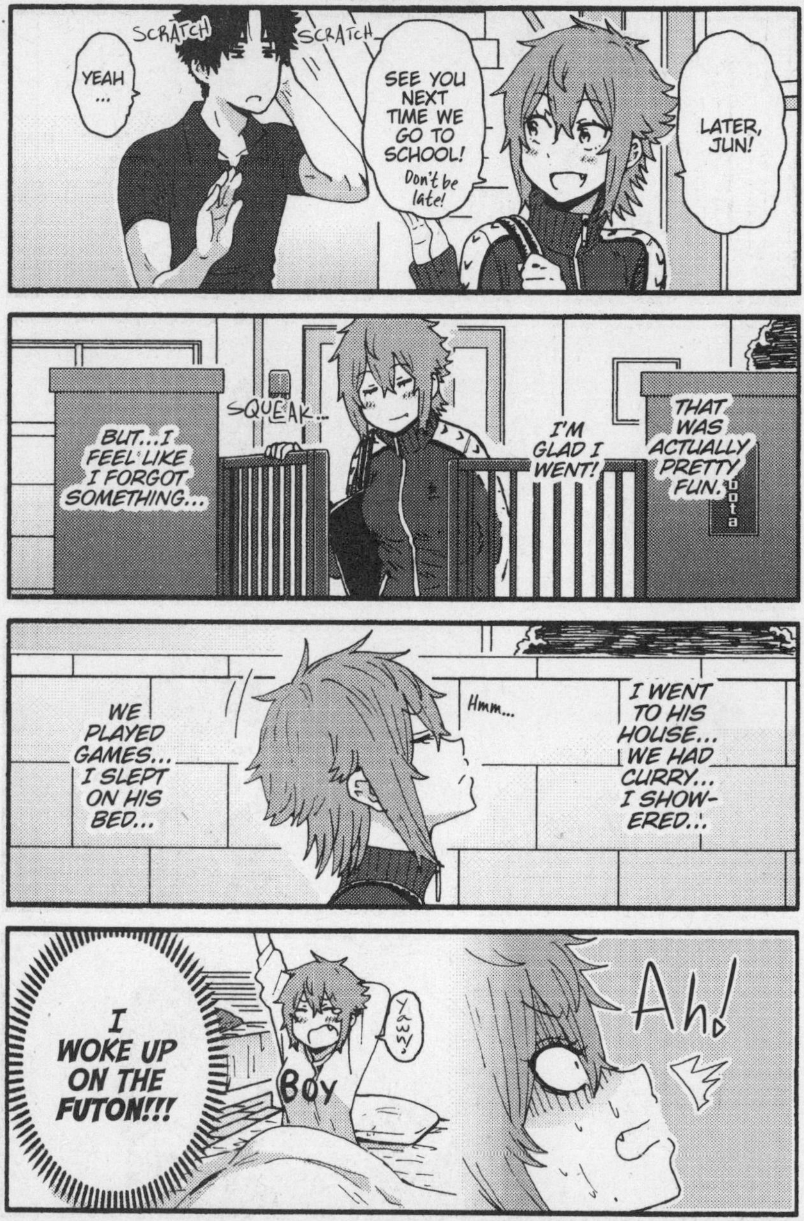
LATER, JUN!
SEE YOU NEXT TIME WE GO TO SCHOOL! Don't be late!
SCRATCH SCRATCH
YEAH...
THAT WAS ACTUALLY PRETTY FUN.
I'M GLAD I WENT!
SQUEAK...
BUT...I FEEL LIKE I FORGOT SOMETHING...
I WENT TO HIS HOUSE... WE HAD CURRY... I SHOWERED...
Hmm...
WE PLAYED GAMES... I SLEPT ON HIS BED...
Ah!
Yawn!
Boy
I WOKE UP ON THE FUTON!!!

Aftermath

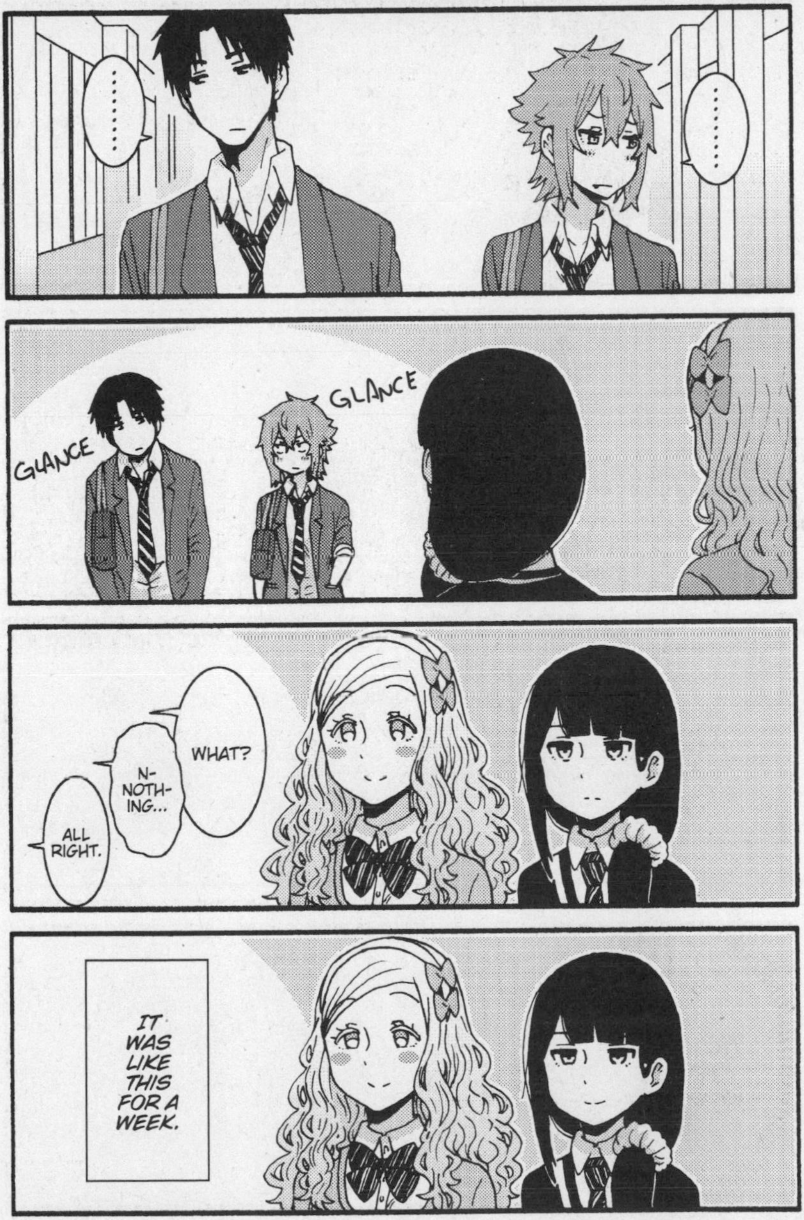
……
……
GLANCE
GLANCE
WHAT?
N-NOTHING...
ALL RIGHT.
IT WAS LIKE THIS FOR A WEEK.

OMAKE

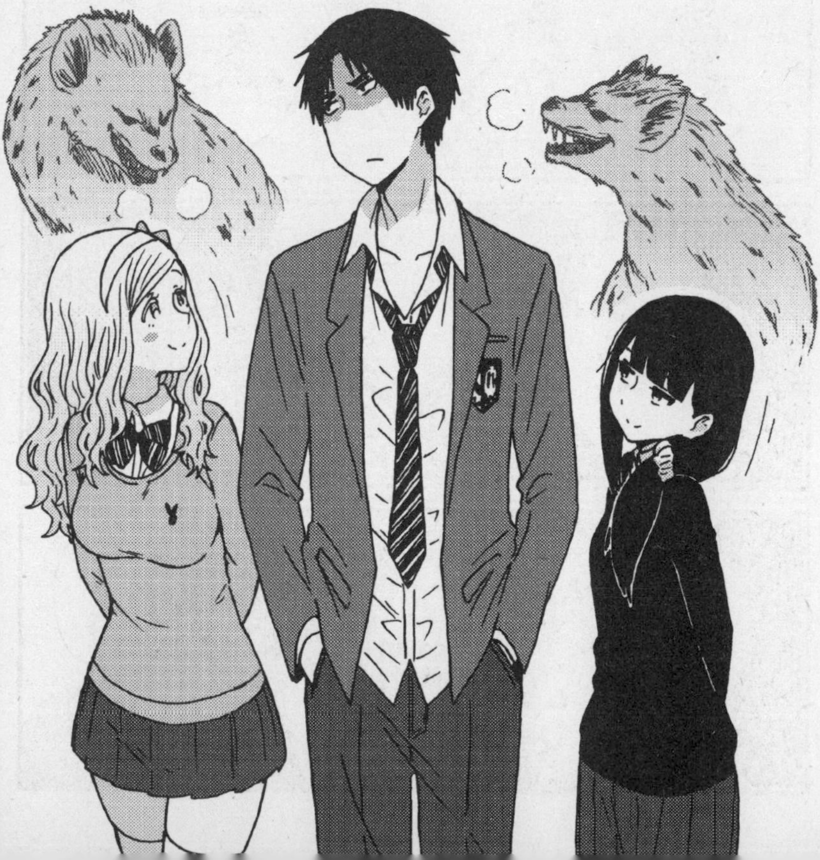

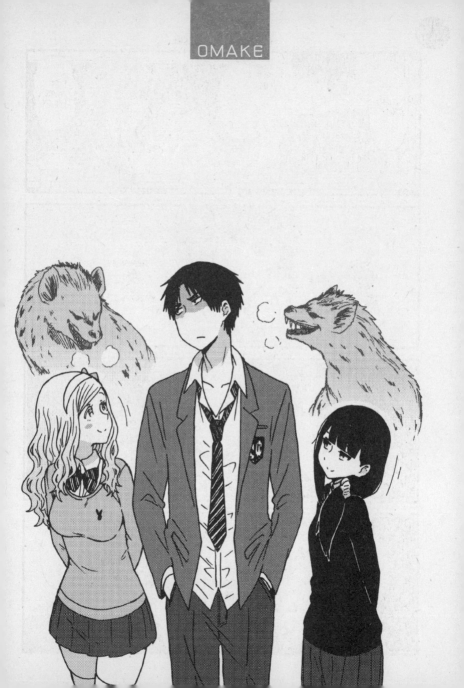

Ch. 21

It's No Joke

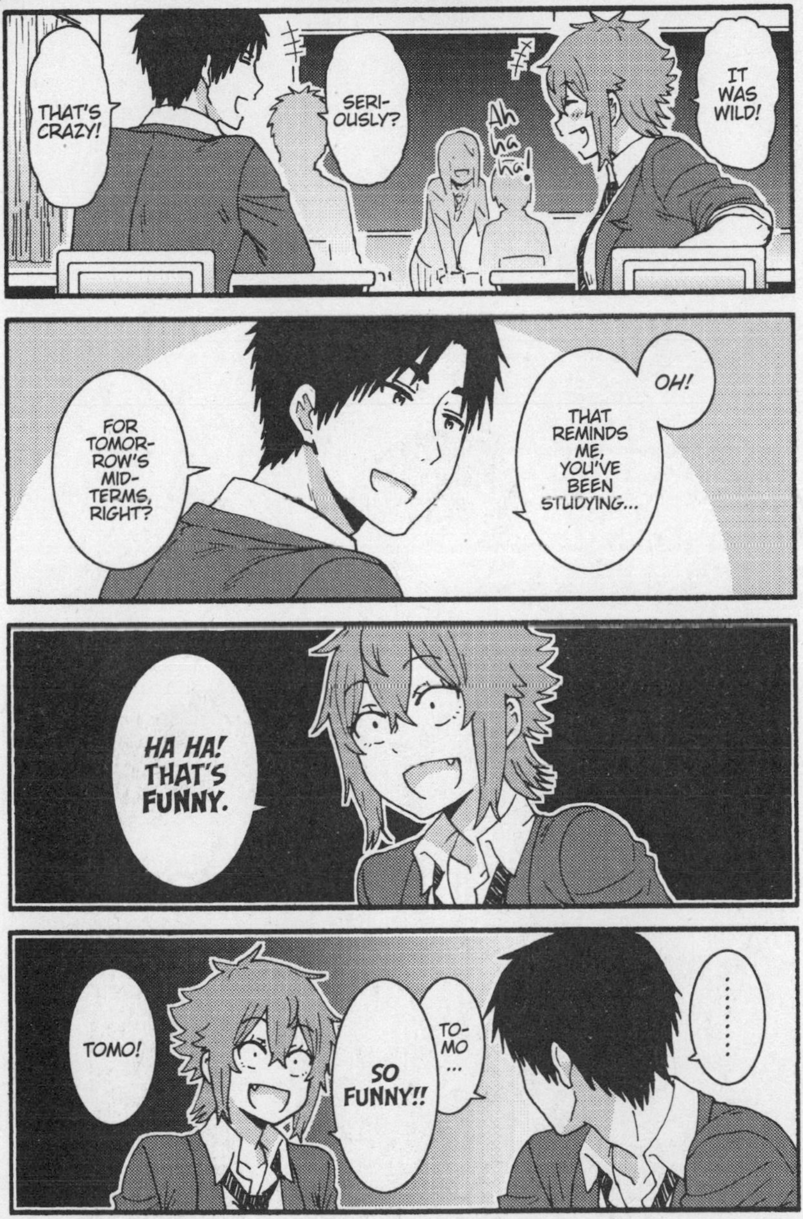

IT WAS WILD!
Ah ha ha!
SERI-OUSLY?
THAT'S CRAZY!
OH!
THAT REMINDS ME, YOU'VE BEEN STUDYING...
FOR TOMOR-ROW'S MID-TERMS, RIGHT?
HA HA! THAT'S FUNNY.
....
TO-MO...
SO FUNNY!!
TOMO!

It's No Joke II

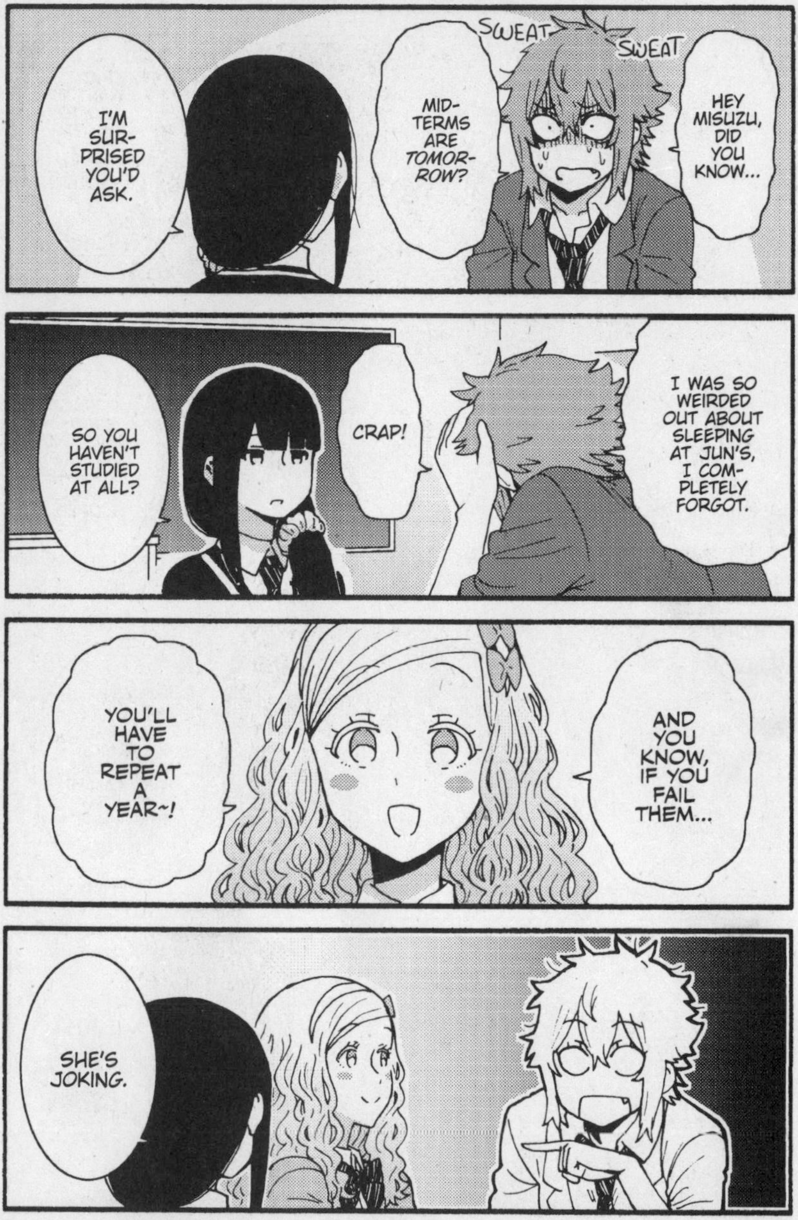
SWEAT SWEAT
HEY MISUZU, DID YOU KNOW...
MID-TERMS ARE TOMORROW?
I'M SUR-PRISED YOU'D ASK.
I WAS SO WEIRDED OUT ABOUT SLEEPING AT JUN'S, I COM-PLETELY FORGOT.
CRAP!
SO YOU HAVEN'T STUDIED AT ALL?
AND YOU KNOW, IF YOU FAIL THEM...
YOU'LL HAVE TO REPEAT A YEAR~!
SHE'S JOKING.

Where'll You Be in Five Years?

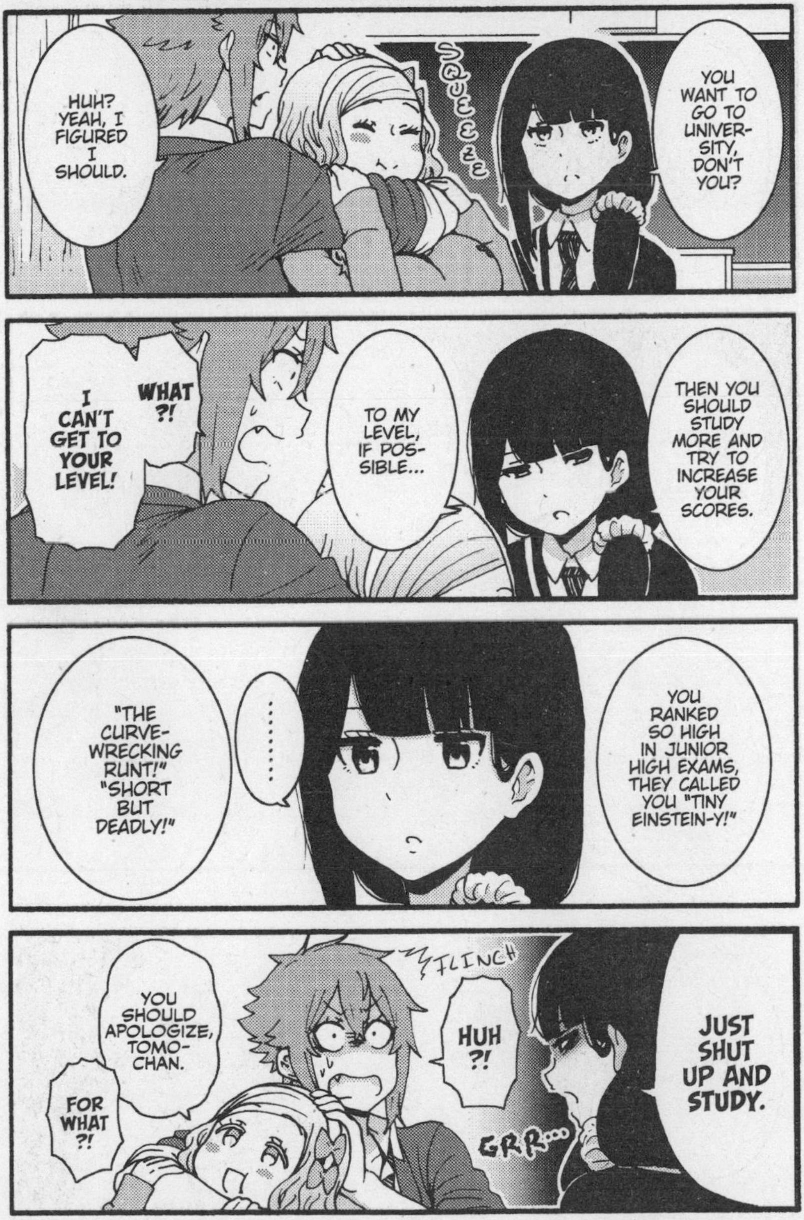
YOU WANT TO GO TO UNIVERSITY, DON'T YOU?
SQUEEZE
HUH? YEAH, I FIGURED I SHOULD.
THEN YOU SHOULD STUDY MORE AND TRY TO INCREASE YOUR SCORES.
TO MY LEVEL, IF POSSIBLE...
WHAT?!
I CAN'T GET TO YOUR LEVEL!
YOU RANKED SO HIGH IN JUNIOR HIGH EXAMS, THEY CALLED YOU "TINY EINSTEIN-Y!"
......
"THE CURVE-WRECKING RUNT!" "SHORT BUT DEADLY!"
JUST SHUT UP AND STUDY.
GRR...
FLINCH
HUH?!
YOU SHOULD APOLOGIZE, TOMO-CHAN.
FOR WHAT?!

You're Ruining My Image

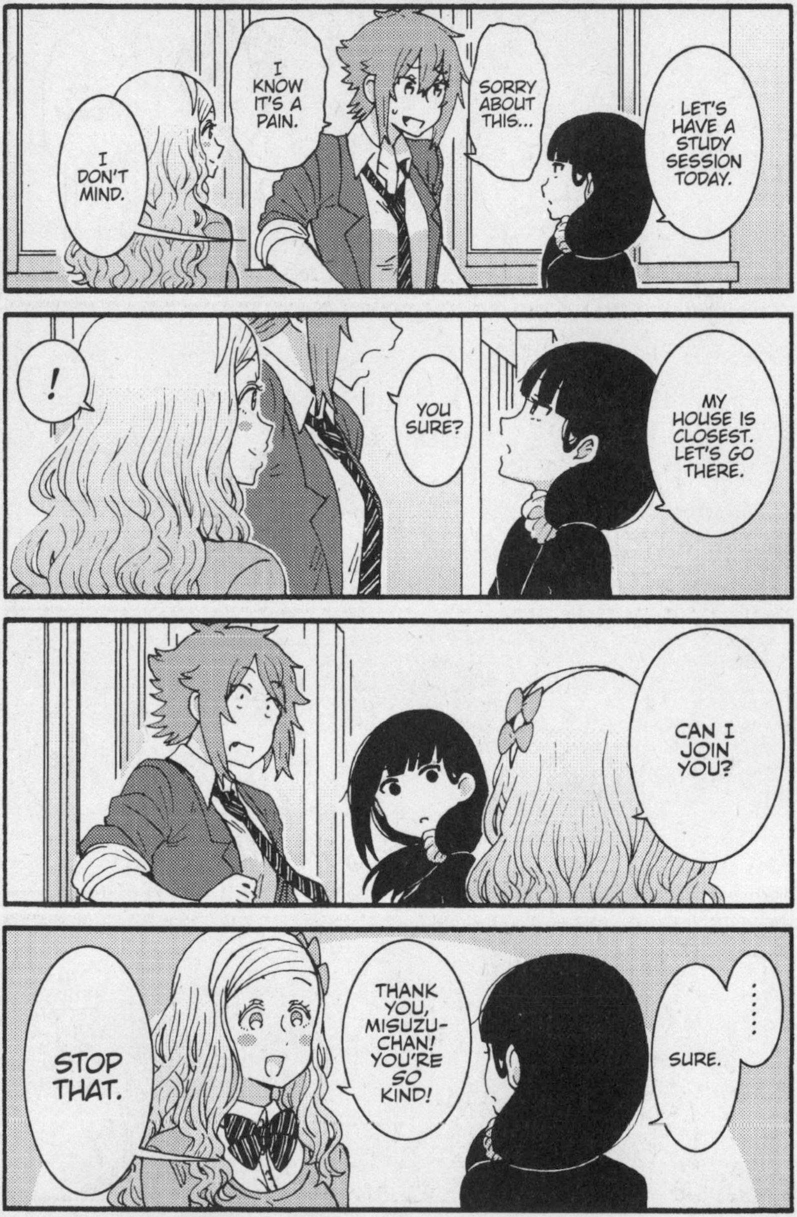
LET'S HAVE A STUDY SESSION TODAY.
SORRY ABOUT THIS...
I KNOW IT'S A PAIN.
I DON'T MIND.
MY HOUSE IS CLOSEST. LET'S GO THERE.
YOU SURE?
!
CAN I JOIN YOU?
......
SURE.
THANK YOU, MISUZU-CHAN! YOU'RE *SO* KIND!
STOP THAT.

Old Labels

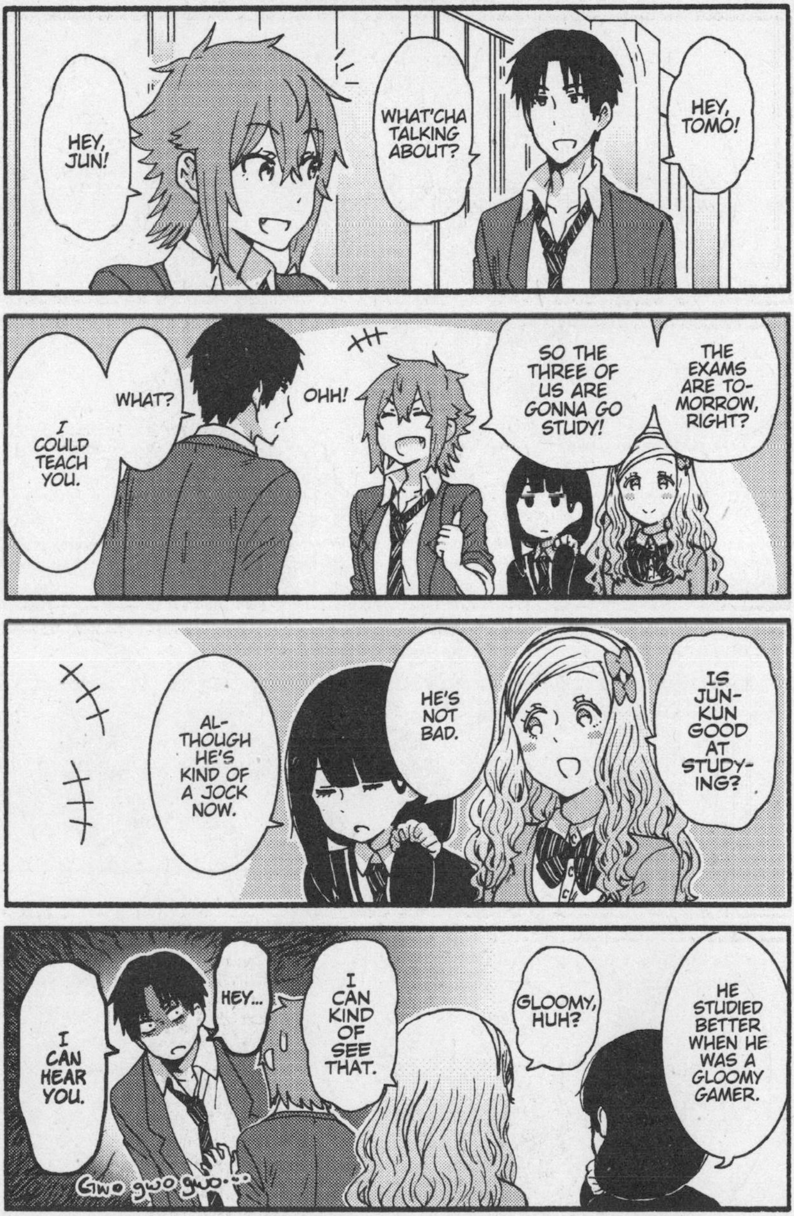
HEY, TOMO!
WHAT'CHA TALKING ABOUT?
HEY, JUN!
THE EXAMS ARE TO-MORROW, RIGHT?
SO THE THREE OF US ARE GONNA GO STUDY!
OHH!
WHAT?
I COULD TEACH YOU.
IS JUN-KUN GOOD AT STUDY-ING?
HE'S NOT BAD.
AL-THOUGH HE'S KIND OF A JOCK NOW.
HE STUDIED BETTER WHEN HE WAS A GLOOMY GAMER.
GLOOMY, HUH?
I CAN KIND OF SEE THAT.
HEY...
I CAN HEAR YOU.
Gwo gwo gwo...

Pulling Rank

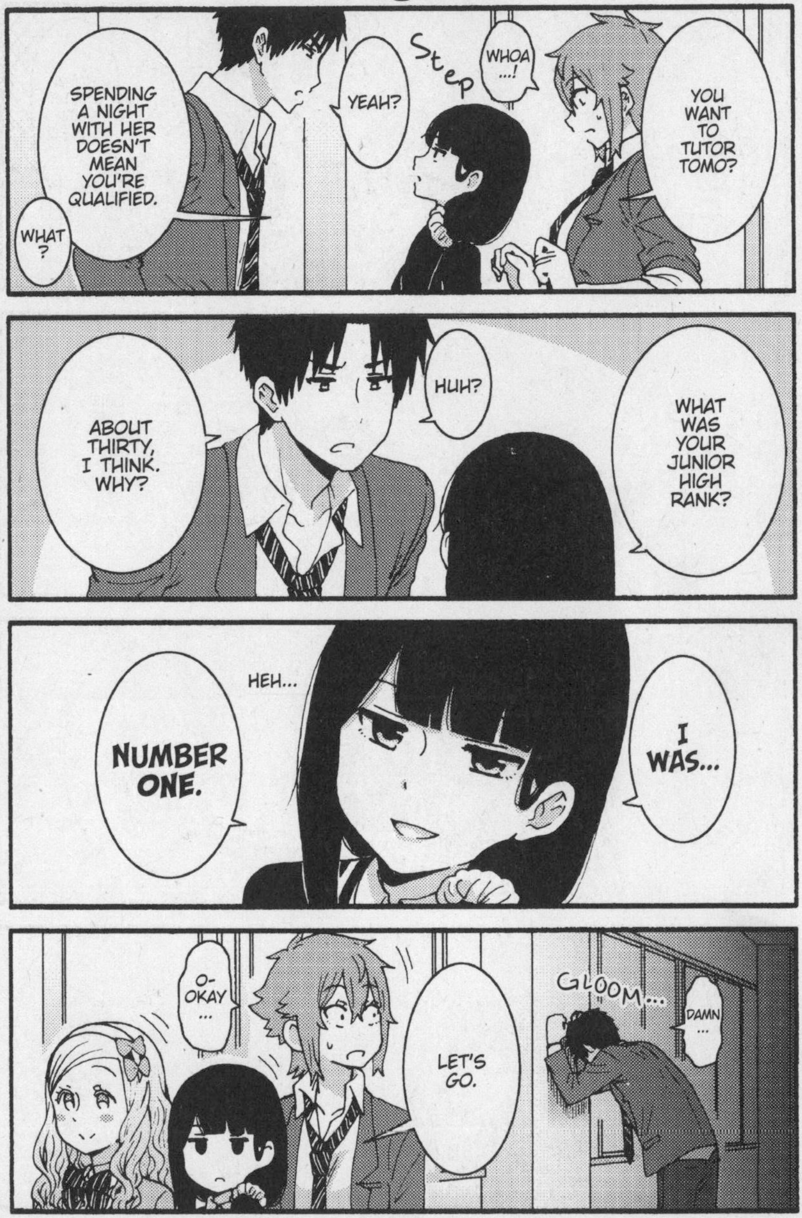
YOU WANT TO TUTOR TOMO?
WHOA ...!
Step
YEAH?
SPENDING A NIGHT WITH HER DOESN'T MEAN YOU'RE QUALIFIED.
WHAT ?
WHAT WAS YOUR JUNIOR HIGH RANK?
HUH?
ABOUT THIRTY, I THINK. WHY?
I WAS...
HEH...
NUMBER ONE.
DAMN ...
GLOOM...
LET'S GO.
O-OKAY ...

Never Gonna Give You Up

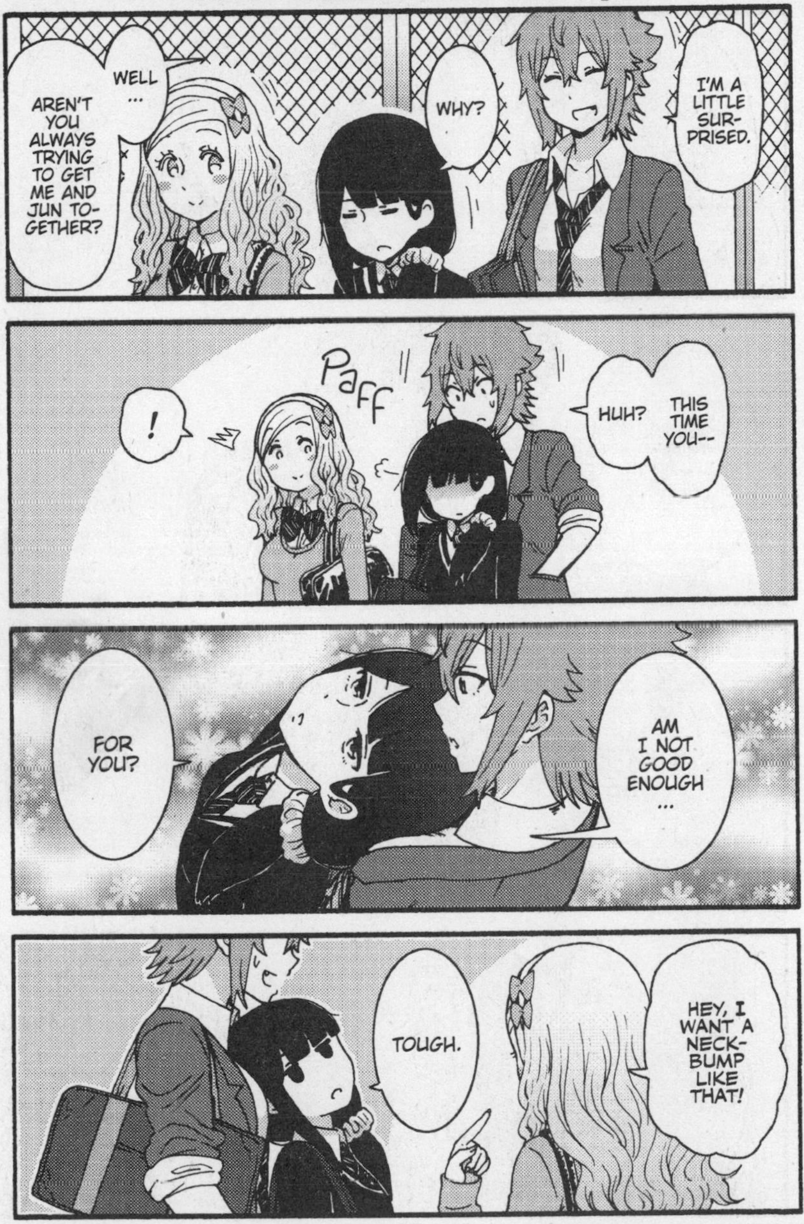
I'M A LITTLE SUR-PRISED.
WHY?
WELL ...
AREN'T YOU ALWAYS TRYING TO GET ME AND JUN TO-GETHER?
THIS TIME YOU--
HUH?
Paff
!
AM I NOT GOOD ENOUGH ...
FOR YOU?
HEY, I WANT A NECK-BUMP LIKE THAT!
TOUGH.

Innocence or Sarcasm?

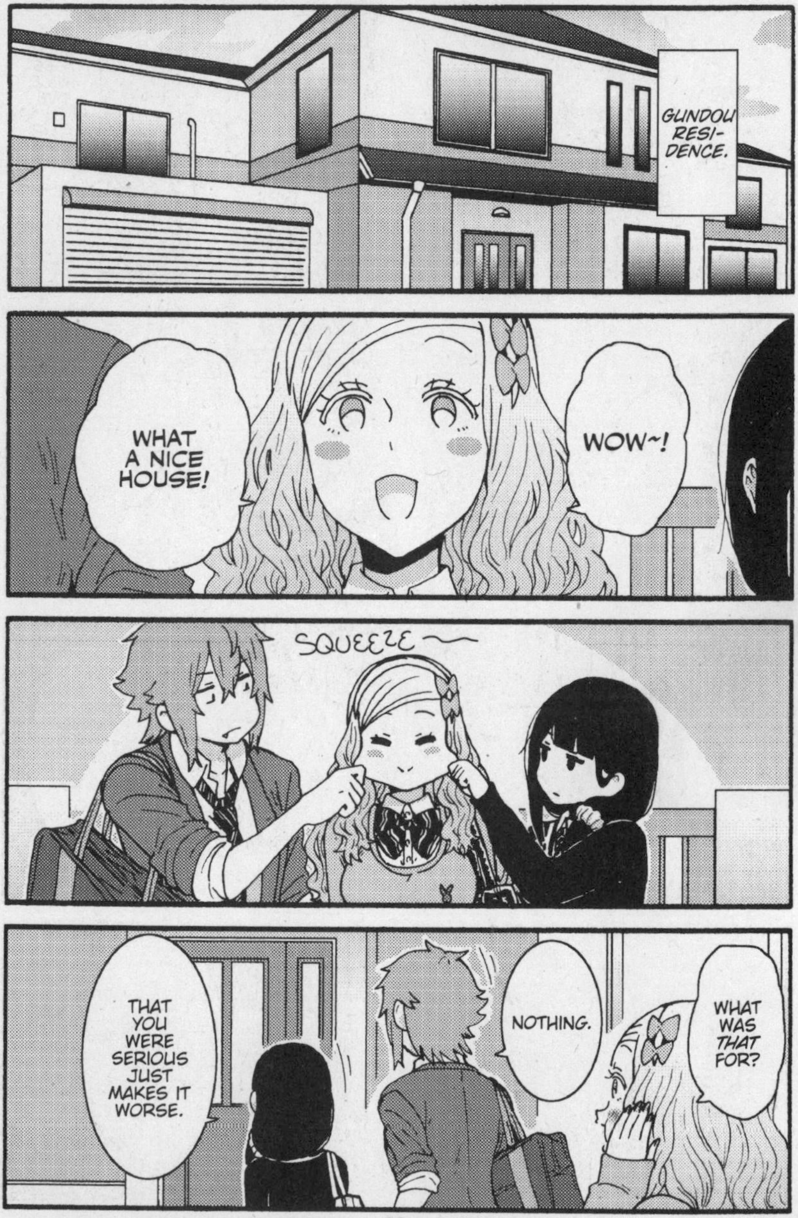
GUNDOU RESI-DENCE.
WOW~!
WHAT A NICE HOUSE!
SQUEEZE~~
WHAT WAS THAT FOR?
NOTHING.
THAT YOU WERE SERIOUS JUST MAKES IT WORSE.

Hurricane Tomo

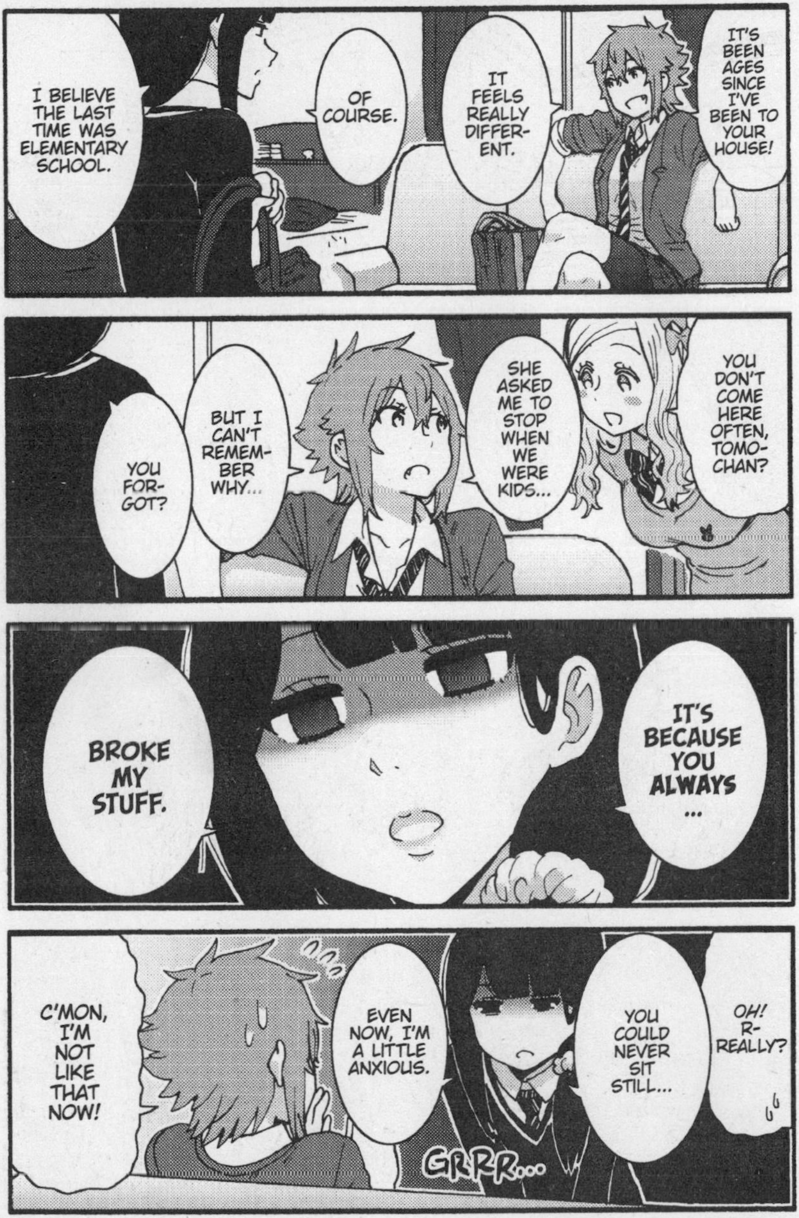
IT'S BEEN AGES SINCE I'VE BEEN TO YOUR HOUSE!
IT FEELS REALLY DIFFERENT.
OF COURSE.
I BELIEVE THE LAST TIME WAS ELEMENTARY SCHOOL.
YOU DON'T COME HERE OFTEN, TOMO-CHAN?
SHE ASKED ME TO STOP WHEN WE WERE KIDS...
BUT I CAN'T REMEMBER WHY...
YOU FORGOT?
IT'S BECAUSE YOU ALWAYS...
BROKE MY STUFF.
OH! R-REALLY?
YOU COULD NEVER SIT STILL...
EVEN NOW, I'M A LITTLE ANXIOUS.
GRRR...
C'MON, I'M NOT LIKE THAT NOW!

Twenty-Six Centimeters

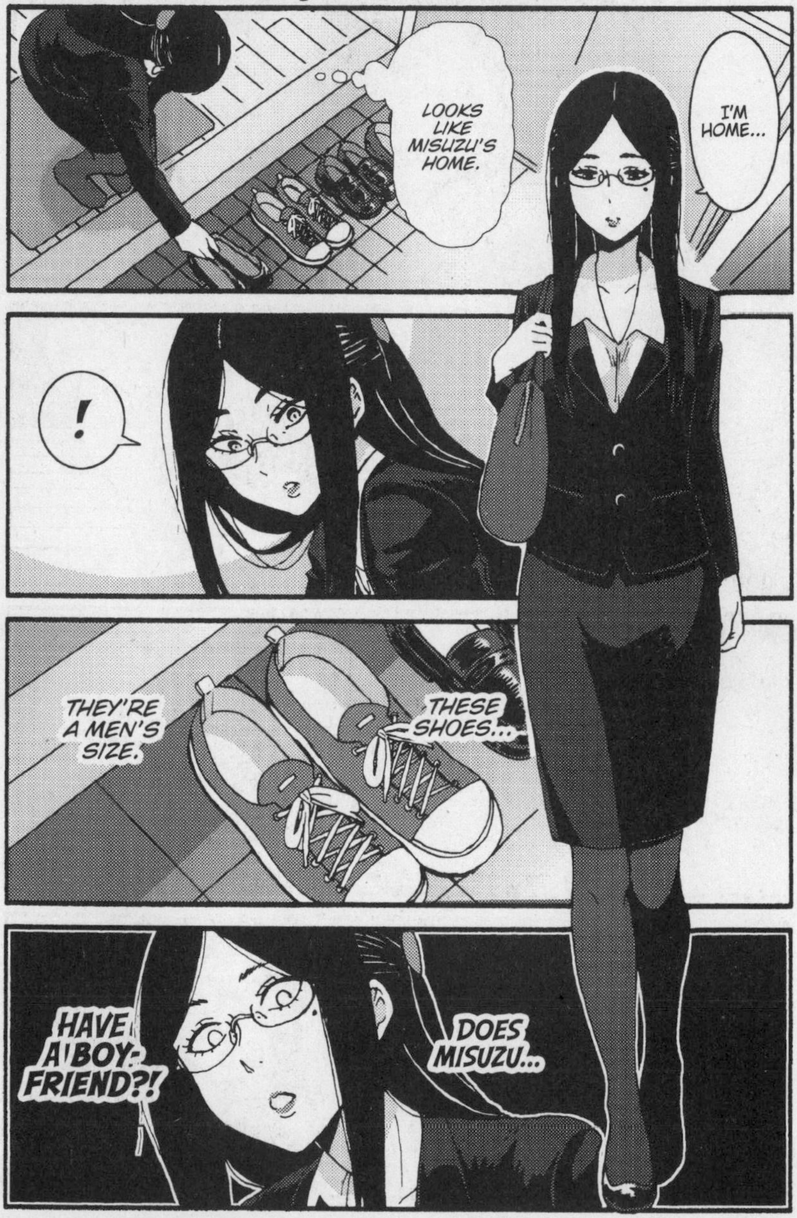
I'M HOME...
LOOKS LIKE MISUZU'S HOME.
!
THESE SHOES...
THEY'RE A MEN'S SIZE.
DOES MISUZU...
HAVE A BOY-FRIEND?!

Spitting Image

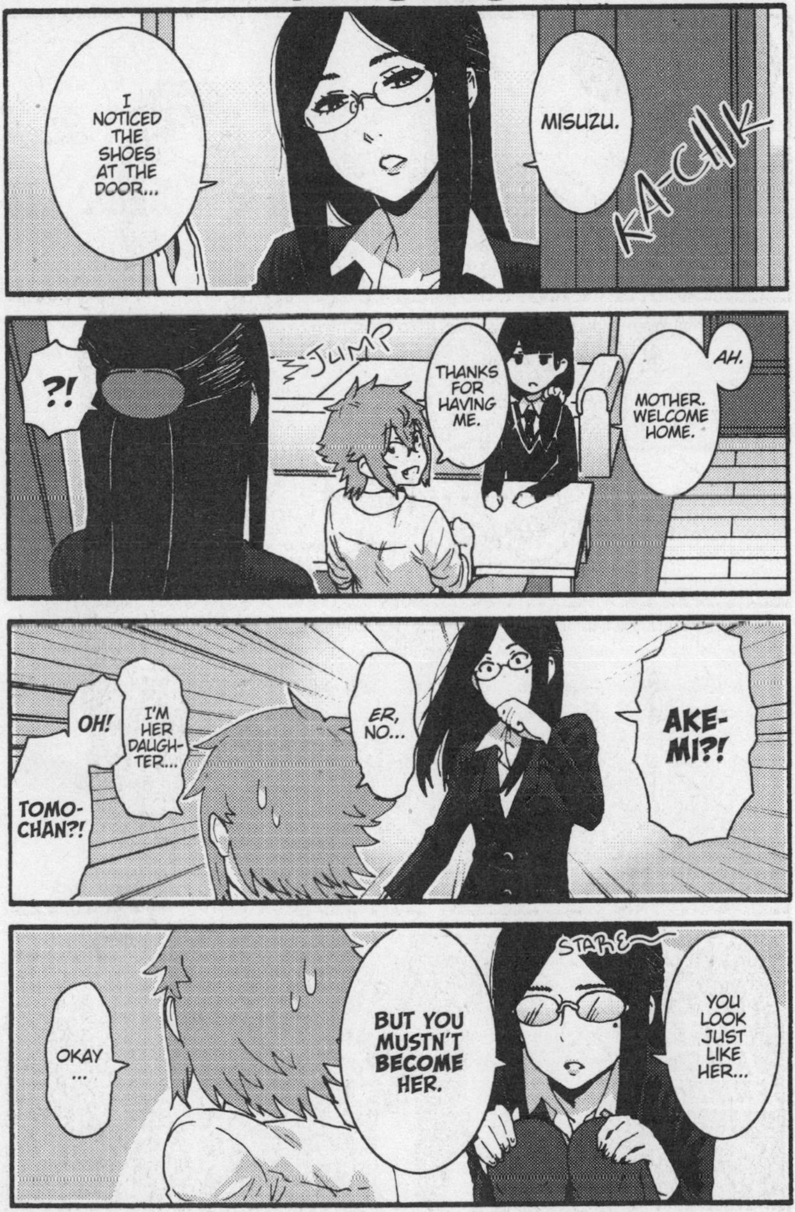
KA-CLIK
MISUZU.
I NOTICED THE SHOES AT THE DOOR...
AH.
MOTHER. WELCOME HOME.
THANKS FOR HAVING ME.
JUMP
?!
AKE-MI?!
ER, NO...
I'M HER DAUGHTER...
OH!
TOMO-CHAN?!
STARE
YOU LOOK JUST LIKE HER...
BUT YOU MUSTN'T BECOME HER.
OKAY...

Uncanny Valley

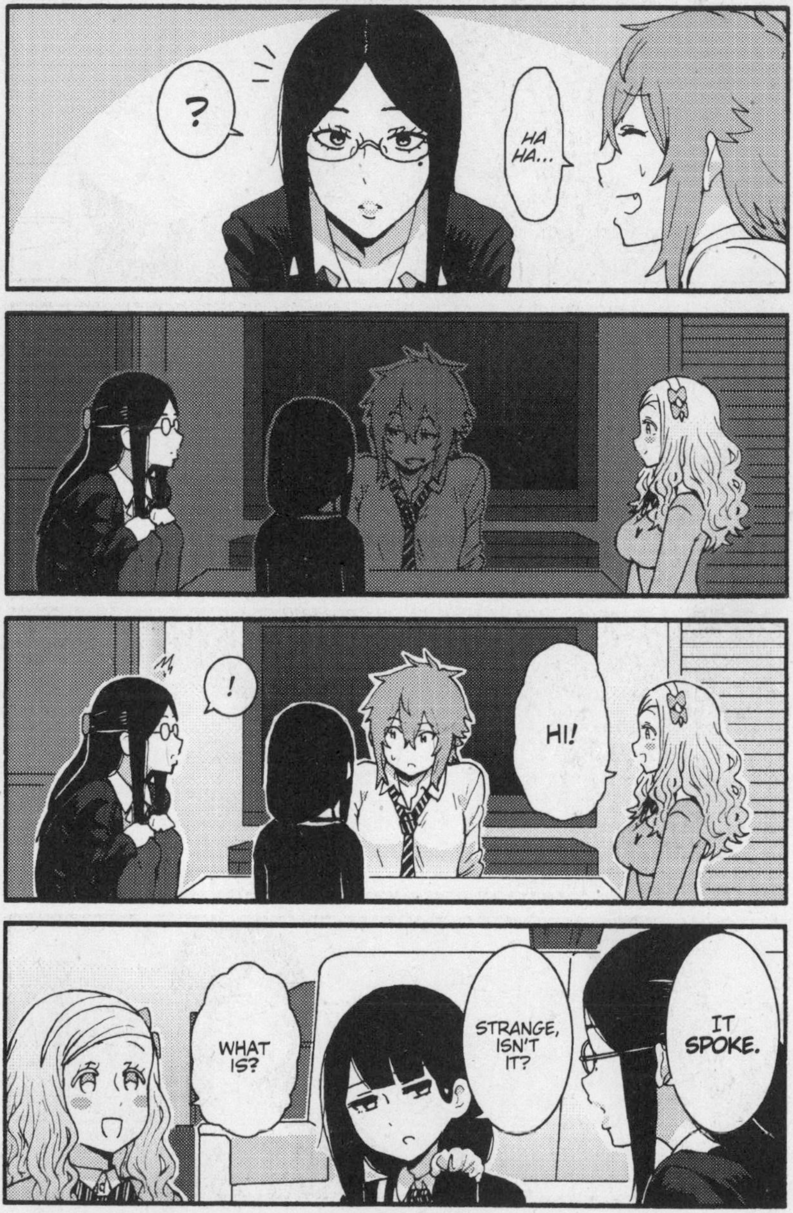
HA HA...
?
HI!
!
IT SPOKE.
STRANGE, ISN'T IT?
WHAT IS?

Like Mother, Like Daughter

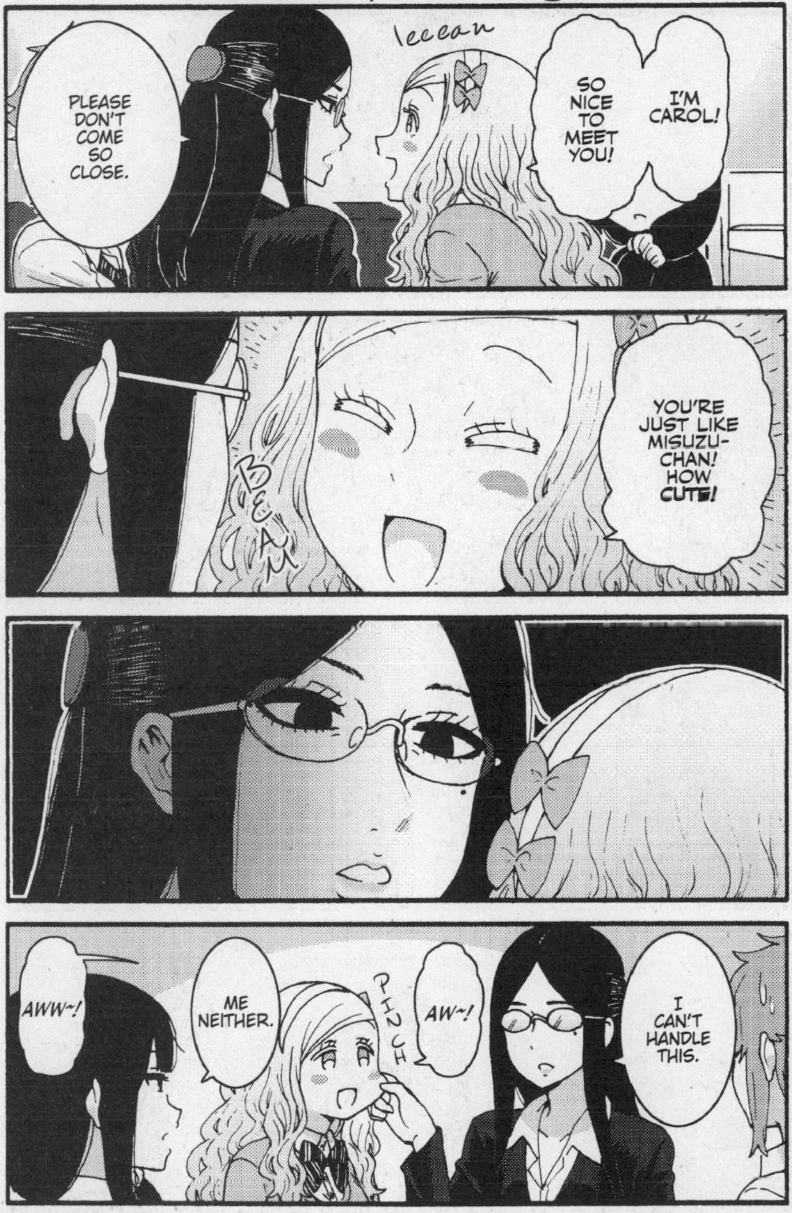
I'M CAROL!
SO NICE TO MEET YOU!
PLEASE DON'T COME SO CLOSE.
YOU'RE JUST LIKE MISUZU-CHAN! HOW CUTE!
BEAM
I CAN'T HANDLE THIS.
AW~!
PINCH
ME NEITHER.
AWW~!

Later, After You Help Me

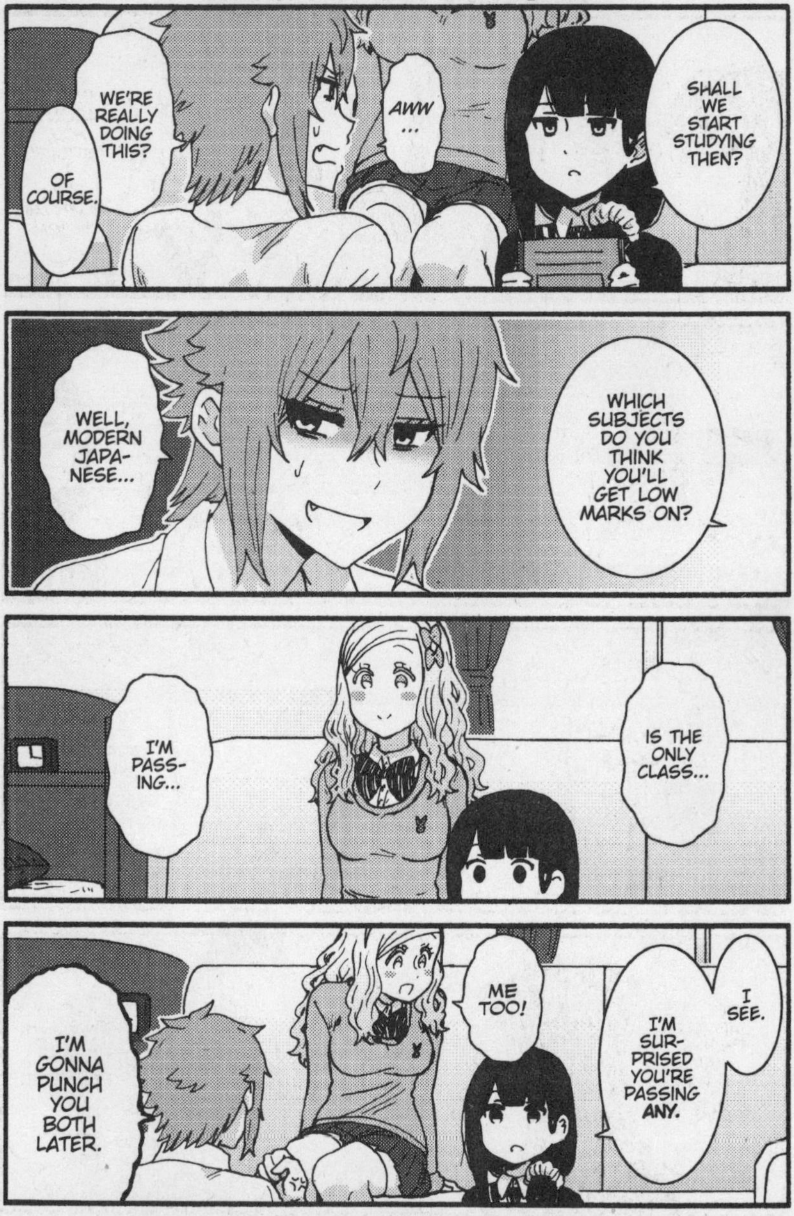
SHALL WE START STUDYING THEN?
AWW...
WE'RE REALLY DOING THIS?
OF COURSE.
WHICH SUBJECTS DO YOU THINK YOU'LL GET LOW MARKS ON?
WELL, MODERN JAPA-NESE...
IS THE ONLY CLASS...
I'M PASS-ING...
I SEE.
I'M SUR-PRISED YOU'RE PASSING ANY.
ME TOO!
I'M GONNA PUNCH YOU BOTH LATER.

At Least You're Fluent

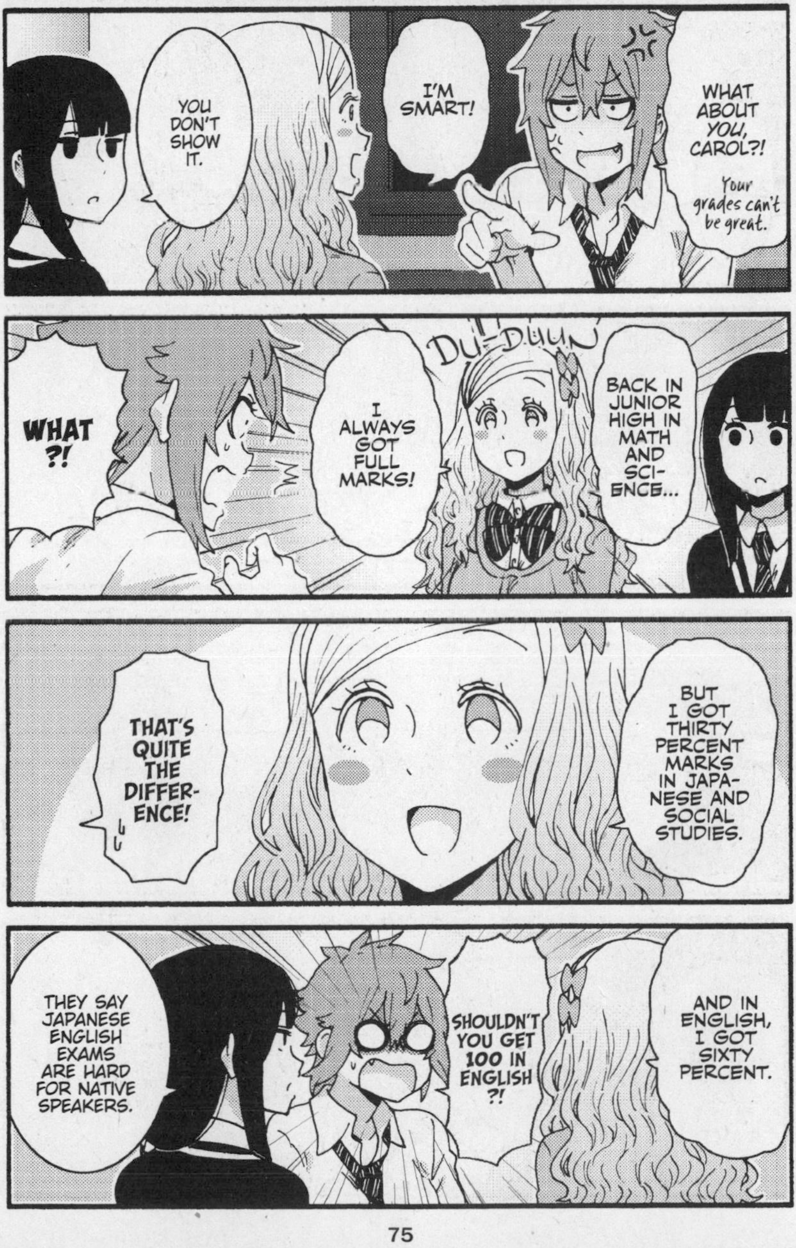
WHAT ABOUT YOU, CAROL?!
Your grades can't be great.
I'M SMART!
YOU DON'T SHOW IT.
BACK IN JUNIOR HIGH IN MATH AND SCI-ENCE...
DU-DUUN
I ALWAYS GOT FULL MARKS!
WHAT?!
BUT I GOT THIRTY PERCENT MARKS IN JAPA-NESE AND SOCIAL STUDIES.
THAT'S QUITE THE DIFFER-ENCE!
AND IN ENGLISH, I GOT SIXTY PERCENT.
SHOULDN'T YOU GET 100 IN ENGLISH?!
THEY SAY JAPANESE ENGLISH EXAMS ARE HARD FOR NATIVE SPEAKERS.

New Math

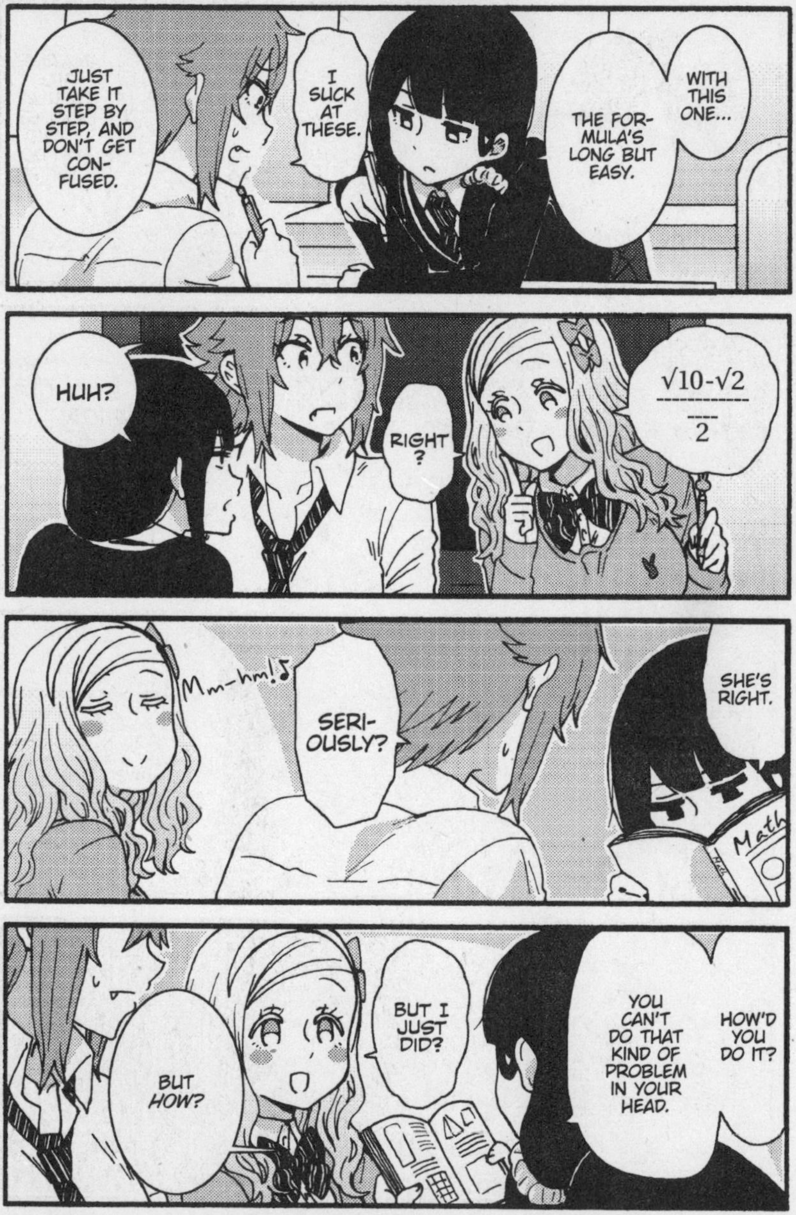

WITH THIS ONE...
THE FORMULA'S LONG BUT EASY.
I SUCK AT THESE.
JUST TAKE IT STEP BY STEP, AND DON'T GET CONFUSED.
$\frac{\sqrt{10}-\sqrt{2}}{2}$
RIGHT?
HUH?
SHE'S RIGHT.
Math
SERIOUSLY?
Mm-hm!♪
HOW'D YOU DO IT?
YOU CAN'T DO THAT KIND OF PROBLEM IN YOUR HEAD.
BUT I JUST DID?
BUT *HOW?*

Intuition

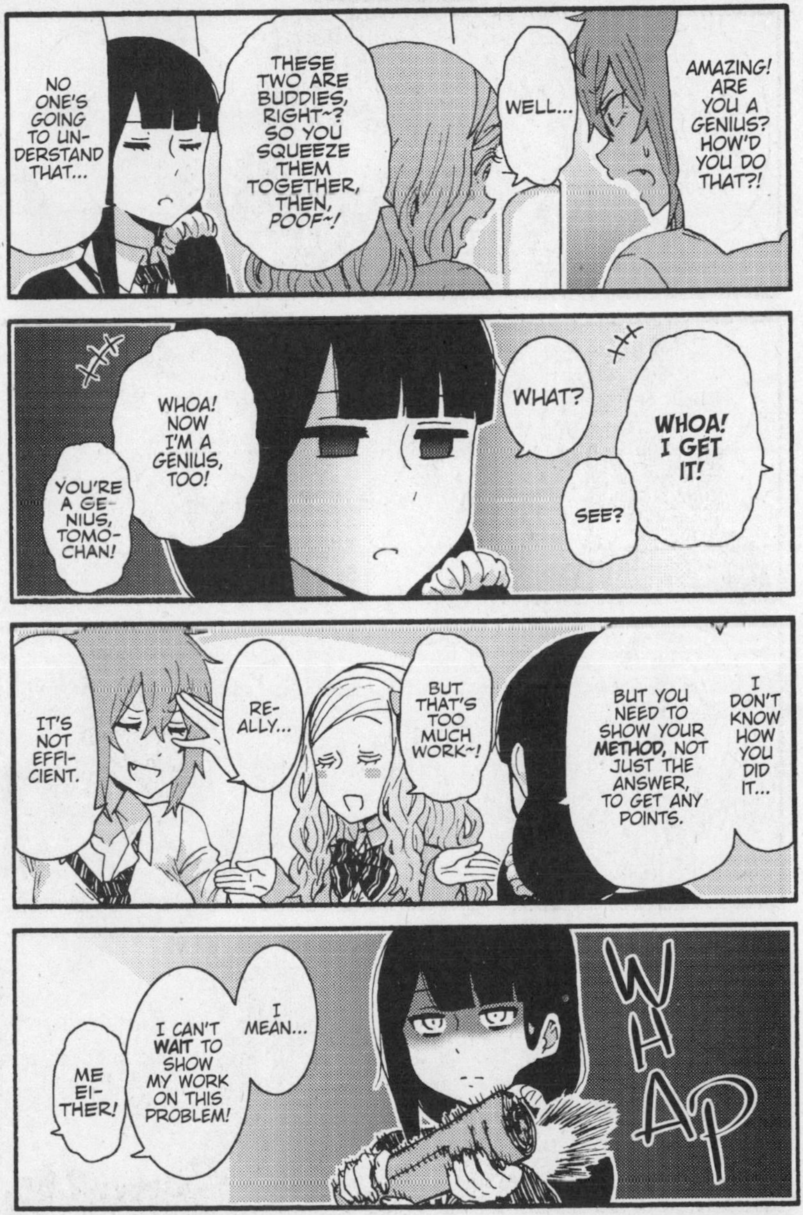

AMAZING! ARE YOU A GENIUS? HOW'D YOU DO THAT?!
WELL...
THESE TWO ARE BUDDIES, RIGHT~? SO YOU SQUEEZE THEM TOGETHER, THEN, *POOF~!*
NO ONE'S GOING TO UNDERSTAND THAT...
WHOA! I GET IT!
WHAT?
SEE?
WHOA! NOW I'M A GENIUS, TOO!
YOU'RE A GENIUS, TOMO-CHAN!
I DON'T KNOW HOW YOU DID IT...
BUT YOU NEED TO SHOW YOUR **METHOD,** NOT JUST THE ANSWER, TO GET ANY POINTS.
BUT THAT'S TOO MUCH WORK~!
REALLY...
IT'S NOT EFFICIENT.
WHAP
I MEAN...
I CAN'T **WAIT** TO SHOW MY WORK ON THIS PROBLEM!
ME EITHER!

And "Quadratic Equation"

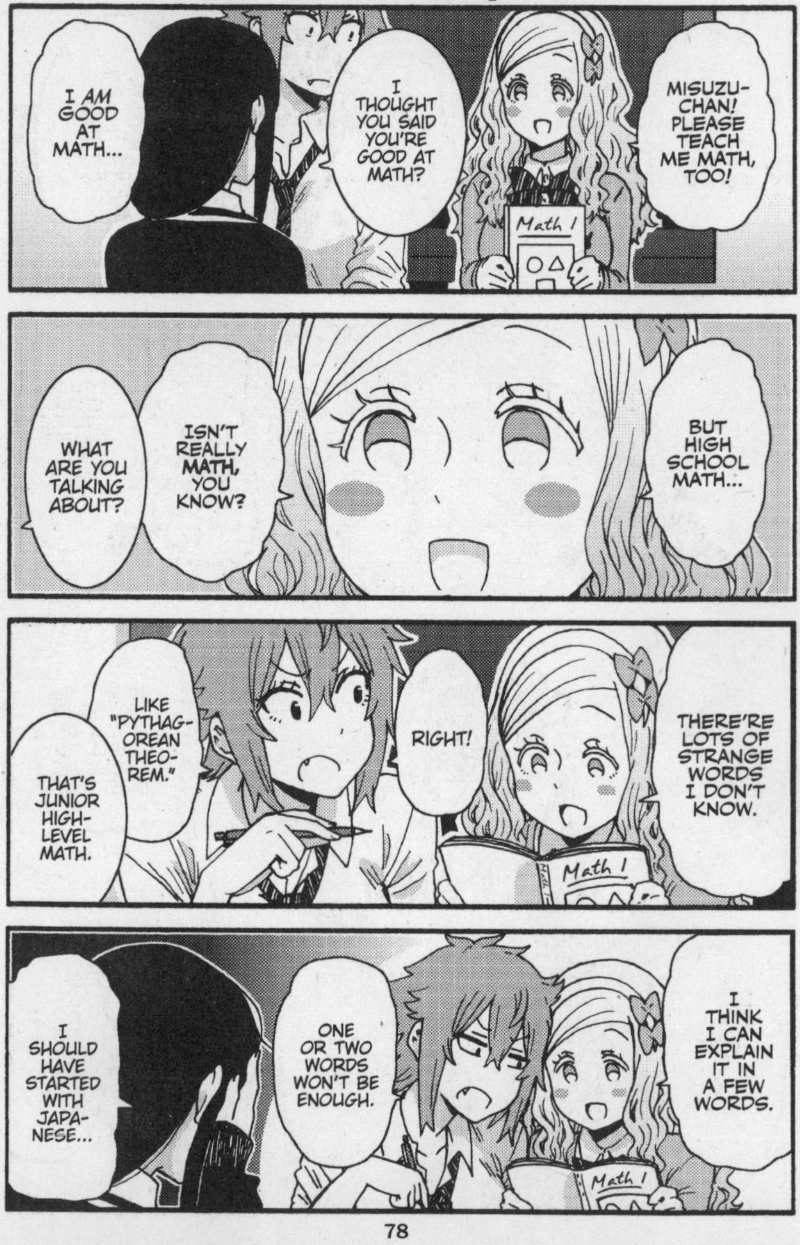
MISUZU-CHAN! PLEASE TEACH ME MATH, TOO!
I THOUGHT YOU SAID YOU'RE GOOD AT MATH?
I AM GOOD AT MATH...
Math 1
BUT HIGH SCHOOL MATH...
ISN'T REALLY **MATH**, YOU KNOW?
WHAT ARE YOU TALKING ABOUT?
THERE'RE LOTS OF STRANGE WORDS I DON'T KNOW.
RIGHT!
LIKE "PYTHAGOREAN THEOREM."
THAT'S JUNIOR HIGH-LEVEL MATH.
Math 1
I THINK I CAN EXPLAIN IT IN A FEW WORDS.
ONE OR TWO WORDS WON'T BE ENOUGH.
I SHOULD HAVE STARTED WITH JAPANESE...
Math 1

Aptitude

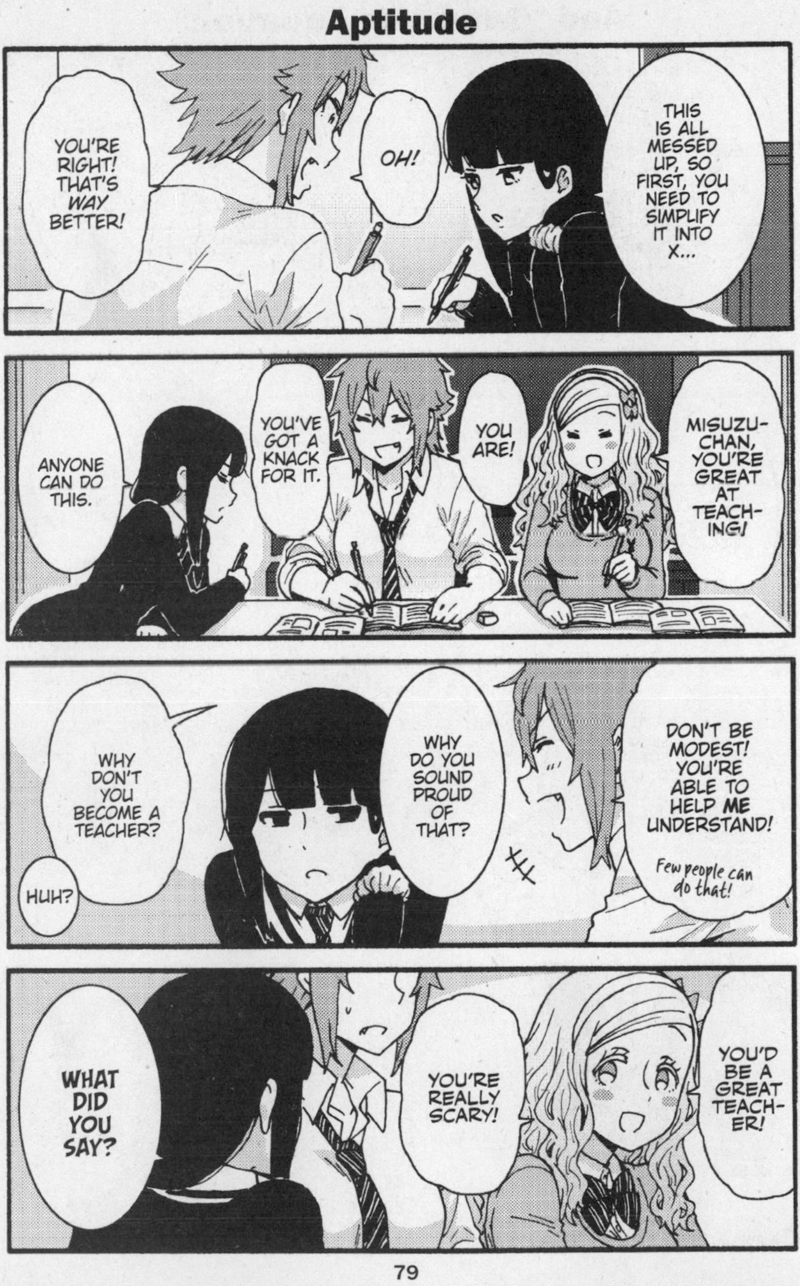
THIS IS ALL MESSED UP, SO FIRST, YOU NEED TO SIMPLIFY IT INTO X...
OH!
YOU'RE RIGHT! THAT'S *WAY* BETTER!
MISUZU-CHAN, YOU'RE GREAT AT TEACHING!
YOU ARE!
YOU'VE GOT A KNACK FOR IT.
ANYONE CAN DO THIS.
DON'T BE MODEST! YOU'RE ABLE TO HELP **ME** UNDERSTAND!
Few people can do that!
WHY DO YOU SOUND PROUD OF THAT?
WHY DON'T YOU BECOME A TEACHER?
HUH?
YOU'D BE A GREAT TEACHER!
YOU'RE REALLY SCARY!
WHAT DID YOU SAY?

Their World

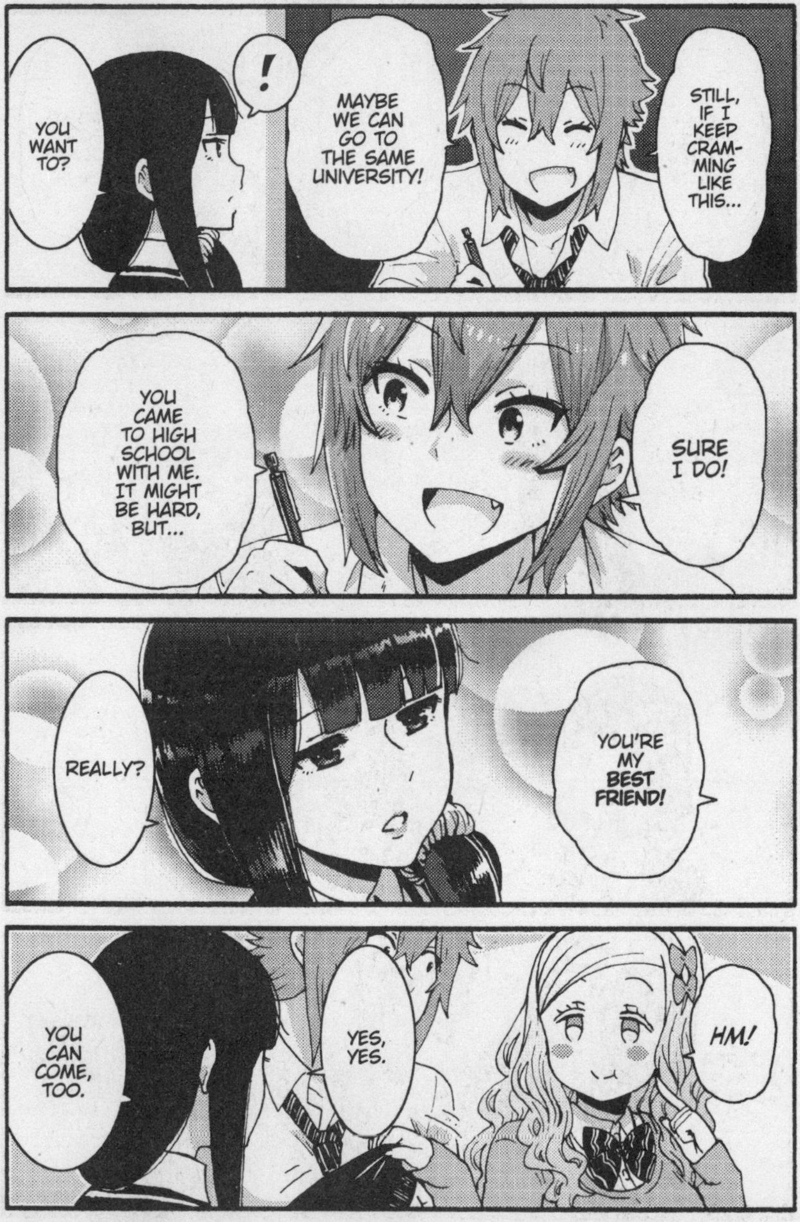
STILL, IF I KEEP CRAMMING LIKE THIS...
MAYBE WE CAN GO TO THE SAME UNIVERSITY!
!
YOU WANT TO?
SURE I DO!
YOU CAME TO HIGH SCHOOL WITH ME. IT MIGHT BE HARD, BUT...
YOU'RE MY BEST FRIEND!
REALLY?
HM!
YES, YES.
YOU CAN COME, TOO.

Opposites Attract

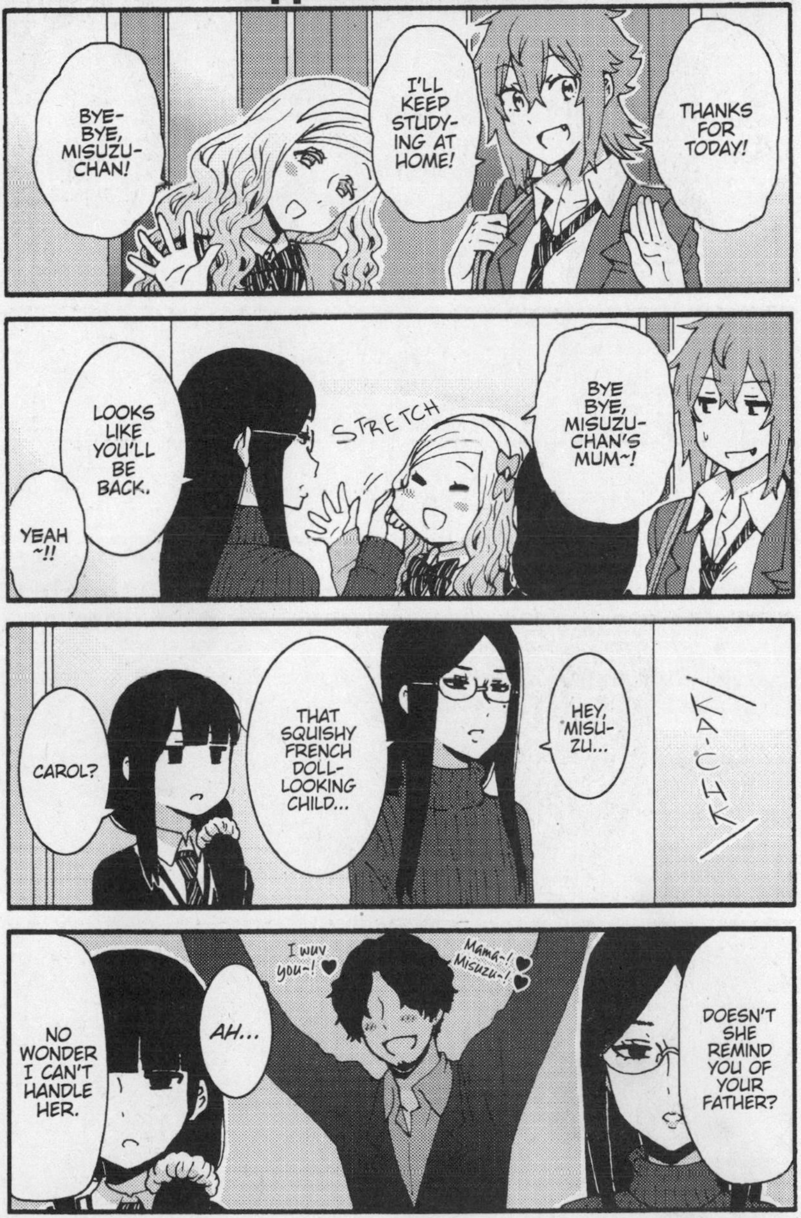
THANKS FOR TODAY!
I'LL KEEP STUDYING AT HOME!
BYE-BYE, MISUZU-CHAN!
BYE BYE, MISUZU-CHAN'S MUM~!
STRETCH
LOOKS LIKE YOU'LL BE BACK.
YEAH ~!!
KA-CHK
HEY, MISUZU...
THAT SQUISHY FRENCH DOLL-LOOKING CHILD...
CAROL?
DOESN'T SHE REMIND YOU OF YOUR FATHER?
Mama~! Misuzu~! ♥
I wuv you~! ♥
AH...
NO WONDER I CAN'T HANDLE HER.

And That's Good?

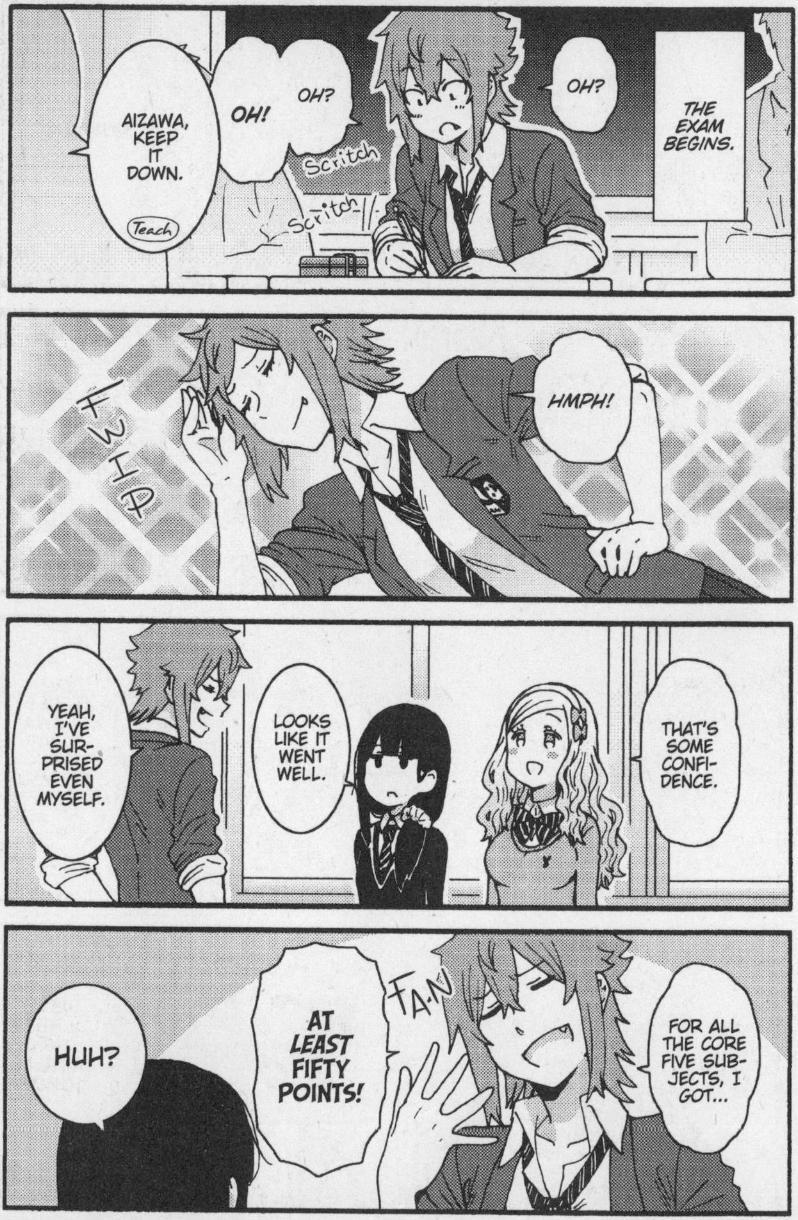
THE EXAM BEGINS.
OH?
OH?
OH!
Scritch
Scritch
AIZAWA, KEEP IT DOWN.
Teach
HMPH!
FWIP
THAT'S SOME CONFIDENCE.
LOOKS LIKE IT WENT WELL.
YEAH, I'VE SURPRISED EVEN MYSELF.
FOR ALL THE CORE FIVE SUBJECTS, I GOT...
FA-N
AT *LEAST* FIFTY POINTS!
HUH?

Out of 150 First Years

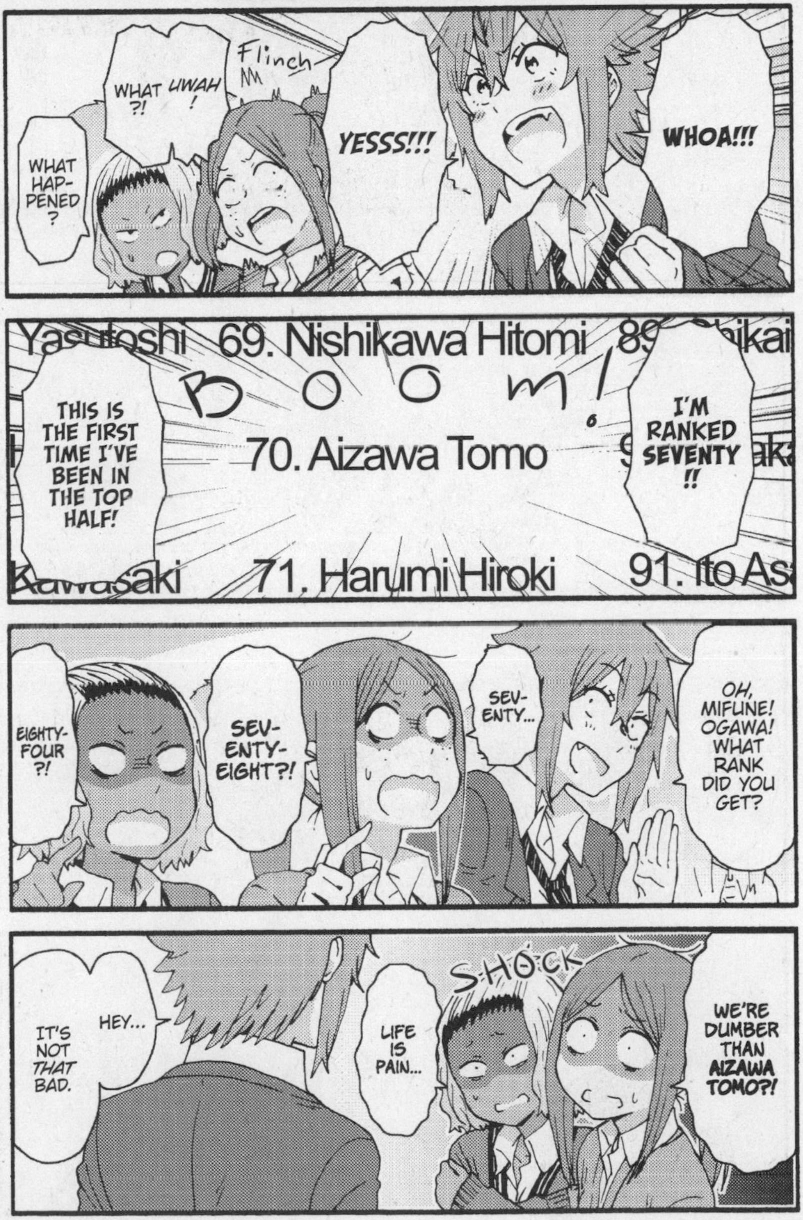
WHOA!!!
YESSS!!!
Flinch
UWAH!
WHAT?!
WHAT HAPPENED?
69. Nishikawa Hitomi
I'M RANKED SEVENTY!!
BOOM!
70. Aizawa Tomo
THIS IS THE FIRST TIME I'VE BEEN IN THE TOP HALF!
71. Harumi Hiroki
OH, MIFUNE! OGAWA! WHAT RANK DID YOU GET?
SEVENTY...
SEVENTY-EIGHT?!
EIGHTY-FOUR?!
WE'RE DUMBER THAN AIZAWA TOMO?!
SHOCK
LIFE IS PAIN...
HEY...
IT'S NOT THAT BAD.

Tomo-chan Had to Get Them Down

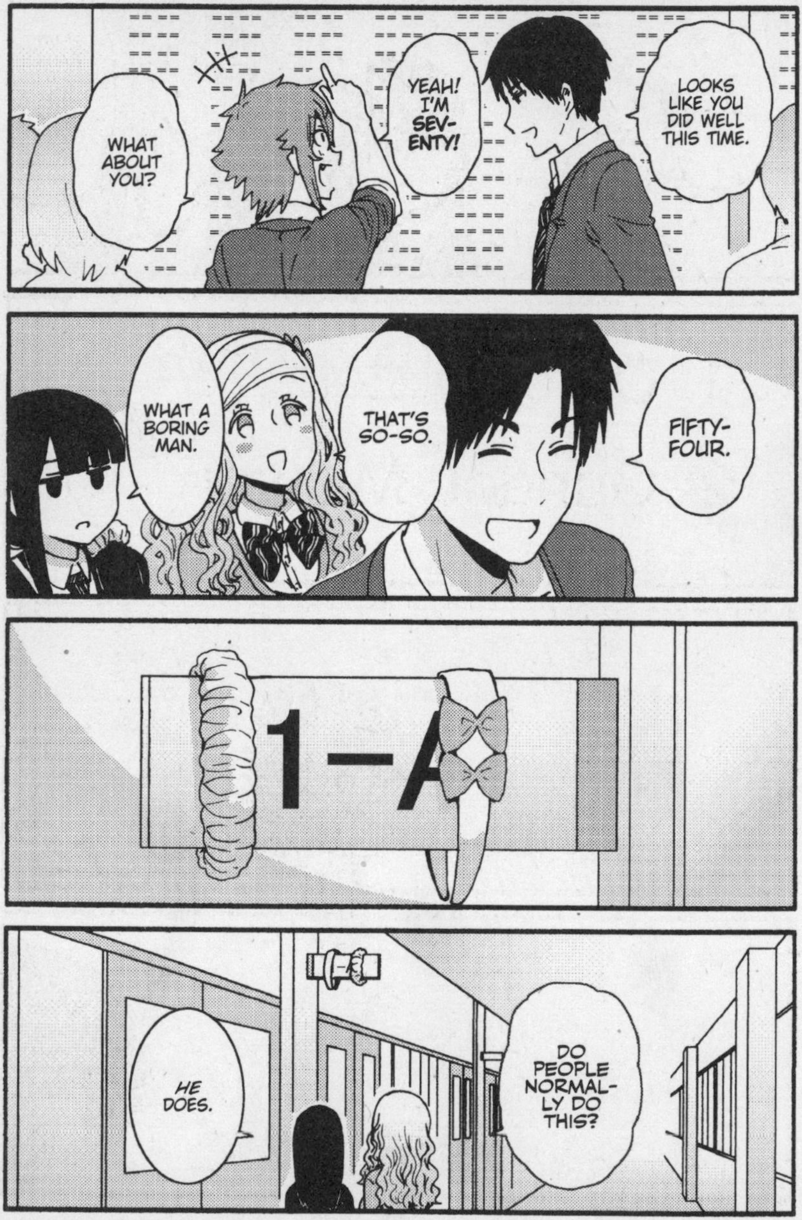
LOOKS LIKE YOU DID WELL THIS TIME.
YEAH! I'M SEV-ENTY!
WHAT ABOUT YOU?
FIFTY-FOUR.
THAT'S SO-SO.
WHAT A BORING MAN.
1-A
DO PEOPLE NORMALLY DO THIS?
HE DOES.

Hard Work Pays Off

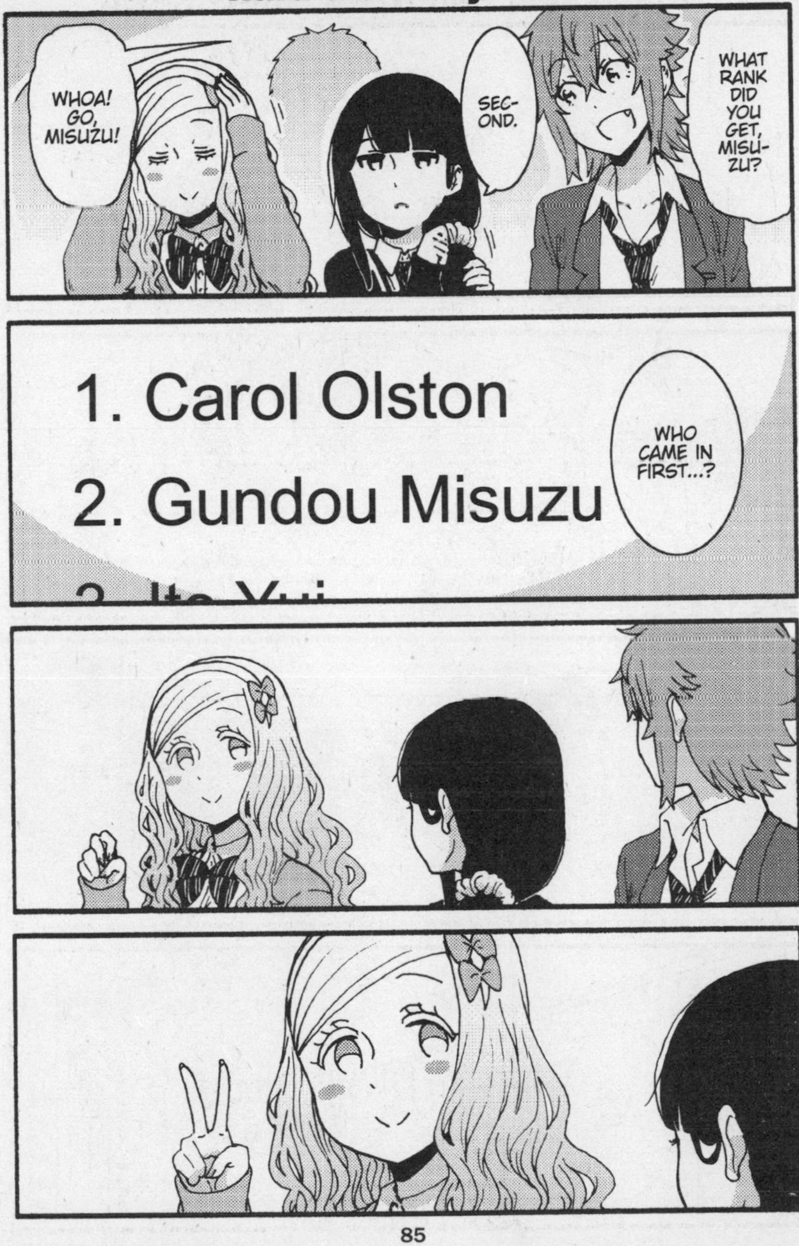
WHAT RANK DID YOU GET, MISUZU?
SECOND.
WHOA! GO, MISUZU!
1. Carol Olston
2. Gundou Misuzu
WHO CAME IN FIRST...?

OMAKE

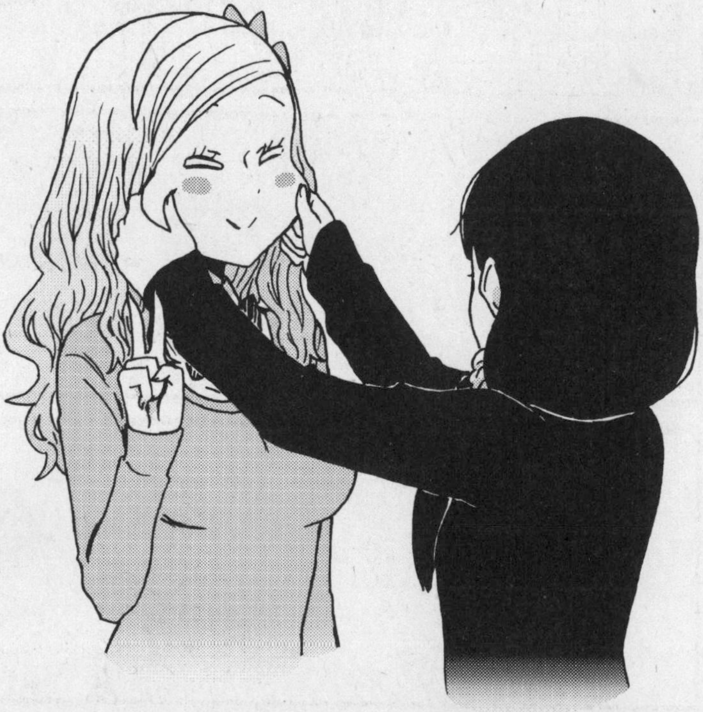

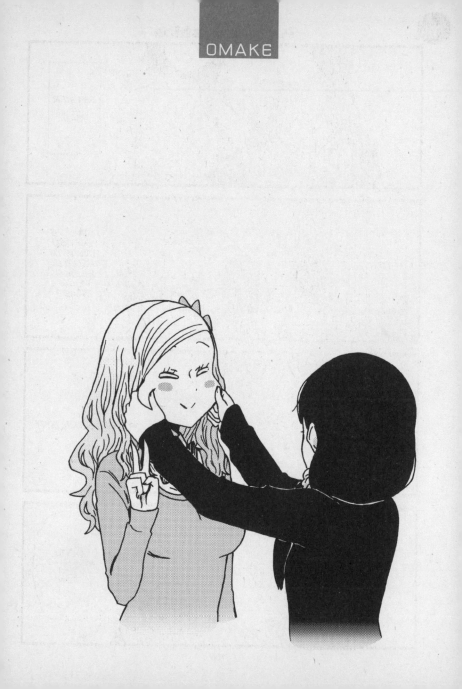

Ch. 22

Summer Fashion

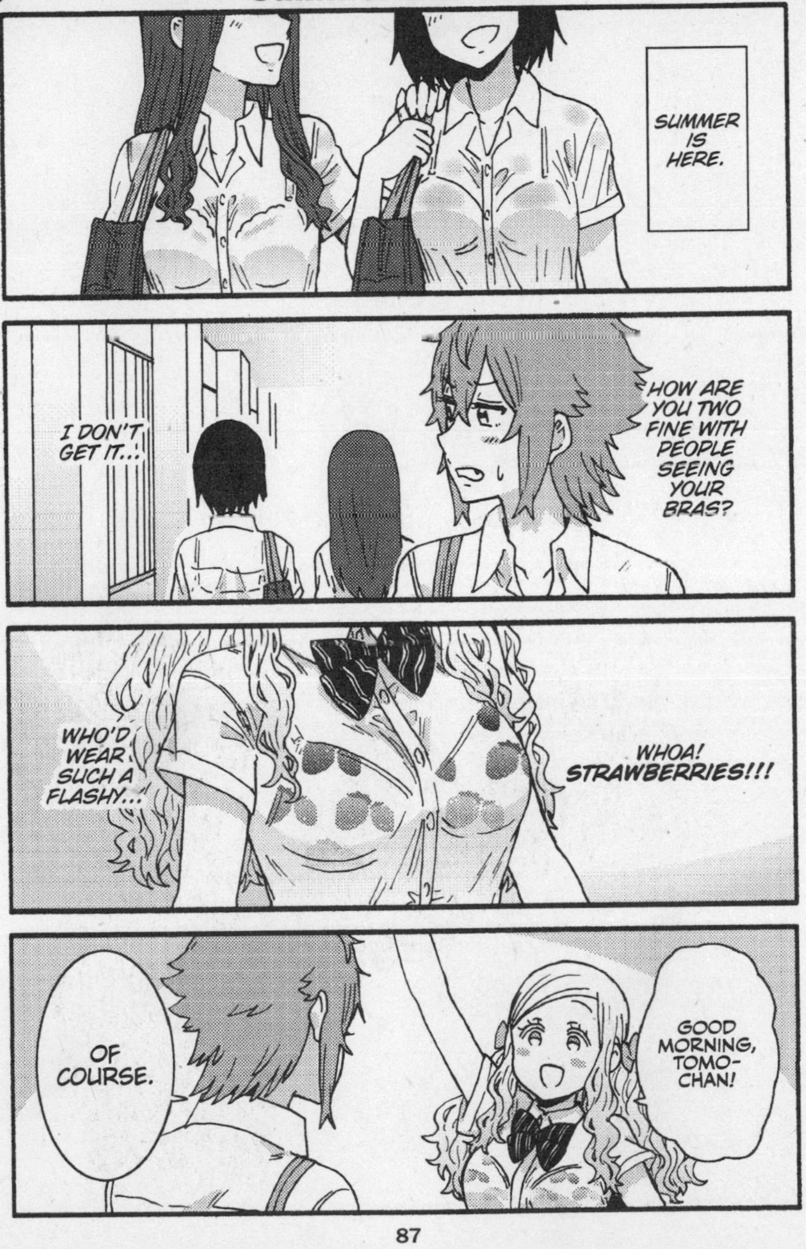
SUMMER IS HERE.
HOW ARE YOU TWO FINE WITH PEOPLE SEEING YOUR BRAS?
I DON'T GET IT...
WHOA! STRAWBERRIES!!!
WHO'D WEAR SUCH A FLASHY...
GOOD MORNING, TOMO-CHAN!
OF COURSE.

That's My Best Friend For You

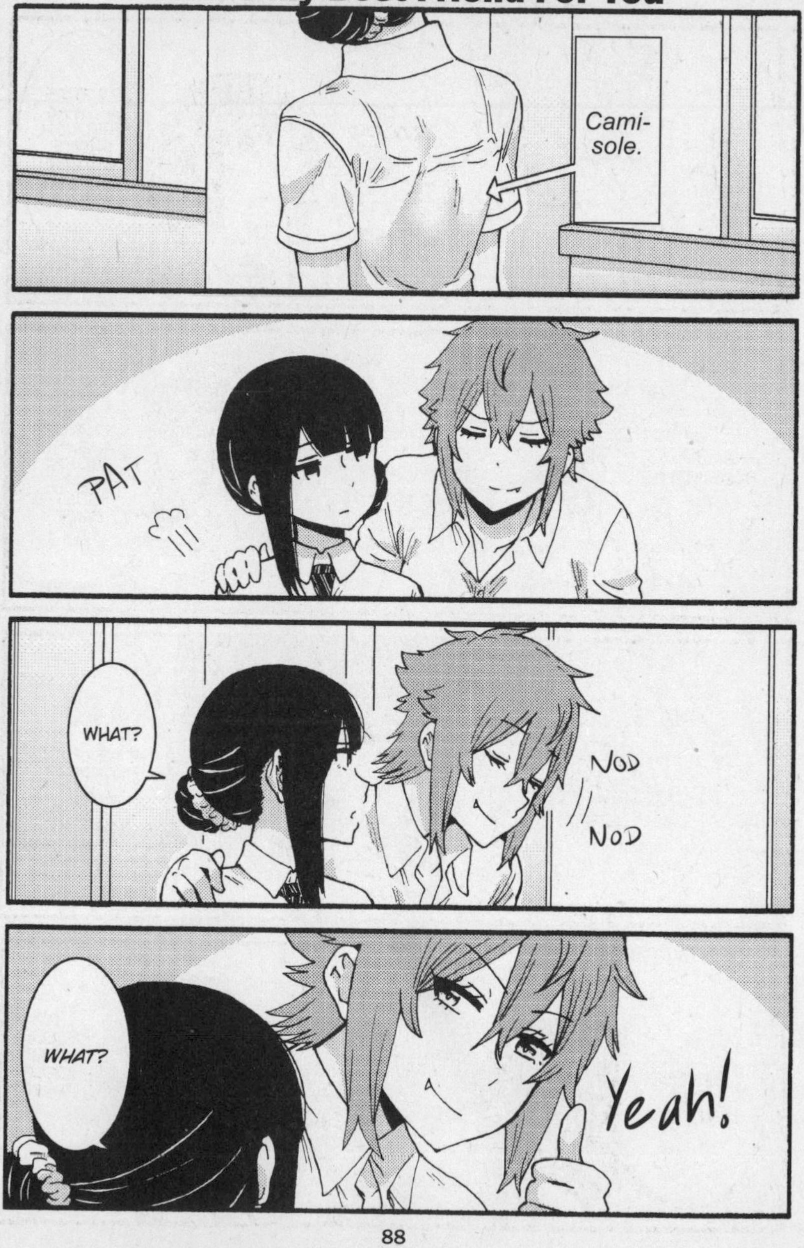
Cami-
sole.
PAT
WHAT?
NOD
NOD
WHAT?
Yeah!

Don't Go to Extremes

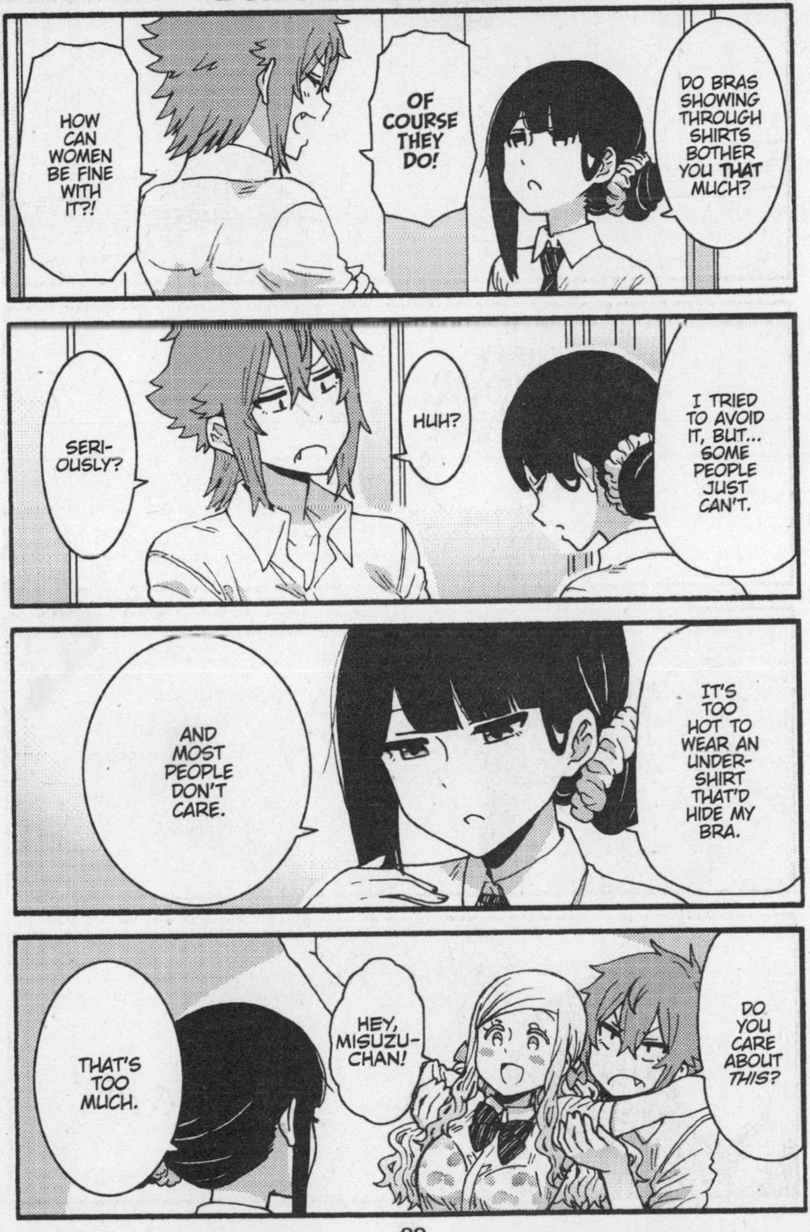
DO BRAS SHOWING THROUGH SHIRTS BOTHER YOU **THAT** MUCH?
OF COURSE THEY DO!
HOW CAN WOMEN BE FINE WITH IT?!
I TRIED TO AVOID IT, BUT... SOME PEOPLE JUST CAN'T.
HUH?
SERI-OUSLY?
IT'S TOO HOT TO WEAR AN UNDER-SHIRT THAT'D HIDE MY BRA.
AND MOST PEOPLE DON'T CARE.
DO YOU CARE ABOUT *THIS*?
HEY, MISUZU-CHAN!
THAT'S TOO MUCH.

Beware!

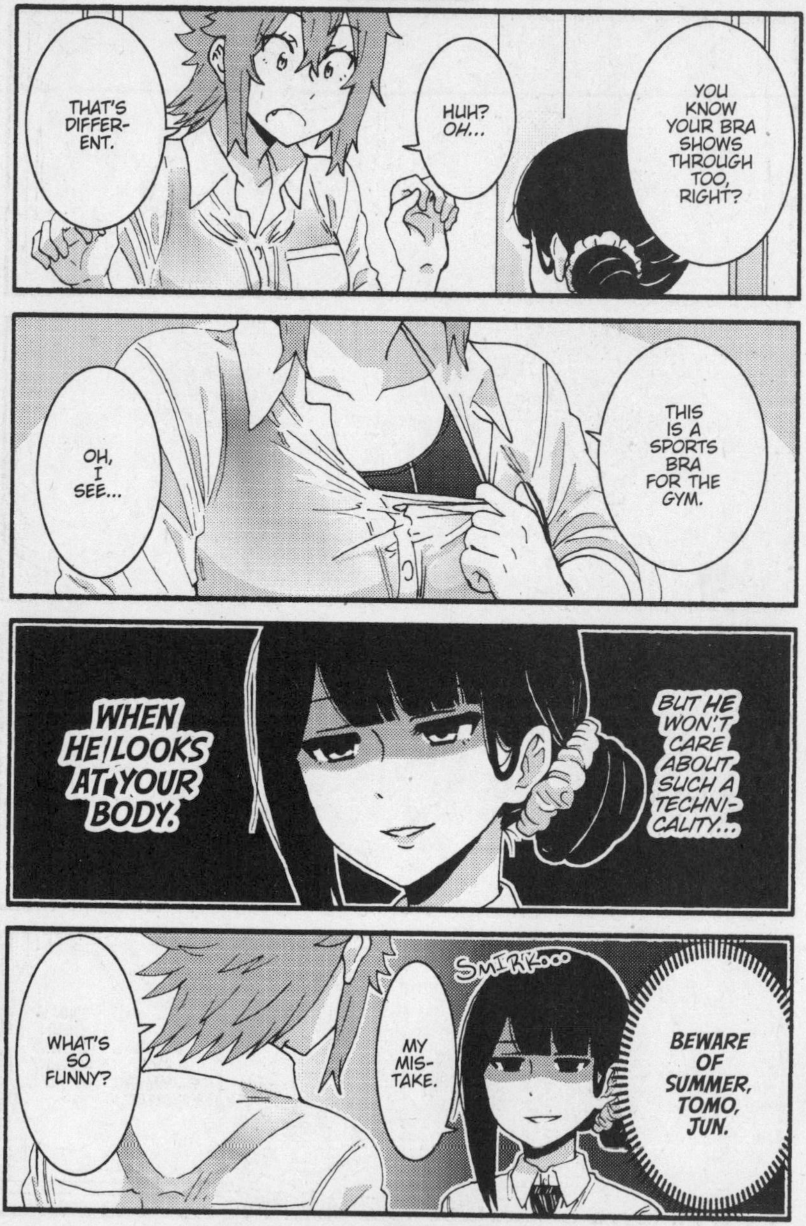

YOU KNOW YOUR BRA SHOWS THROUGH TOO, RIGHT?
HUH? OH...
THAT'S DIFFER-ENT.
THIS IS A SPORTS BRA FOR THE GYM.
OH, I SEE...
BUT HE WON'T CARE ABOUT SUCH A TECHNI-CALITY...
WHEN HE LOOKS AT YOUR BODY.
BEWARE OF SUMMER, TOMO, JUN.
SMIRK...
MY MIS-TAKE.
WHAT'S SO FUNNY?

So Hot

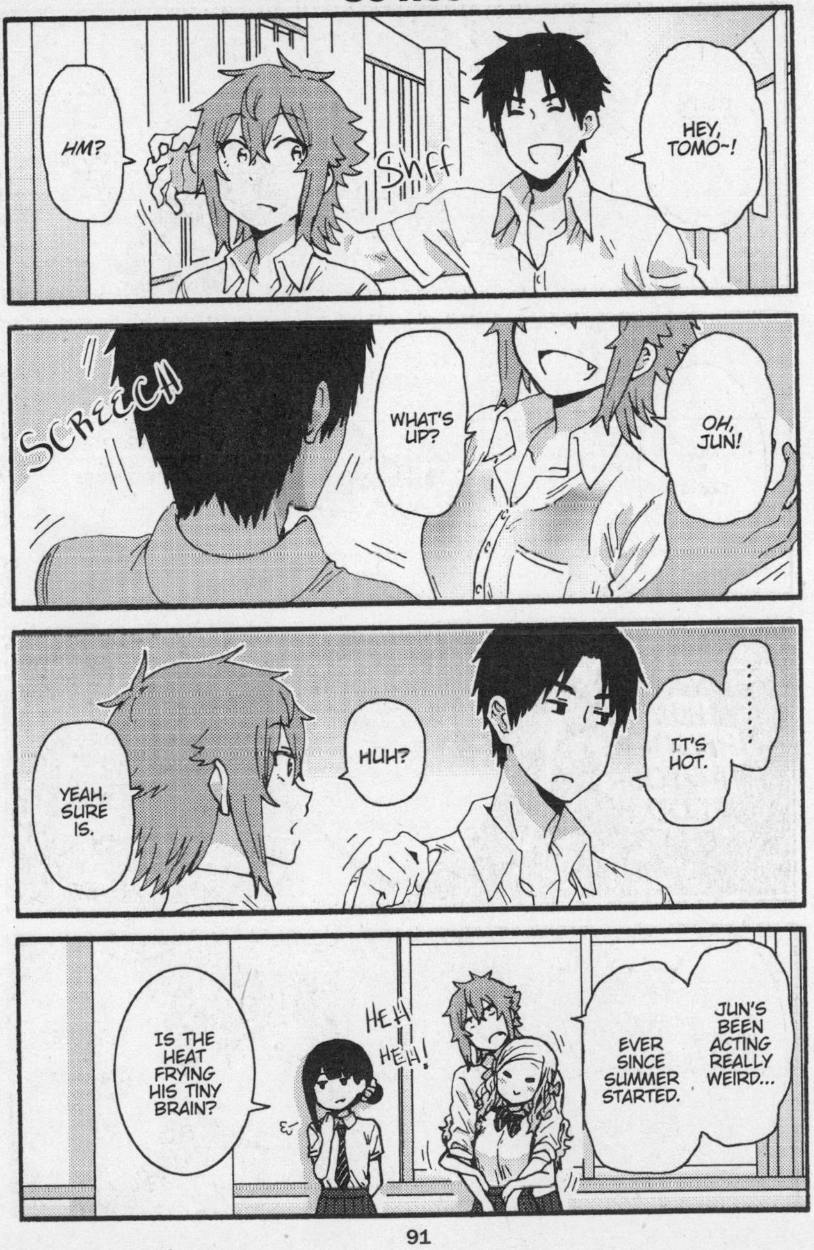
HEY, TOMO~!
SHFF
HM?
OH, JUN!
WHAT'S UP?
SCREECH
......
IT'S HOT.
HUH?
YEAH. SURE IS.
JUN'S BEEN ACTING REALLY WEIRD...
EVER SINCE SUMMER STARTED.
HEH HEH!
IS THE HEAT FRYING HIS TINY BRAIN?

Blind or Blinding?

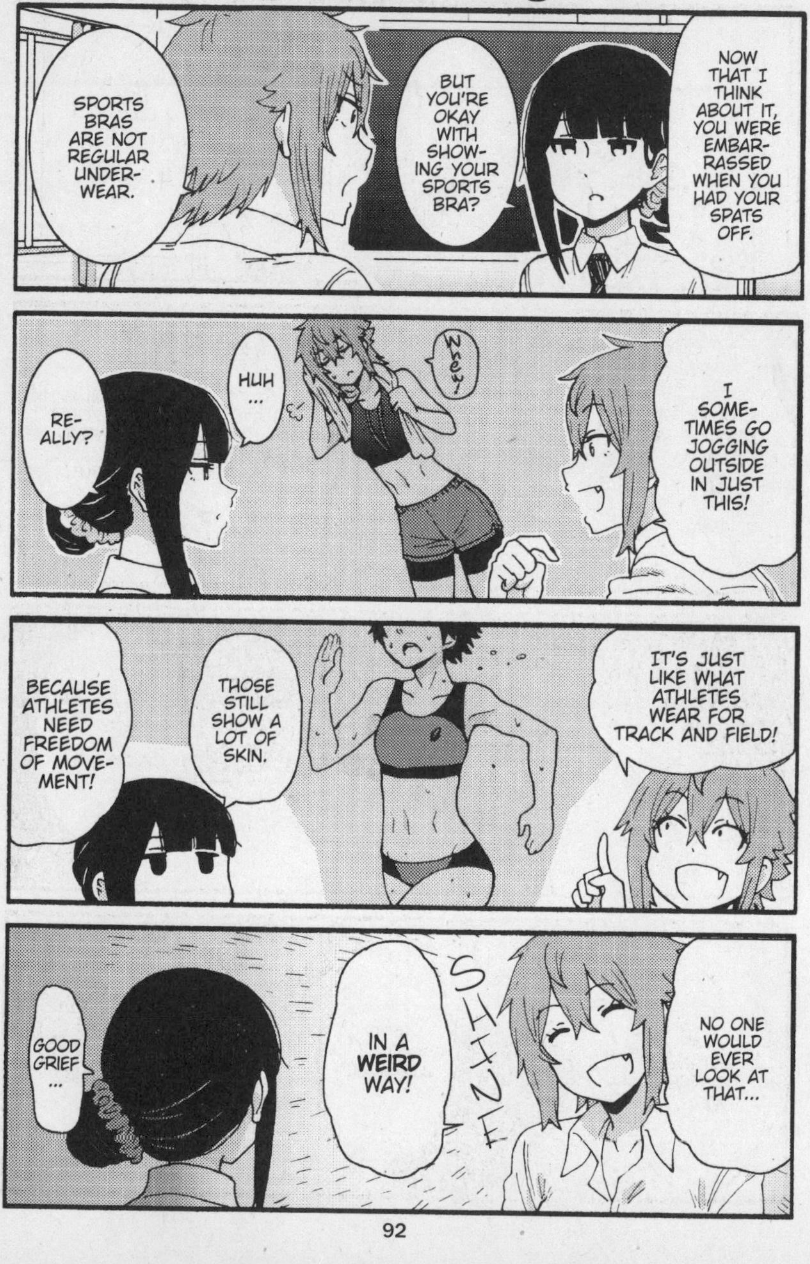
NOW THAT I THINK ABOUT IT, YOU WERE EMBARRASSED WHEN YOU HAD YOUR SPATS OFF.
BUT YOU'RE OKAY WITH SHOWING YOUR SPORTS BRA?
SPORTS BRAS ARE NOT REGULAR UNDERWEAR.
I SOMETIMES GO JOGGING OUTSIDE IN JUST THIS!
Whew!
HUH ...
REALLY?
IT'S JUST LIKE WHAT ATHLETES WEAR FOR TRACK AND FIELD!
THOSE STILL SHOW A LOT OF SKIN.
BECAUSE ATHLETES NEED FREEDOM OF MOVEMENT!
NO ONE WOULD EVER LOOK AT THAT...
SHINE
IN A WEIRD WAY!
GOOD GRIEF ...

He's an Aesthete

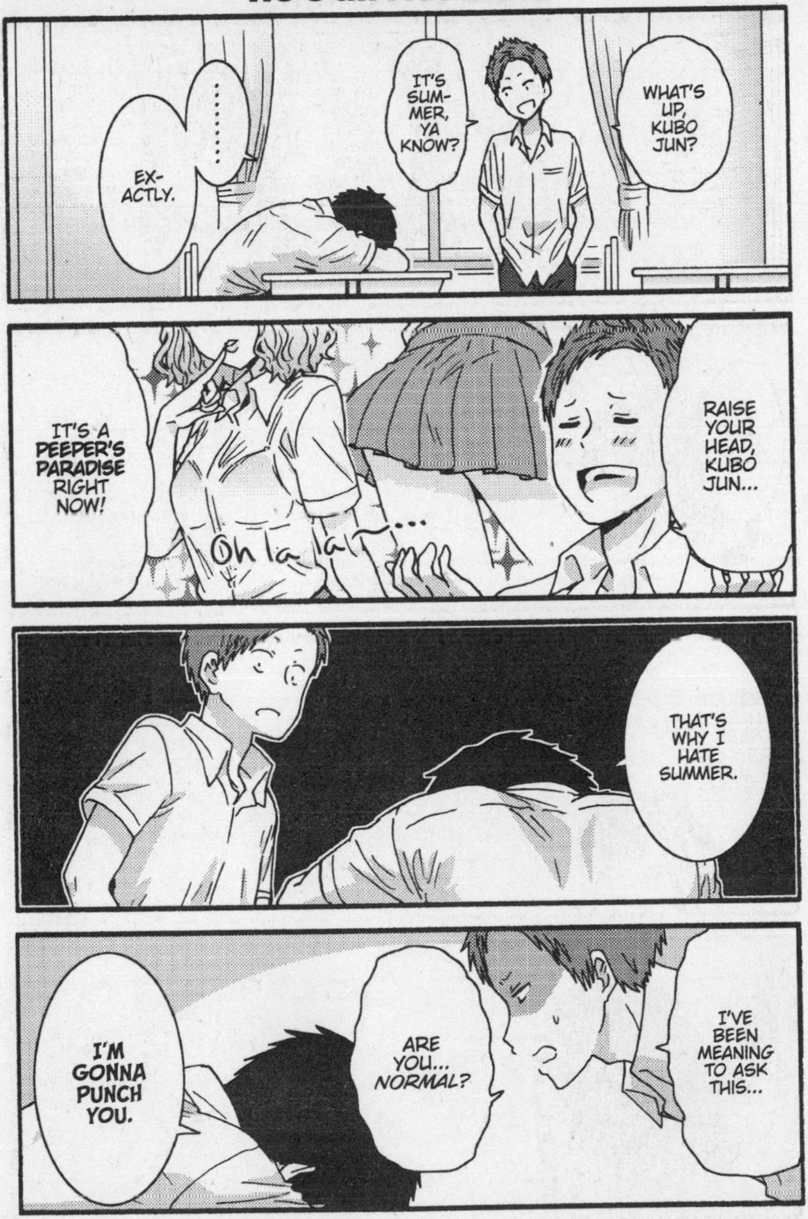
WHAT'S UP, KUBO JUN?
IT'S SUMMER, YA KNOW?
......
EXACTLY.
RAISE YOUR HEAD, KUBO JUN...
IT'S A PEEPER'S PARADISE RIGHT NOW!
Oh la la~...
THAT'S WHY I HATE SUMMER.
I'VE BEEN MEANING TO ASK THIS...
ARE YOU... *NORMAL?*
I'M GONNA PUNCH YOU.

Triggered

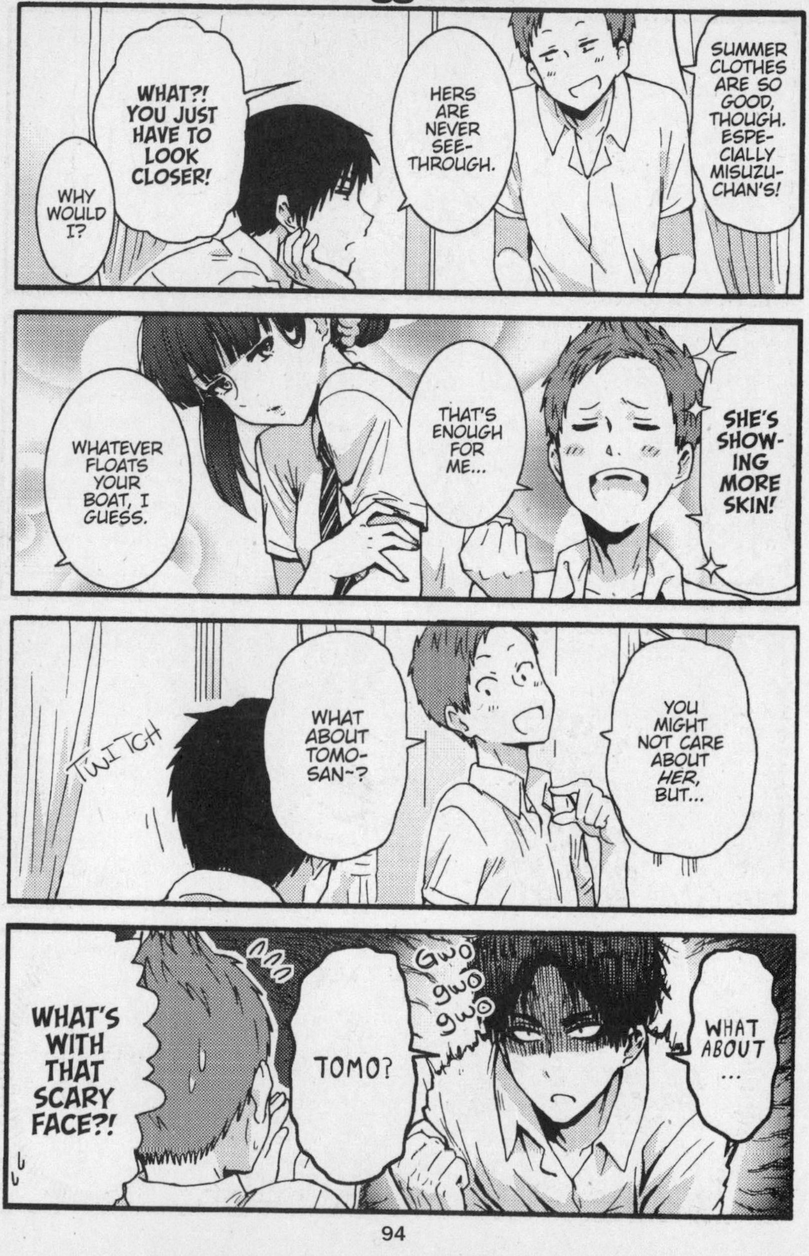
SUMMER CLOTHES ARE SO GOOD, THOUGH. ESPECIALLY MISUZU-CHAN'S!
HERS ARE NEVER SEE-THROUGH.
WHAT?! YOU JUST HAVE TO LOOK CLOSER!
WHY WOULD I?
SHE'S SHOWING MORE SKIN!
THAT'S ENOUGH FOR ME...
WHATEVER FLOATS YOUR BOAT, I GUESS.
YOU MIGHT NOT CARE ABOUT *HER*, BUT...
WHAT ABOUT TOMO-SAN~?
TWITCH
WHAT ABOUT ...
GWO GWO GWO
TOMO?
WHAT'S WITH THAT SCARY FACE?!

Sports Bra Incident

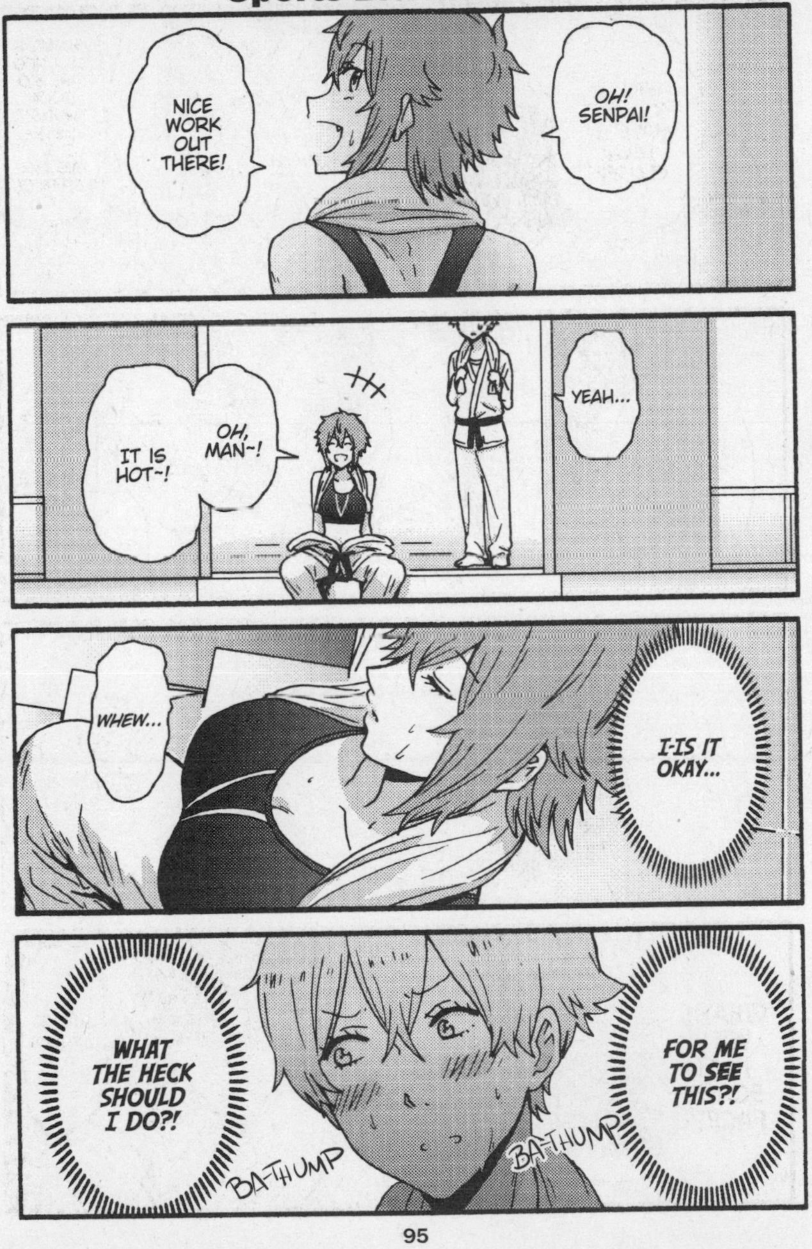
OH! SENPAI!
NICE WORK OUT THERE!
YEAH...
OH, MAN~!
IT IS HOT~!
I-IS IT OKAY...
WHEW...
FOR ME TO SEE THIS?!
BA-THUMP
WHAT THE HECK SHOULD I DO?!
BA-THUMP

Sports Bra Incident II

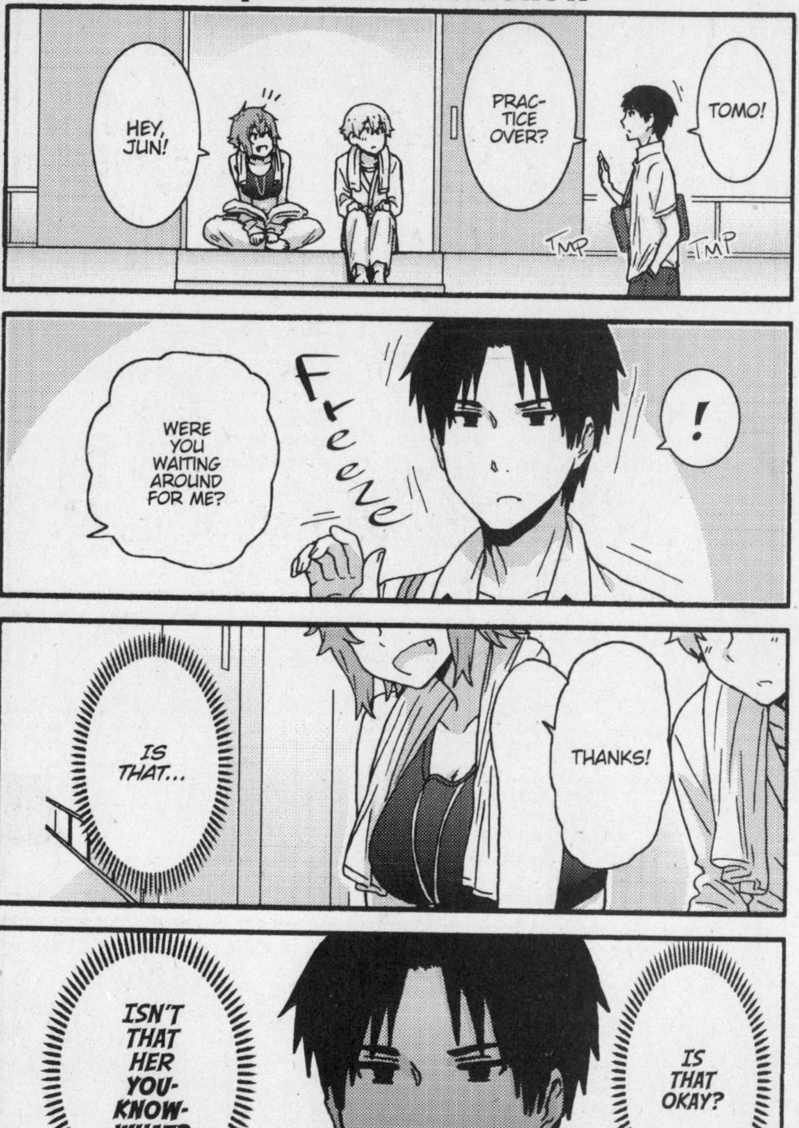
TOMO!
TMP
TMP
PRAC-TICE OVER?
HEY, JUN!
!
Freeze
WERE YOU WAITING AROUND FOR ME?
THANKS!
IS THAT...
IS THAT OKAY?
ISN'T THAT HER YOU-KNOW-WHAT?

Loser Has to Tell Her

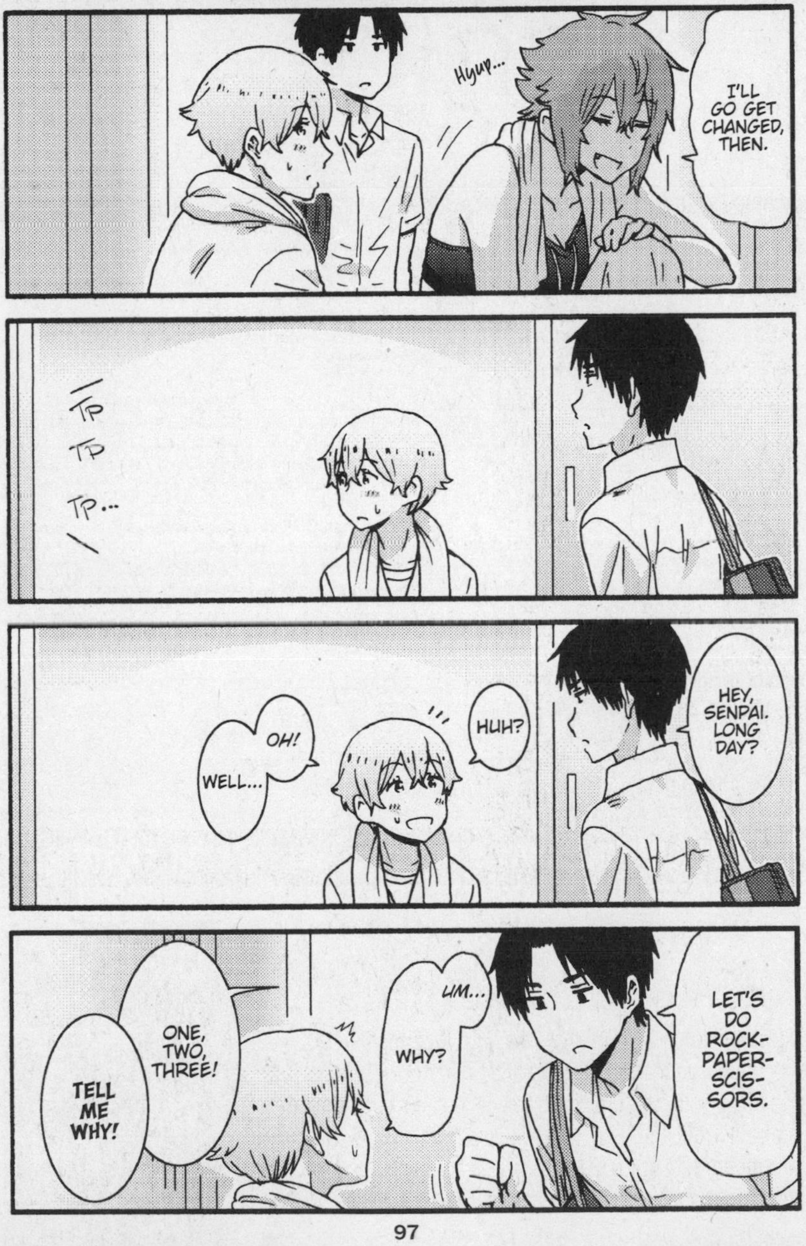
I'LL GO GET CHANGED, THEN.
Hyup...
TP
TP
TP...
HEY, SENPAI. LONG DAY?
HUH?
OH!
WELL...
LET'S DO ROCK-PAPER-SCISSORS.
UM...
WHY?
ONE, TWO, THREE!
TELL ME WHY!

How Would That Even Work?

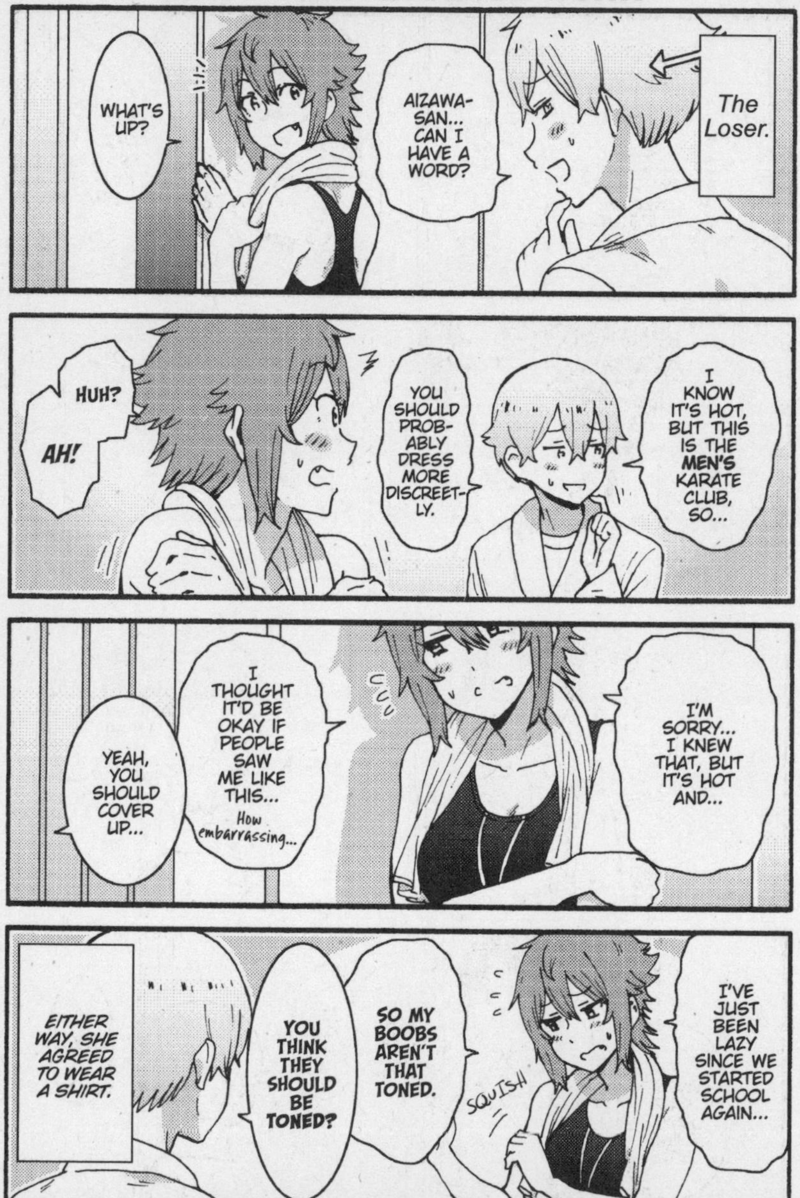
The Loser.
AIZAWA-SAN... CAN I HAVE A WORD?
WHAT'S UP?
I KNOW IT'S HOT, BUT THIS IS THE **MEN'S** KARATE CLUB, SO...
YOU SHOULD PROBABLY DRESS MORE DISCREETLY.
HUH? AH!
I'M SORRY... I KNEW THAT, BUT IT'S HOT AND...
I THOUGHT IT'D BE OKAY IF PEOPLE SAW ME LIKE THIS... How embarrassing...
YEAH, YOU SHOULD COVER UP...
I'VE JUST BEEN LAZY SINCE WE STARTED SCHOOL AGAIN...
SQUISH
SO MY BOOBS AREN'T THAT TONED.
YOU THINK THEY SHOULD BE TONED?
EITHER WAY, SHE AGREED TO WEAR A SHIRT.

Not At All

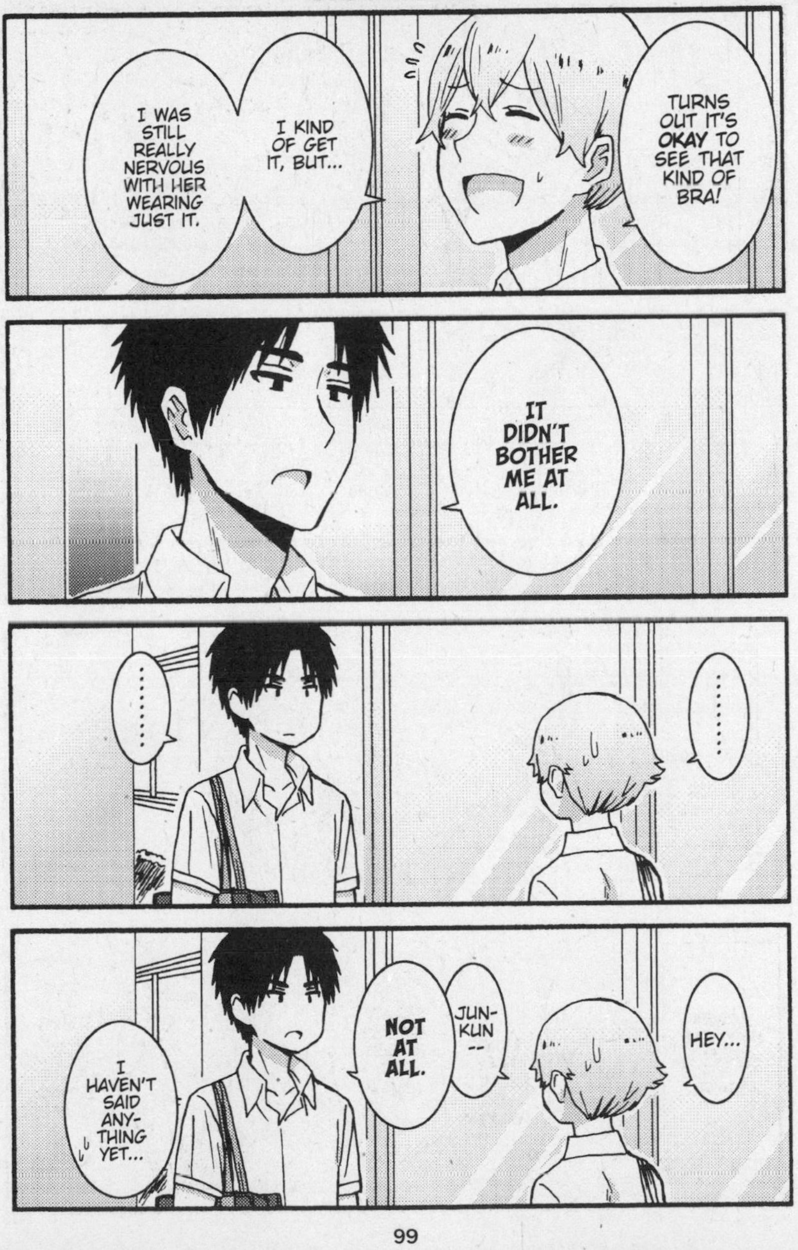
TURNS OUT IT'S **OKAY** TO SEE THAT KIND OF BRA!
I KIND OF GET IT, BUT...
I WAS STILL REALLY NERVOUS WITH HER WEARING JUST IT.
IT DIDN'T BOTHER ME AT ALL.
....
....
HEY...
JUN-KUN--
NOT AT ALL.
I HAVEN'T SAID ANY-THING YET...

His Personal Victory

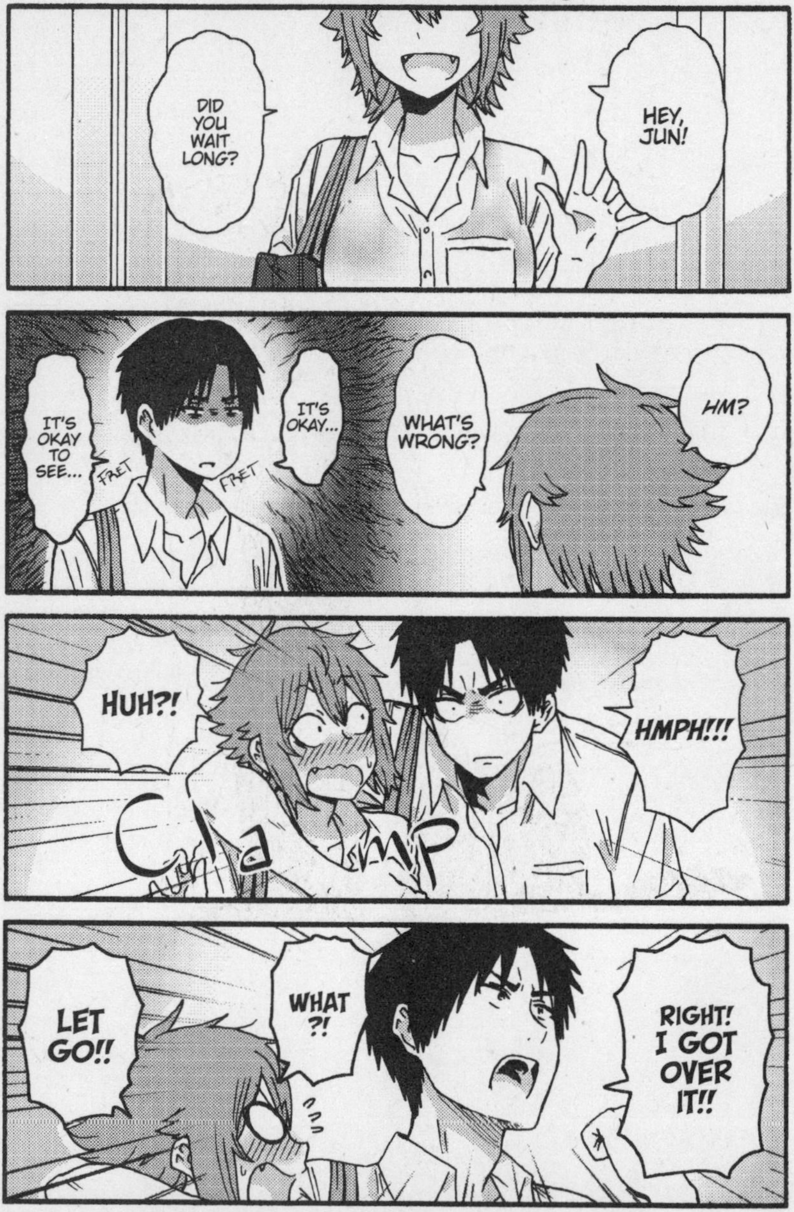
HEY, JUN!
DID YOU WAIT LONG?
HM?
WHAT'S WRONG?
IT'S OKAY...
FRET
FRET
IT'S OKAY TO SEE...
HMPH!!!
HUH?!
CLAMP
RIGHT! I GOT OVER IT!!
WHAT ?!
LET GO!!

OMAKE

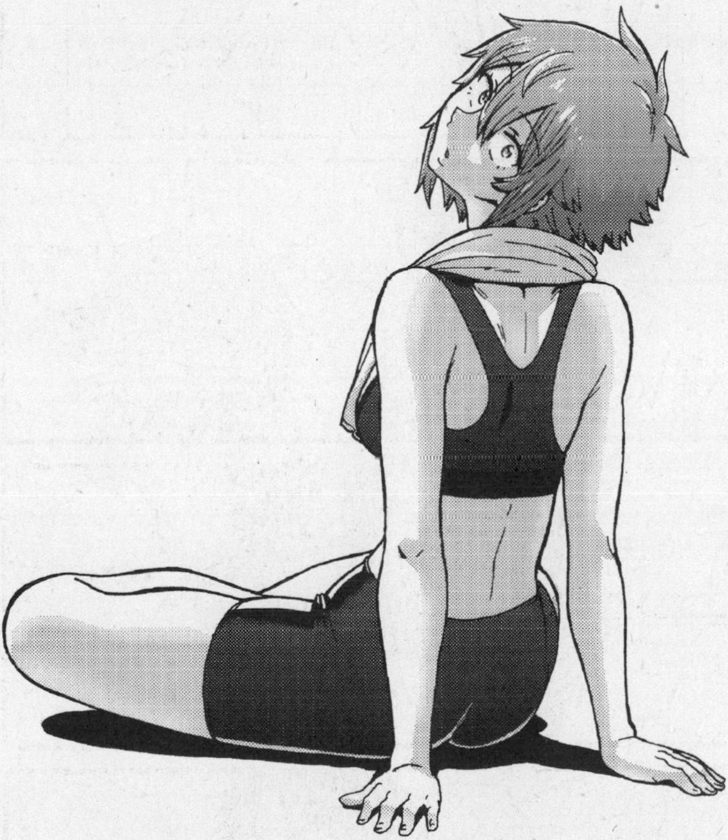

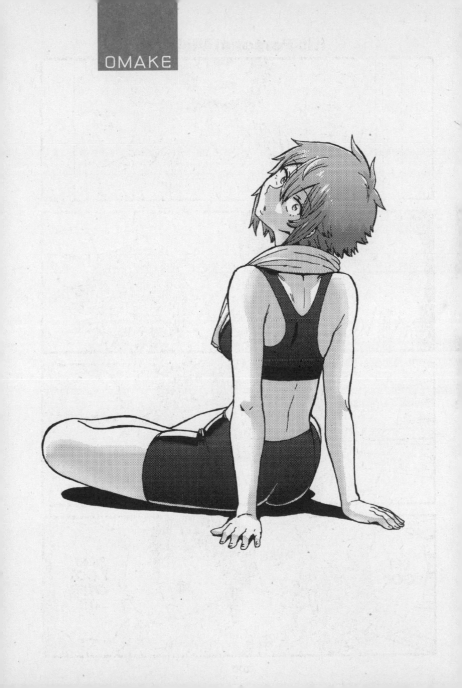

TOMO-CHAN
IS A GIRL!

Ch. 23

Tomo-chan Is a Leo

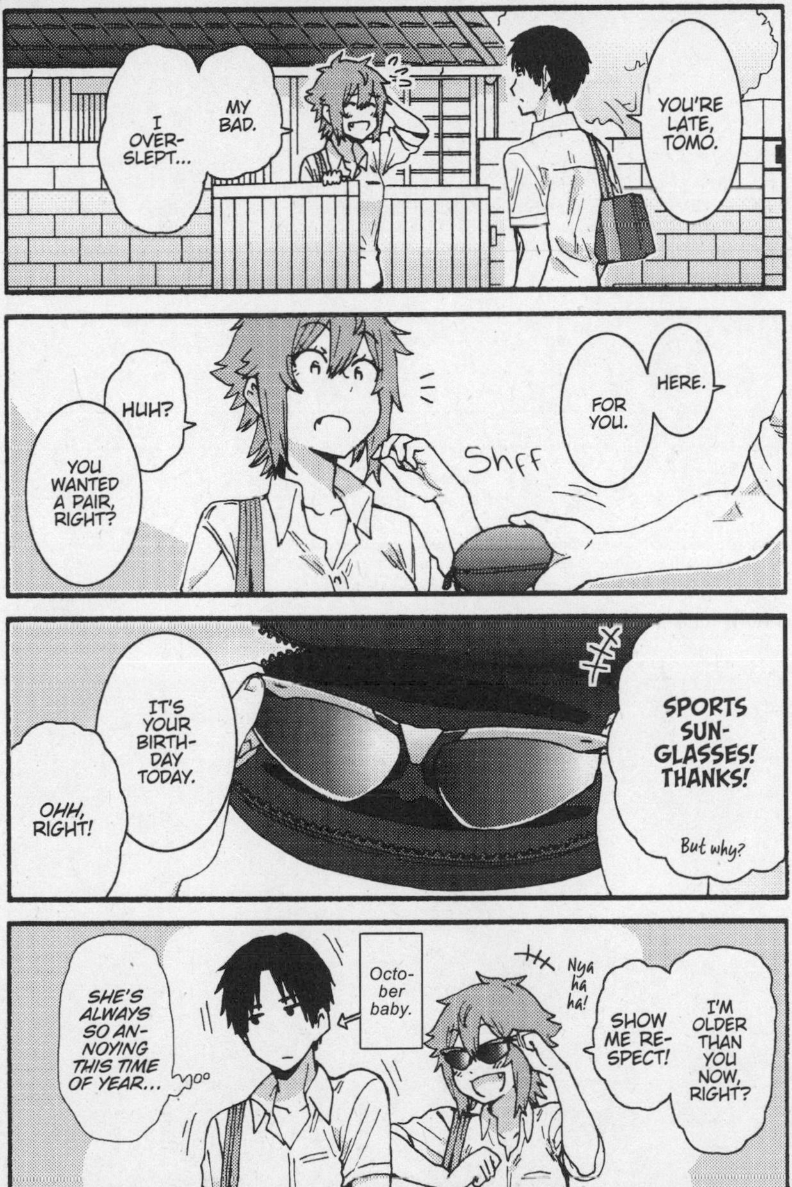
YOU'RE LATE, TOMO.
MY BAD.
I OVER-SLEPT...
HERE.
FOR YOU.
Shff
HUH?
YOU WANTED A PAIR, RIGHT?
SPORTS SUN-GLASSES! THANKS!
But why?
IT'S YOUR BIRTH-DAY TODAY.
OHH, RIGHT!
I'M OLDER THAN YOU NOW, RIGHT?
SHOW ME RE-SPECT!
Nya ha ha!
Octo-ber baby.
SHE'S ALWAYS SO AN-NOYING THIS TIME OF YEAR...

Annoying as Only a Friend Can Be

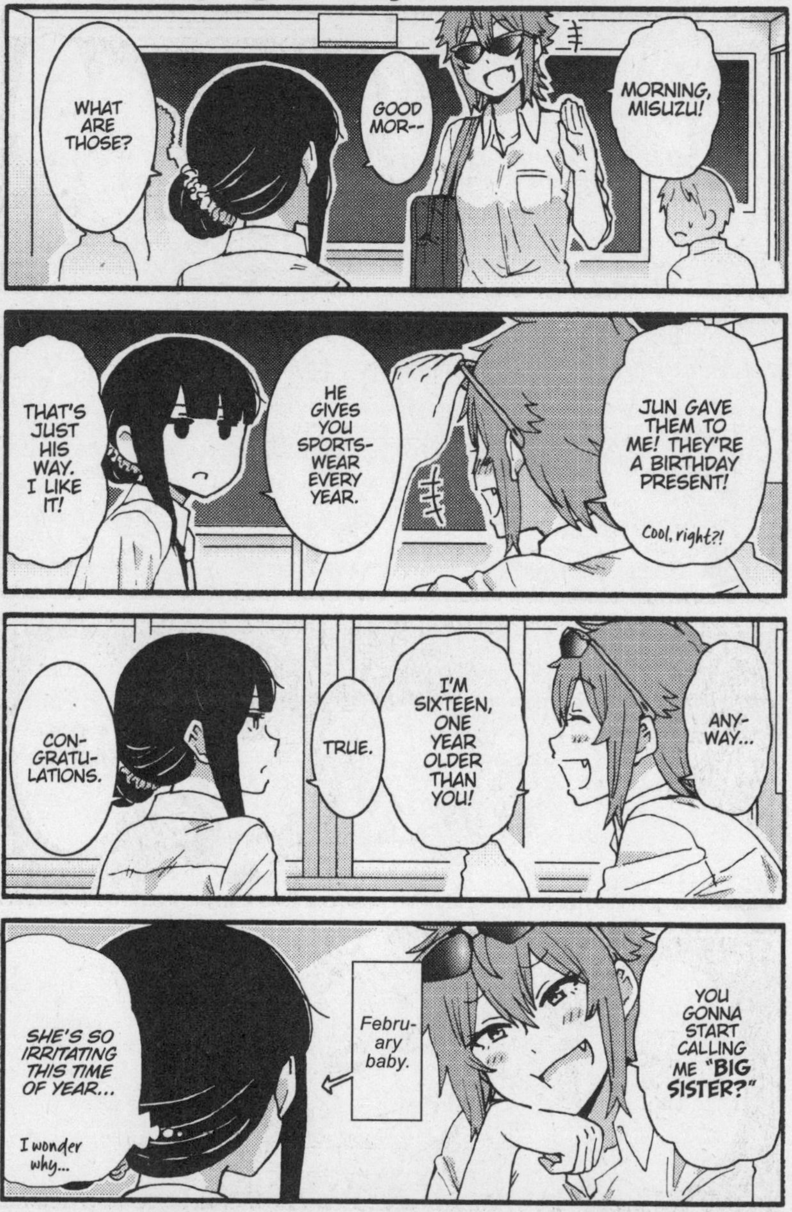
MORNING, MISUZU!
GOOD MOR--
WHAT ARE THOSE?
JUN GAVE THEM TO ME! THEY'RE A BIRTHDAY PRESENT!
Cool, right?!
HE GIVES YOU SPORTS-WEAR EVERY YEAR.
THAT'S JUST HIS WAY. I LIKE IT!
ANY-WAY...
I'M SIXTEEN, ONE YEAR OLDER THAN YOU!
TRUE.
CON-GRATU-LATIONS.
YOU GONNA START CALLING ME "BIG SISTER?"
February baby.
SHE'S SO IRRITATING THIS TIME OF YEAR...
I wonder why...

It's Practical

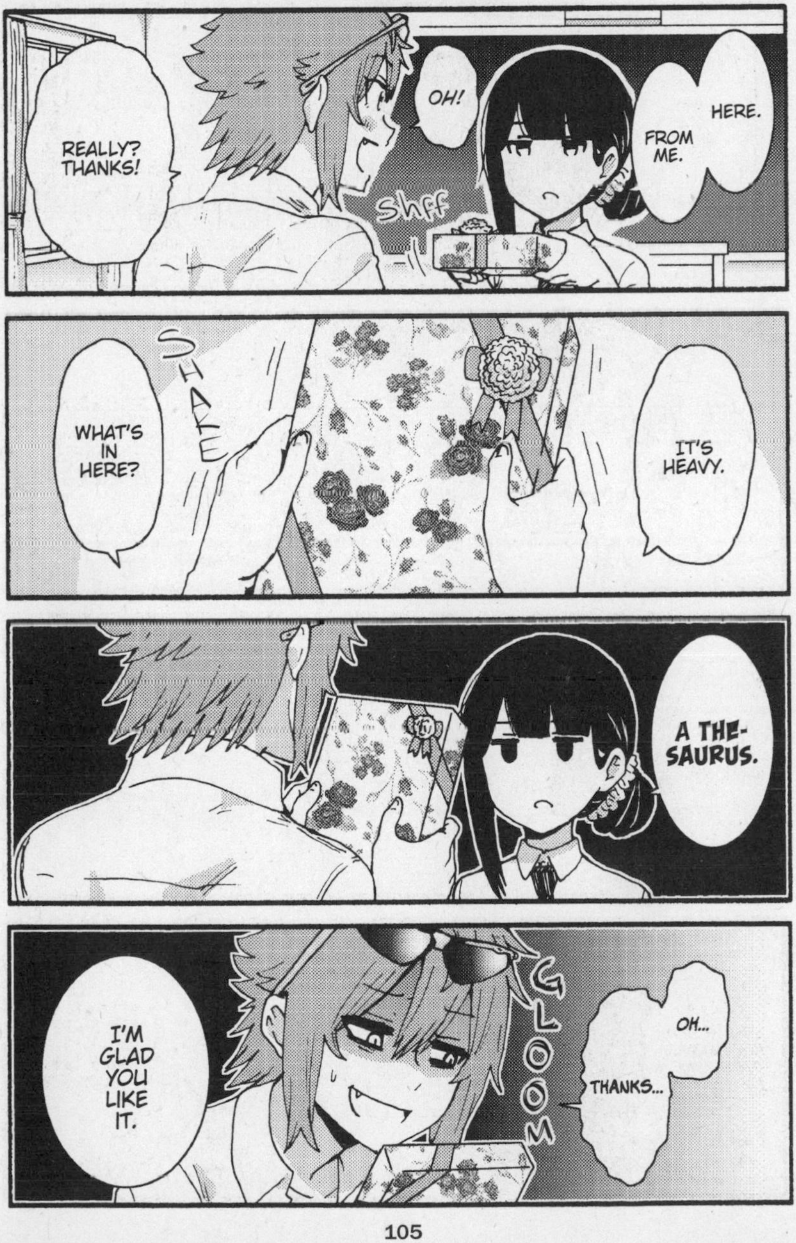

HERE.
FROM ME.
OH!
Shff
REALLY? THANKS!
IT'S HEAVY.
SHAKE
WHAT'S IN HERE?
A THE-SAURUS.
OH...
THANKS...
GLOOM
I'M GLAD YOU LIKE IT.

A Song and Three Bars

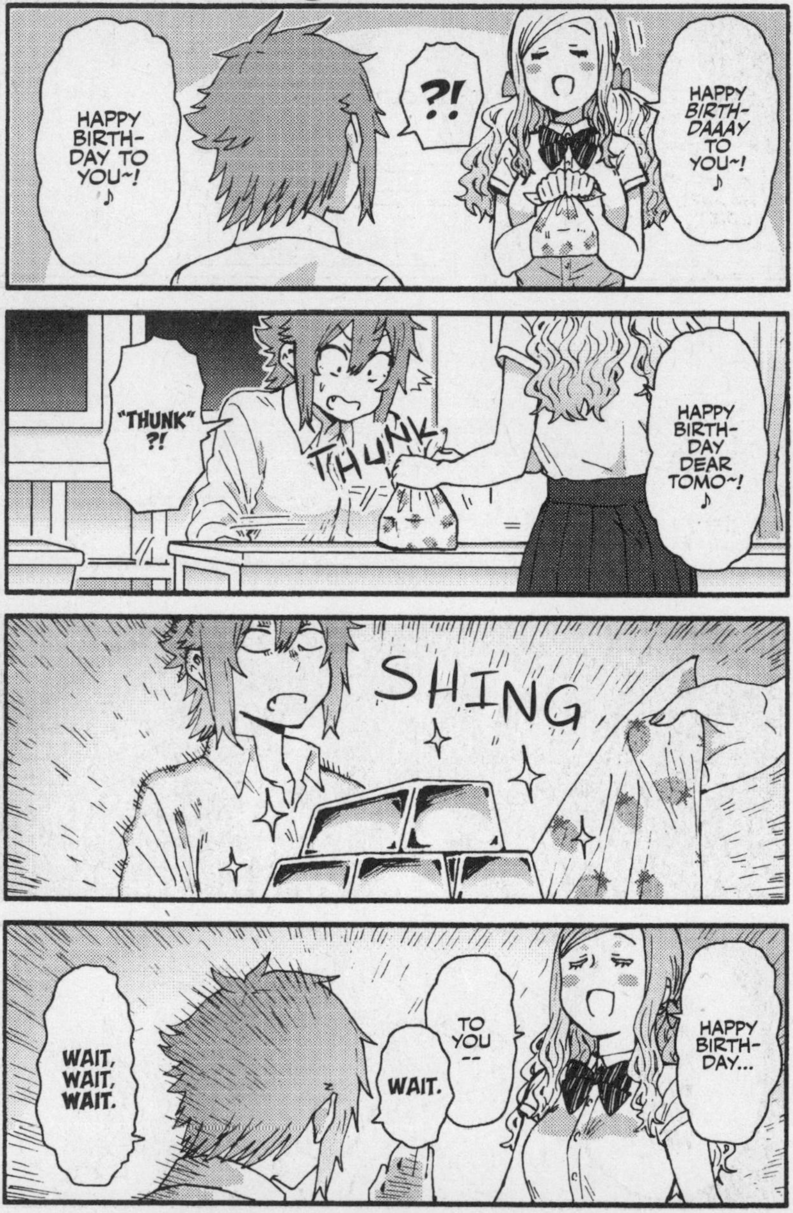
HAPPY BIRTH-DAAAY TO YOU~! ♪
?!
HAPPY BIRTH-DAY TO YOU~! ♪
HAPPY BIRTH-DAY DEAR TOMO~! ♪
THUNK
"THUNK" ?!
SHING
HAPPY BIRTH-DAY...
TO YOU --
WAIT.
WAIT, WAIT, WAIT.

Sounds Legit

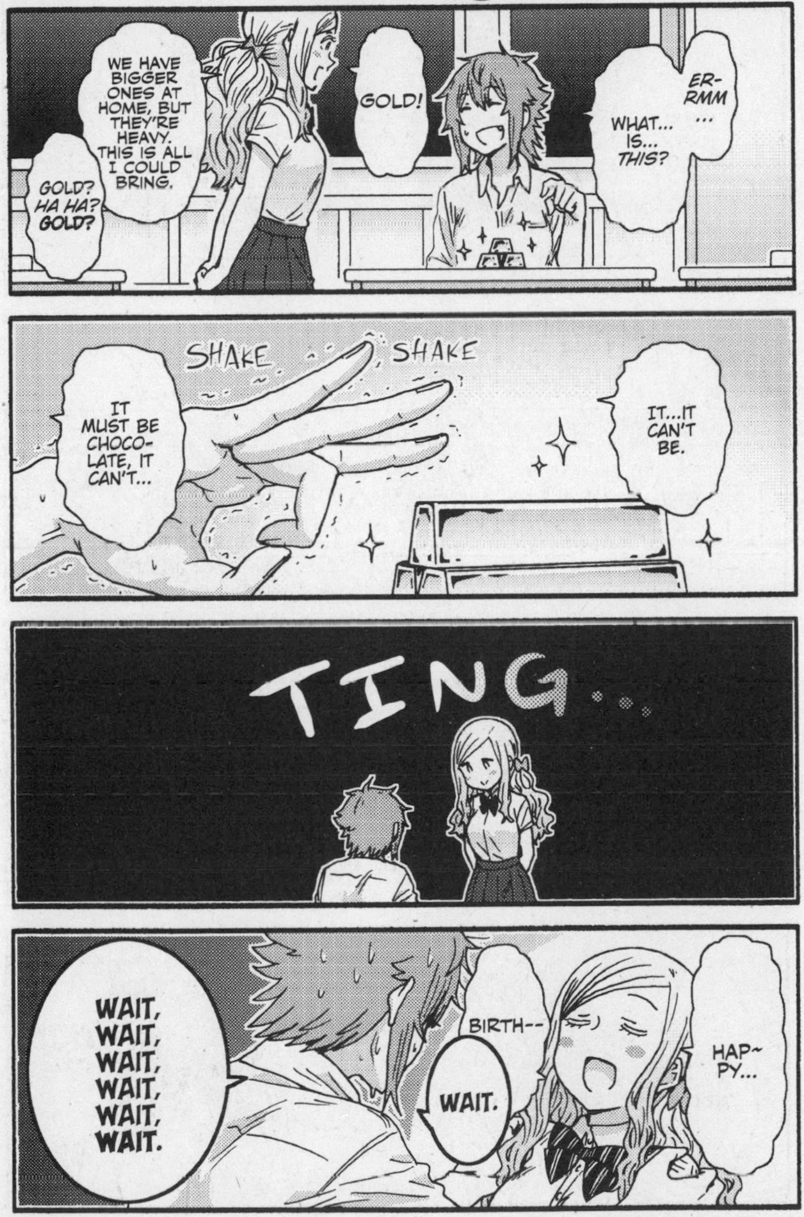
ER-RMM...
WHAT... IS... THIS?
GOLD!
WE HAVE BIGGER ONES AT HOME, BUT THEY'RE HEAVY. THIS IS ALL I COULD BRING.
GOLD? HA HA? GOLD?
SHAKE
SHAKE
IT...IT CAN'T BE.
IT MUST BE CHOCO-LATE, IT CAN'T...
TING...
HAP~PY...
BIRTH--
WAIT.
WAIT, WAIT, WAIT, WAIT, WAIT, WAIT.

Guide

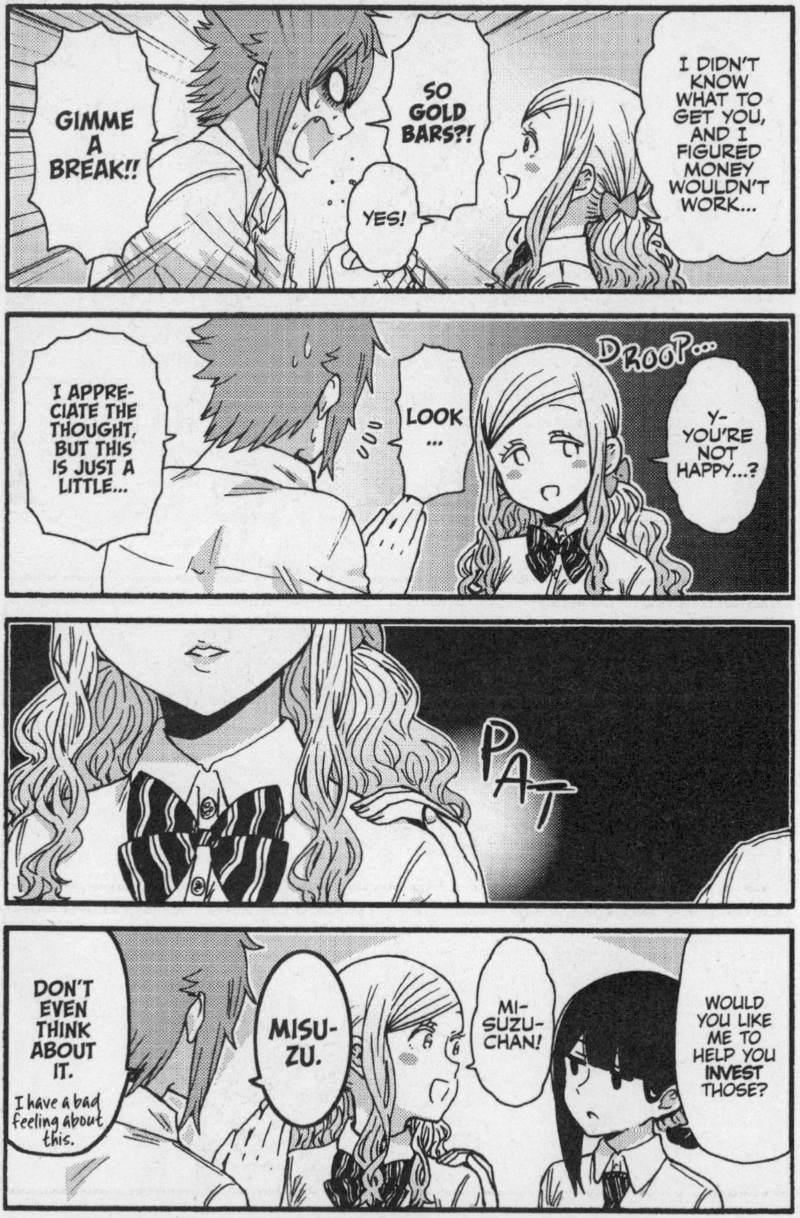

I DIDN'T KNOW WHAT TO GET YOU, AND I FIGURED MONEY WOULDN'T WORK...
SO GOLD BARS?!
YES!
GIMME A BREAK!!
DROOP...
Y-YOU'RE NOT HAPPY...?
LOOK...
I APPRECIATE THE THOUGHT, BUT THIS IS JUST A LITTLE...
PAT
WOULD YOU LIKE ME TO HELP YOU INVEST THOSE?
MI-SUZU-CHAN!
MISU-ZU.
DON'T EVEN THINK ABOUT IT.
I have a bad feeling about this.

Open Secret

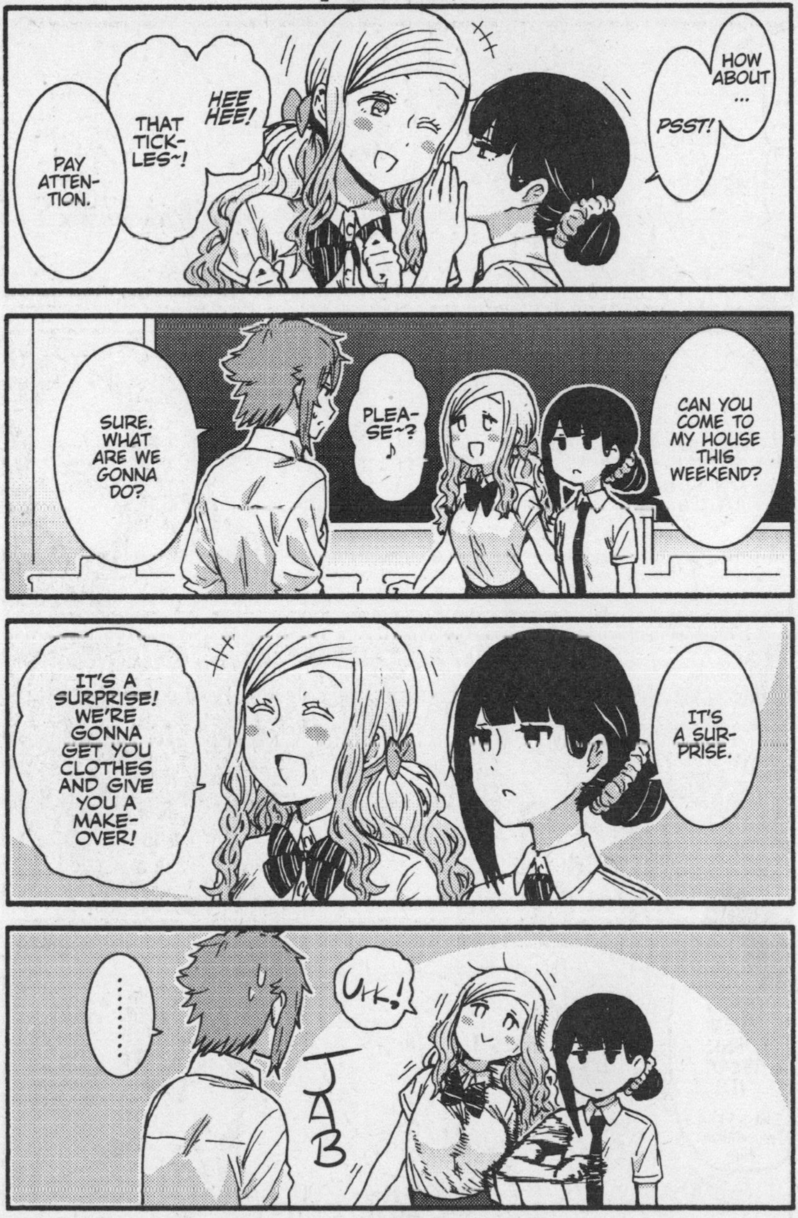

HOW ABOUT ... PSST!
HEE HEE!
THAT TICKLES~!
PAY ATTENTION.
CAN YOU COME TO MY HOUSE THIS WEEKEND?
PLEASE~? ♪
SURE. WHAT ARE WE GONNA DO?
IT'S A SURPRISE.
IT'S A SURPRISE! WE'RE GONNA GET YOU CLOTHES AND GIVE YOU A MAKEOVER!
Urk!
JAB
....

It's Just "Dressing"

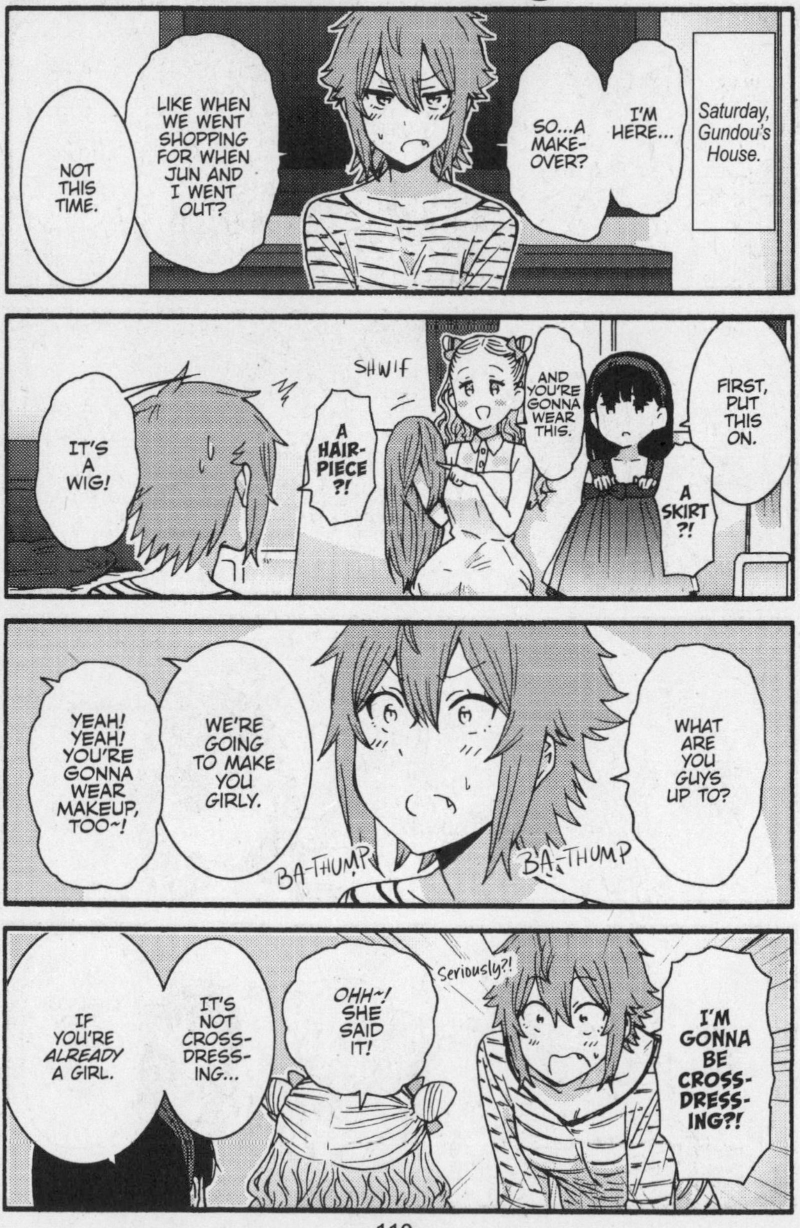
Saturday, Gundou's House.
I'M HERE...
SO...A MAKE-OVER?
LIKE WHEN WE WENT SHOPPING FOR WHEN JUN AND I WENT OUT?
NOT THIS TIME.
FIRST, PUT THIS ON.
A SKIRT?!
AND YOU'RE GONNA WEAR THIS.
SHWIF
A HAIRPIECE?!
IT'S A WIG!
WHAT ARE YOU GUYS UP TO?
BA-THUMP
BA-THUMP
WE'RE GOING TO MAKE YOU GIRLY.
YEAH! YEAH! YOU'RE GONNA WEAR MAKEUP, TOO~!
I'M GONNA BE CROSS-DRESSING?!
Seriously?!
OHH~! SHE SAID IT!
IT'S NOT CROSS-DRESSING...
IF YOU'RE *ALREADY* A GIRL.

About One-Third

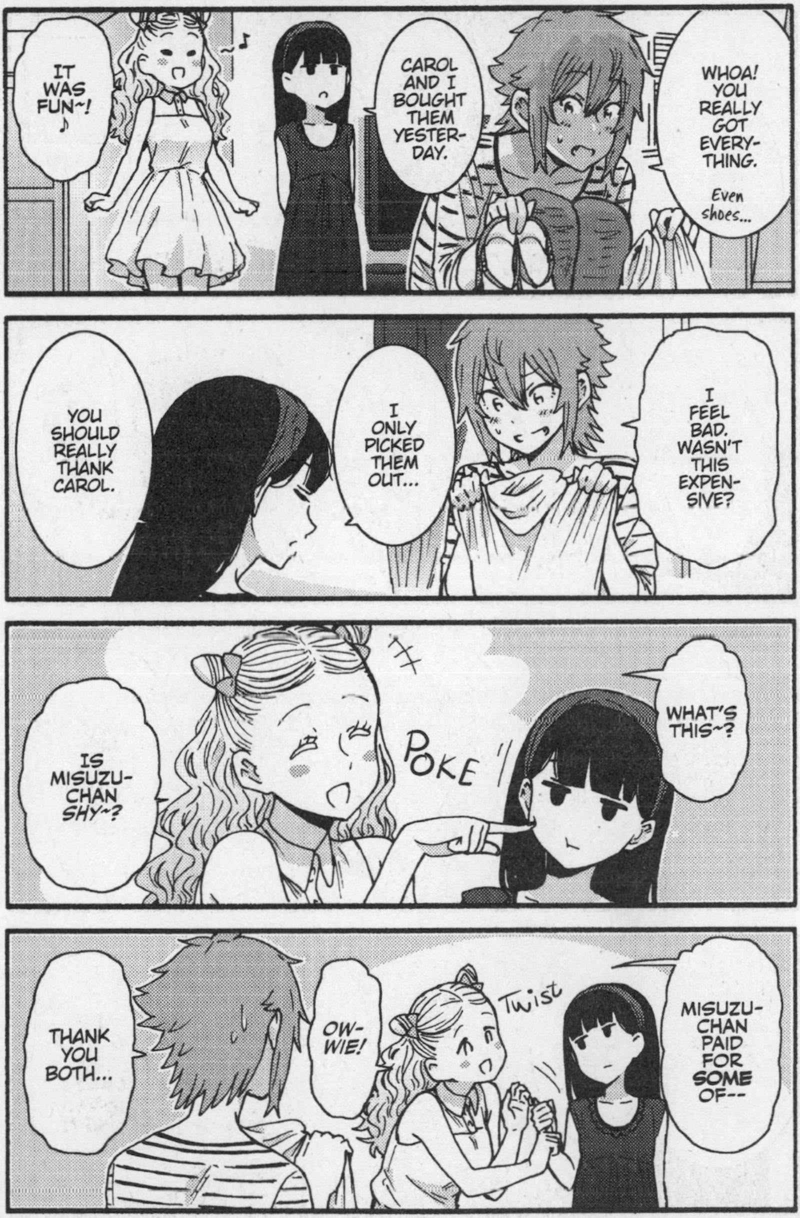
WHOA! YOU REALLY GOT EVERYTHING.
Even shoes...
CAROL AND I BOUGHT THEM YESTER-DAY.
IT WAS FUN~! ♪
I FEEL BAD. WASN'T THIS EXPEN-SIVE?
I ONLY PICKED THEM OUT...
YOU SHOULD REALLY THANK CAROL.
WHAT'S THIS~?
POKE
IS MISUZU-CHAN SHY~?
MISUZU-CHAN PAID FOR SOME OF--
Twist
OW-WIE!
THANK YOU BOTH...

Tap In, Carol

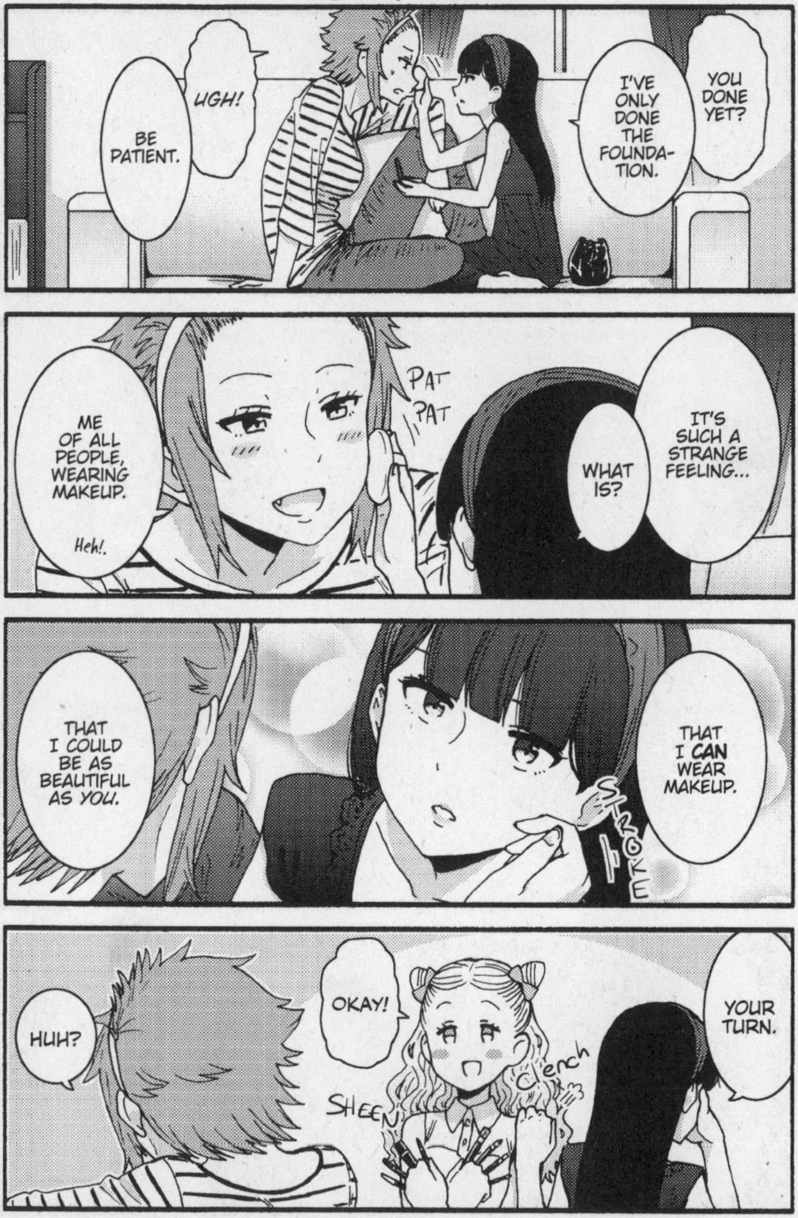
YOU DONE YET?
I'VE ONLY DONE THE FOUNDATION.
UGH!
BE PATIENT.
IT'S SUCH A STRANGE FEELING...
WHAT IS?
PAT PAT
ME OF ALL PEOPLE, WEARING MAKEUP.
Heh!.
THAT I **CAN** WEAR MAKEUP.
STROKE
THAT I COULD BE AS BEAUTIFUL AS *YOU*.
YOUR TURN.
Clench
OKAY!
SHEEN
HUH?

Impossible Not to Tease

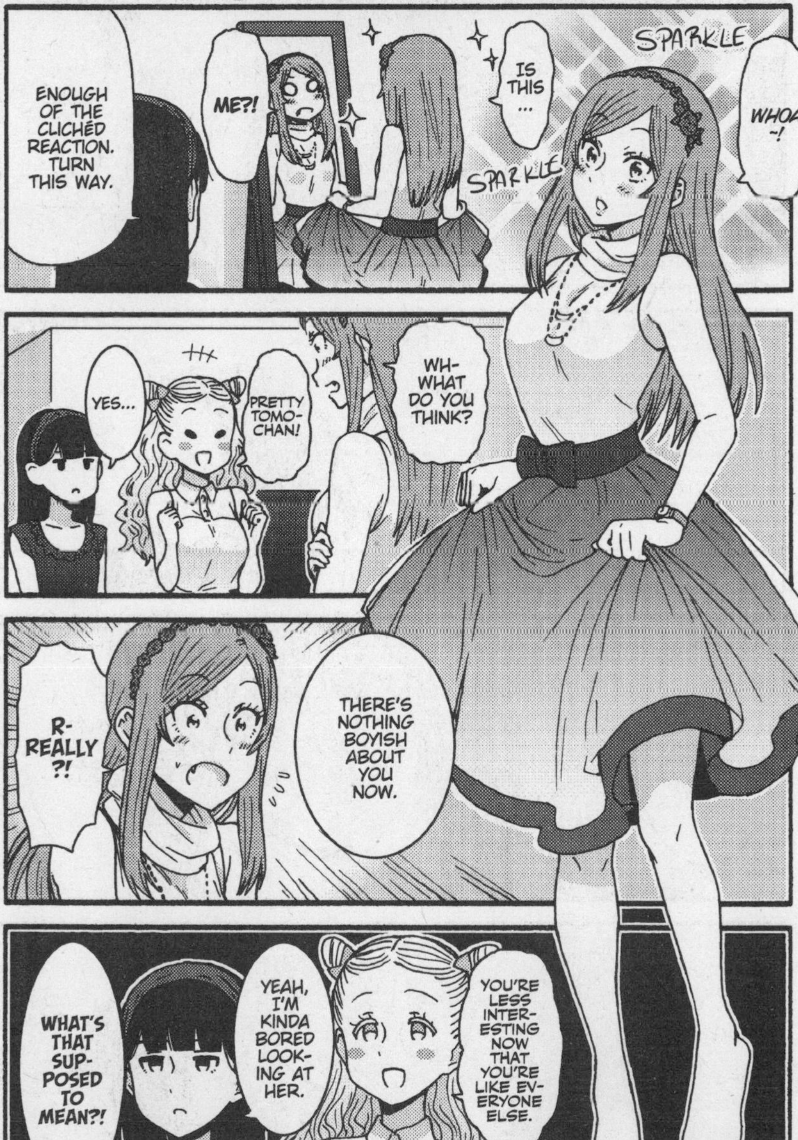
WHOA ~!
SPARKLE
IS THIS ...
SPARKLE
ME?!
ENOUGH OF THE CLICHÉD REACTION. TURN THIS WAY.
WH-WHAT DO YOU THINK?
PRETTY TOMO-CHAN!
YES...
THERE'S NOTHING BOYISH ABOUT YOU NOW.
R-REALLY?!
YOU'RE LESS INTER-ESTING NOW THAT YOU'RE LIKE EV-ERYONE ELSE.
YEAH, I'M KINDA BORED LOOKING AT HER.
WHAT'S THAT SUP-POSED TO MEAN?!

To Be Perfectly Honest

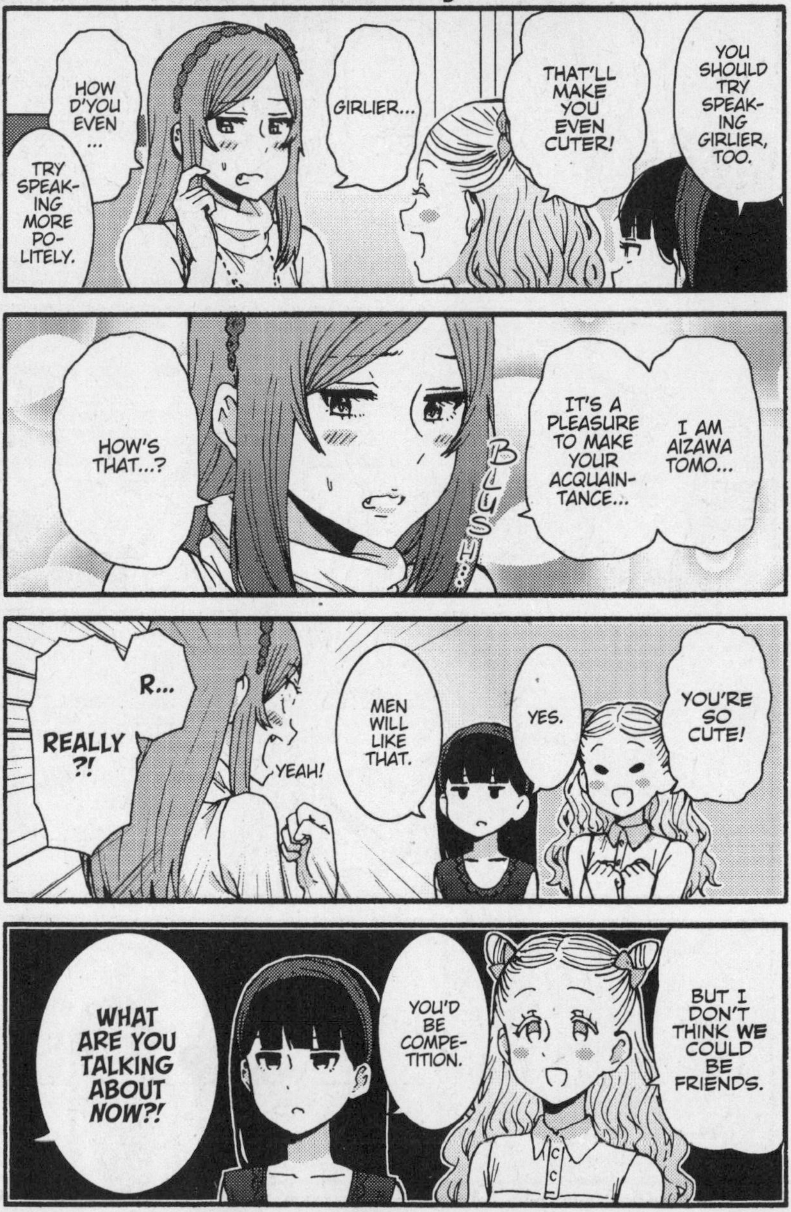
YOU SHOULD TRY SPEAKING GIRLIER, TOO.
THAT'LL MAKE YOU EVEN CUTER!
GIRLIER...
HOW D'YOU EVEN ...
TRY SPEAKING MORE POLITELY.
I AM AIZAWA TOMO...
IT'S A PLEASURE TO MAKE YOUR ACQUAINTANCE...
BLUSH...
HOW'S THAT...?
YOU'RE SO CUTE!
YES.
MEN WILL LIKE THAT.
YEAH!
R... REALLY?!
BUT I DON'T THINK WE COULD BE FRIENDS.
YOU'D BE COMPETITION.
WHAT ARE YOU TALKING ABOUT NOW?!

The Trap Is Sprung

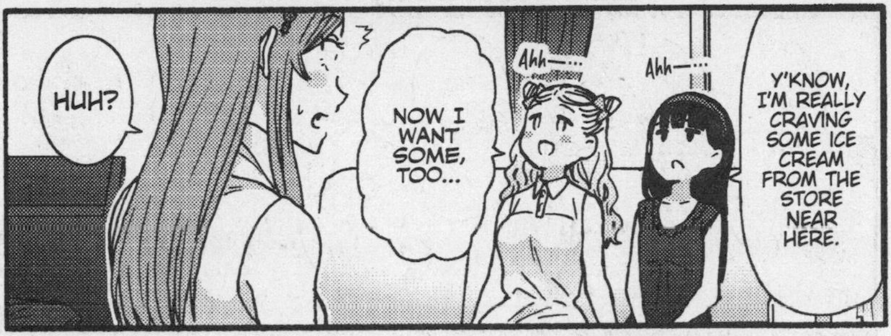

Y'KNOW, I'M REALLY CRAVING SOME ICE CREAM FROM THE STORE NEAR HERE.
Ahh—...
Ahh—...
NOW I WANT SOME, TOO...
HUH?

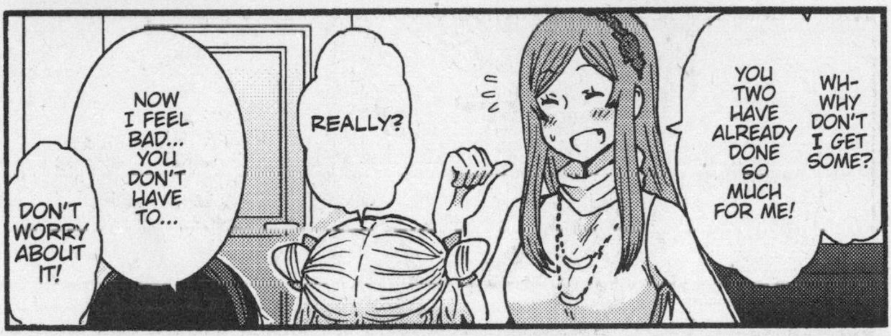

WH- WHY DON'T I GET SOME?
YOU TWO HAVE ALREADY DONE SO MUCH FOR ME!
REALLY?
NOW I FEEL BAD... YOU DON'T HAVE TO...
DON'T WORRY ABOUT IT!

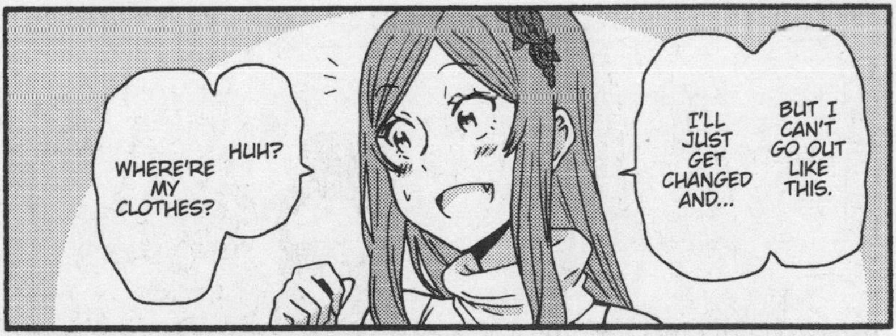

BUT I CAN'T GO OUT LIKE THIS.
I'LL JUST GET CHANGED AND...
HUH?
WHERE'RE MY CLOTHES?

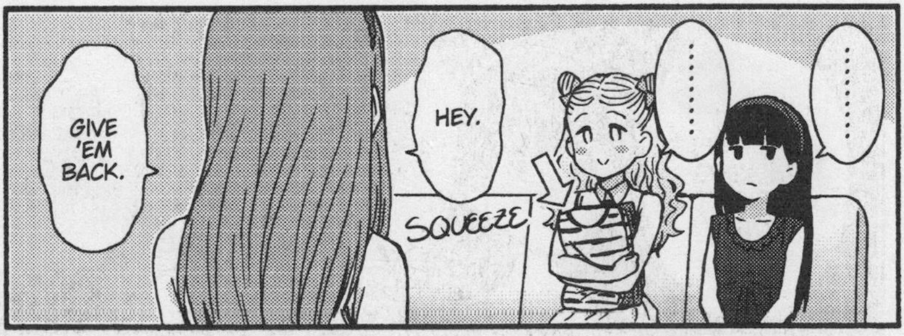

......
......
HEY.
SQUEEZE
GIVE 'EM BACK.

Strangers' Glances

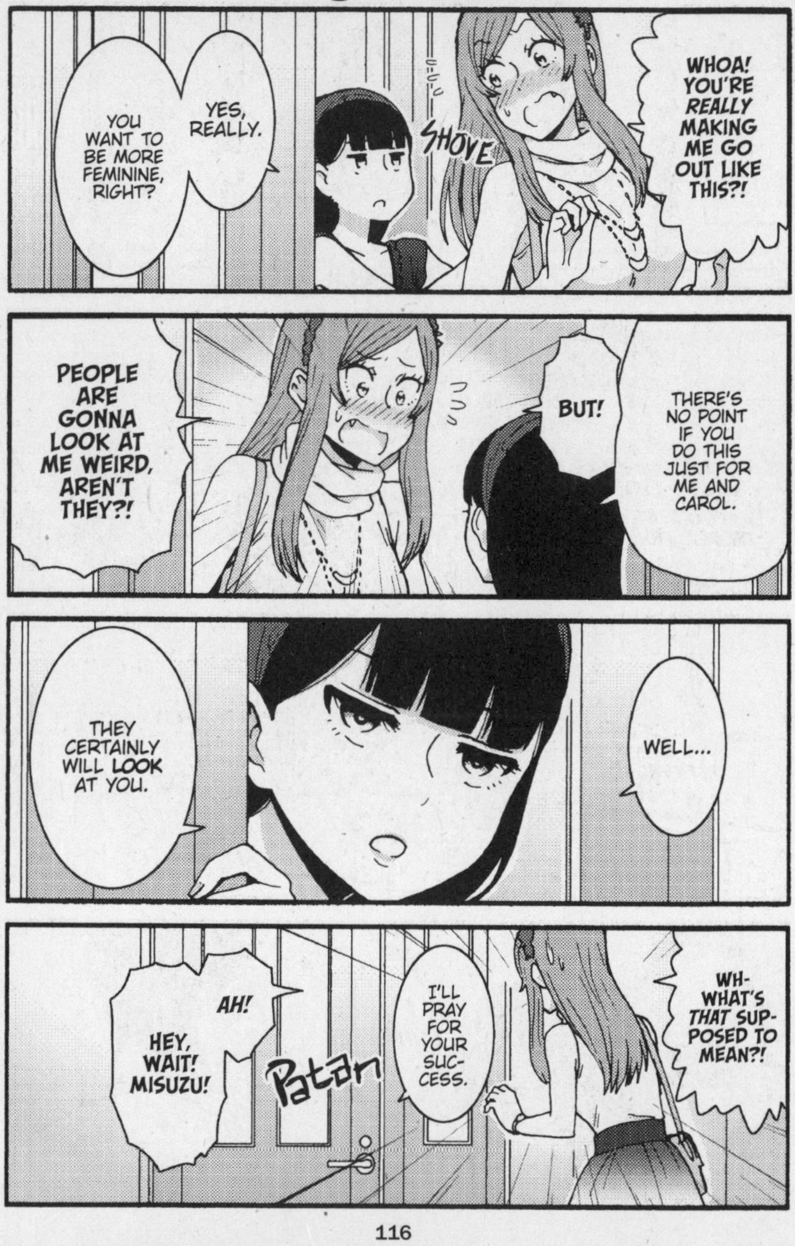

WHOA! YOU'RE *REALLY* MAKING ME GO OUT LIKE THIS?!
SHOVE
YES, REALLY.
YOU WANT TO BE MORE FEMININE, RIGHT?
THERE'S NO POINT IF YOU DO THIS JUST FOR ME AND CAROL.
BUT!
PEOPLE ARE GONNA LOOK AT ME WEIRD, AREN'T THEY?!
WELL...
THEY CERTAINLY WILL **LOOK** AT YOU.
WH- WHAT'S *THAT* SUP-POSED TO MEAN?!
I'LL PRAY FOR YOUR SUC-CESS.
Patan
AH!
HEY, WAIT! MISUZU!

A Familiar Face

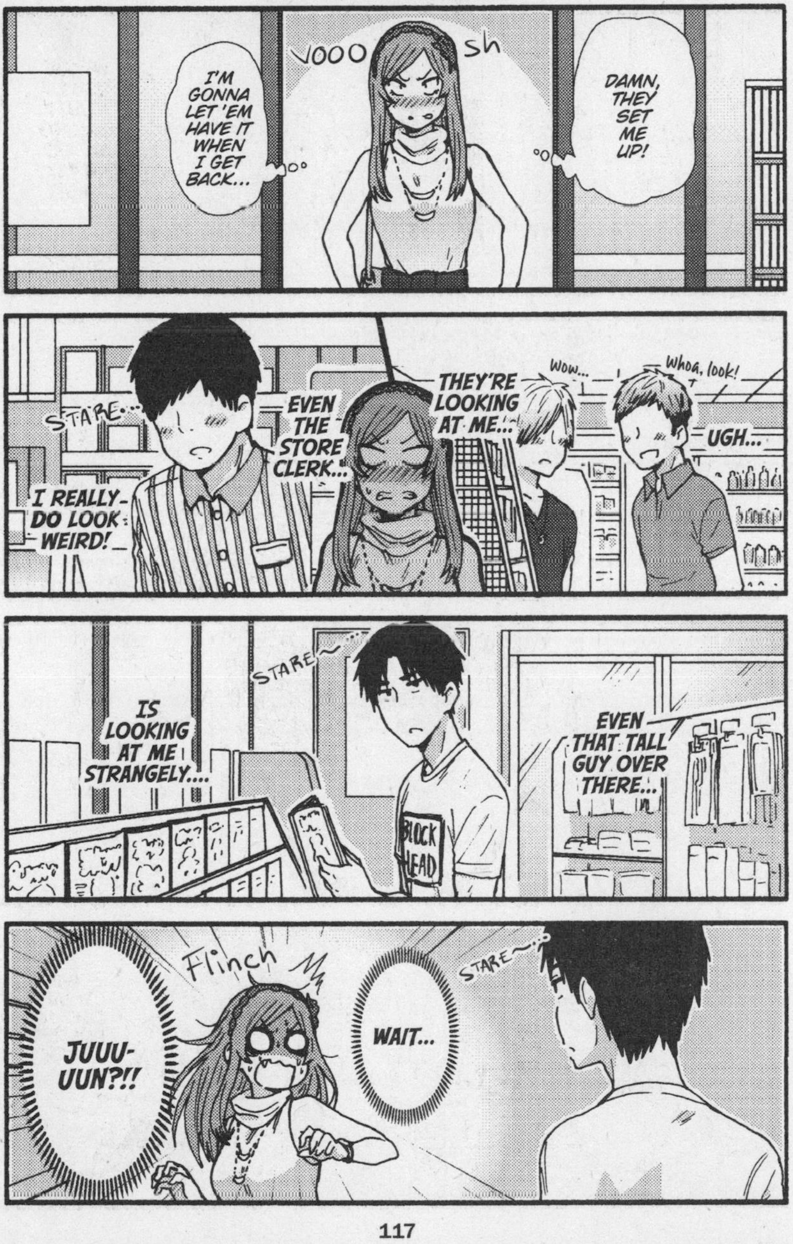
DAMN, THEY SET ME UP!
VOOOsh
I'M GONNA LET 'EM HAVE IT WHEN I GET BACK...
Whoa, look!
UGH...
WOW...
THEY'RE LOOKING AT ME...
EVEN THE STORE CLERK...
STARE...
I REALLY DO LOOK WEIRD!
EVEN THAT TALL GUY OVER THERE...
STARE~...
IS LOOKING AT ME STRANGELY....
BLOCK HEAD
STARE~...
WAIT...
Flinch
JUUU-UUN?!!

Deciding It's His Imagination

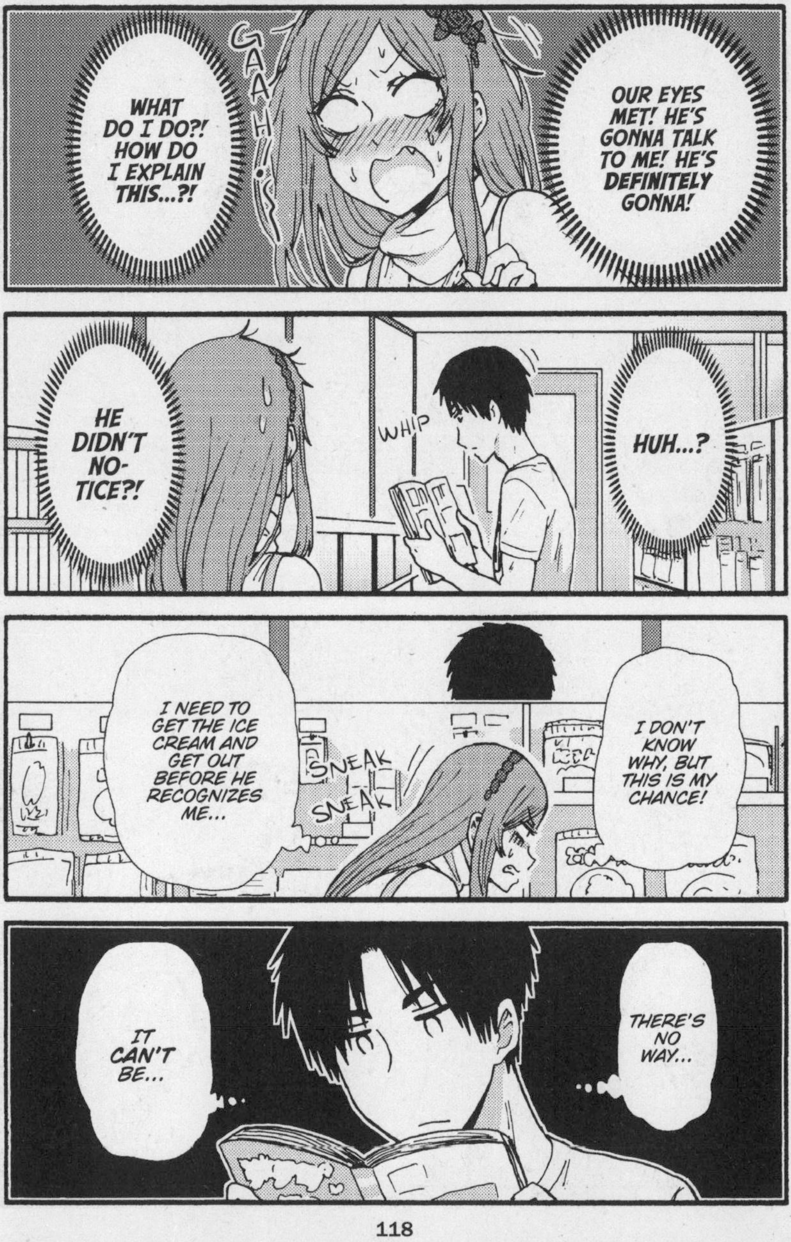

OUR EYES MET! HE'S GONNA TALK TO ME! HE'S DEFINITELY GONNA!
GAAAH!
WHAT DO I DO?! HOW DO I EXPLAIN THIS...?!
HUH...?
WHIP
HE DIDN'T NO-TICE?!
I DON'T KNOW WHY, BUT THIS IS MY CHANCE!
SNEAK SNEAK
I NEED TO GET THE ICE CREAM AND GET OUT BEFORE HE RECOGNIZES ME...
THERE'S NO WAY...
IT CAN'T BE...

Nobody Tell Her About Stilettos

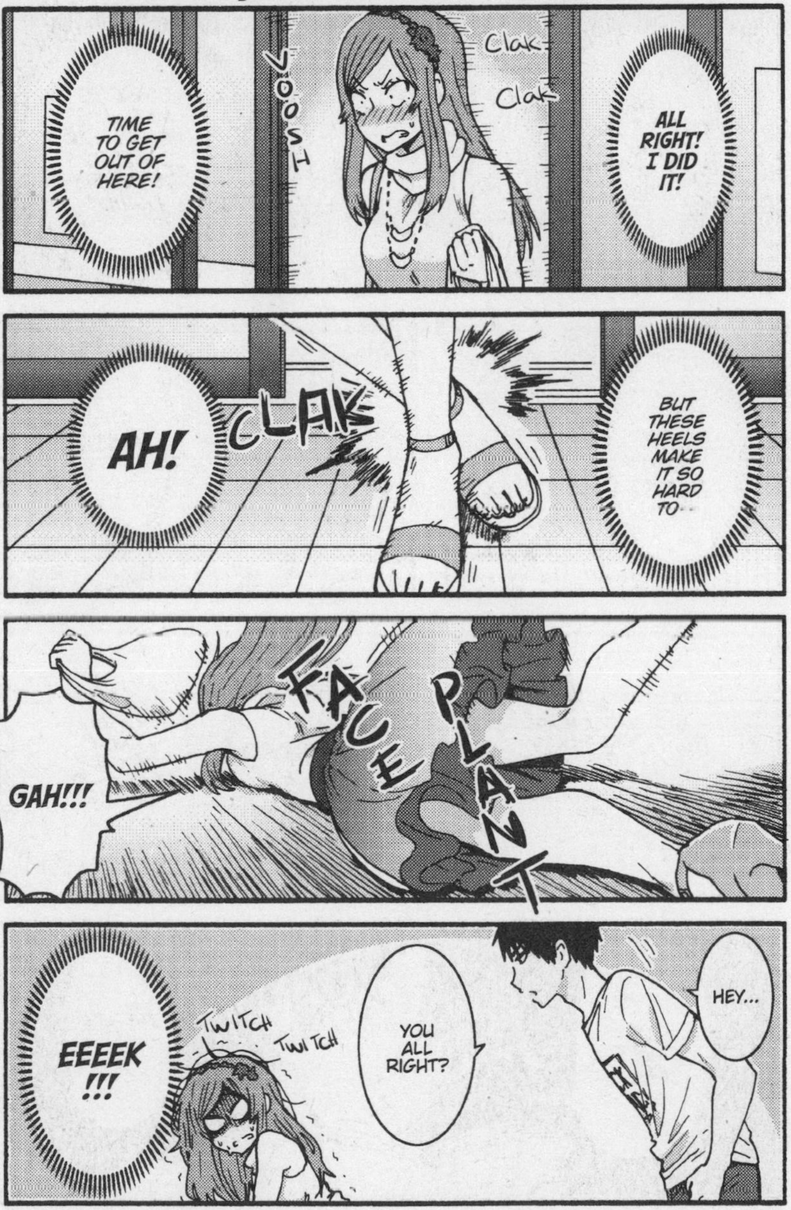
ALL RIGHT! I DID IT!
Clak
Clak
VOOSH
TIME TO GET OUT OF HERE!
BUT THESE HEELS MAKE IT SO HARD TO...
CLAK
AH!
FACE PLANT
GAH!!!
HEY...
YOU ALL RIGHT?
TWITCH
TWITCH
EEEEK!!!

Cognitive Dissonance

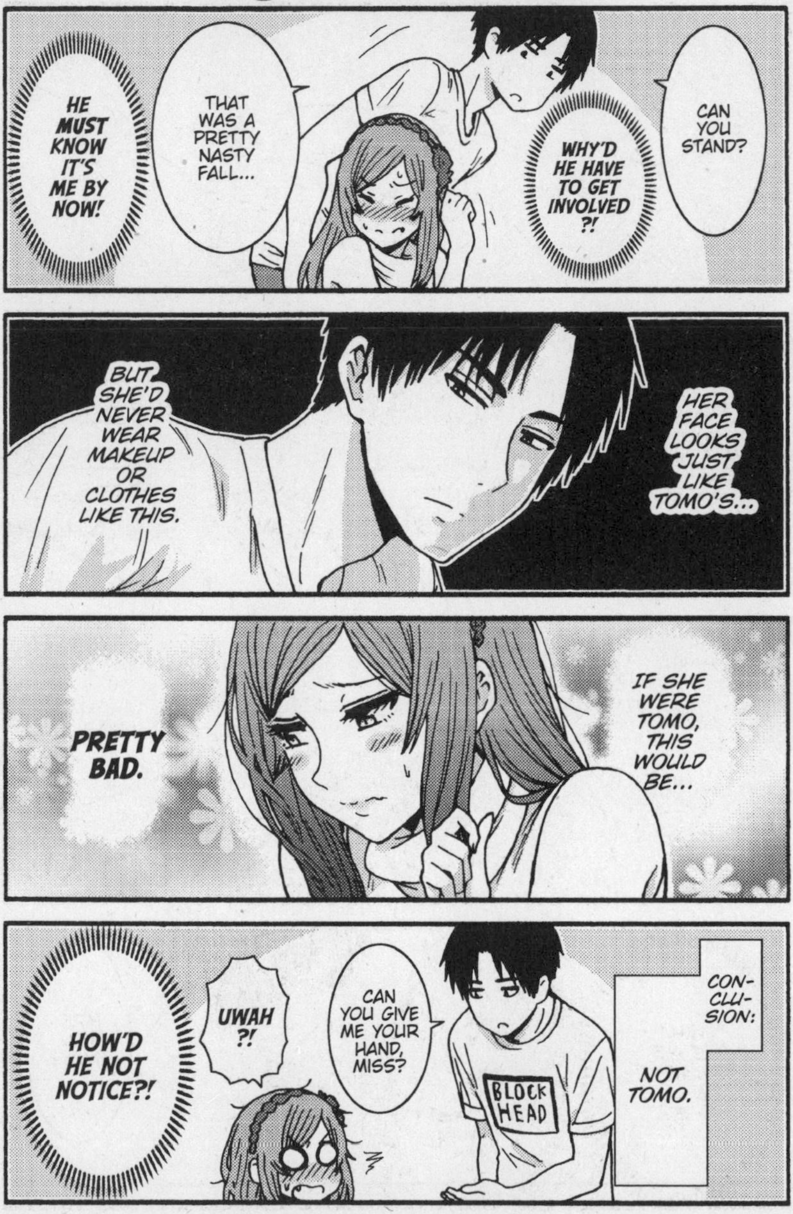
CAN YOU STAND?
WHY'D HE HAVE TO GET INVOLVED?!
THAT WAS A PRETTY NASTY FALL...
HE MUST KNOW IT'S ME BY NOW!
HER FACE LOOKS JUST LIKE TOMO'S...
BUT SHE'D NEVER WEAR MAKEUP OR CLOTHES LIKE THIS.
IF SHE WERE TOMO, THIS WOULD BE...
PRETTY BAD.
CON-CLU-SION:
NOT TOMO.
BLOCK HEAD
CAN YOU GIVE ME YOUR HAND, MISS?
UWAH?!
HOW'D HE NOT NOTICE?!

Is Anything Broken?

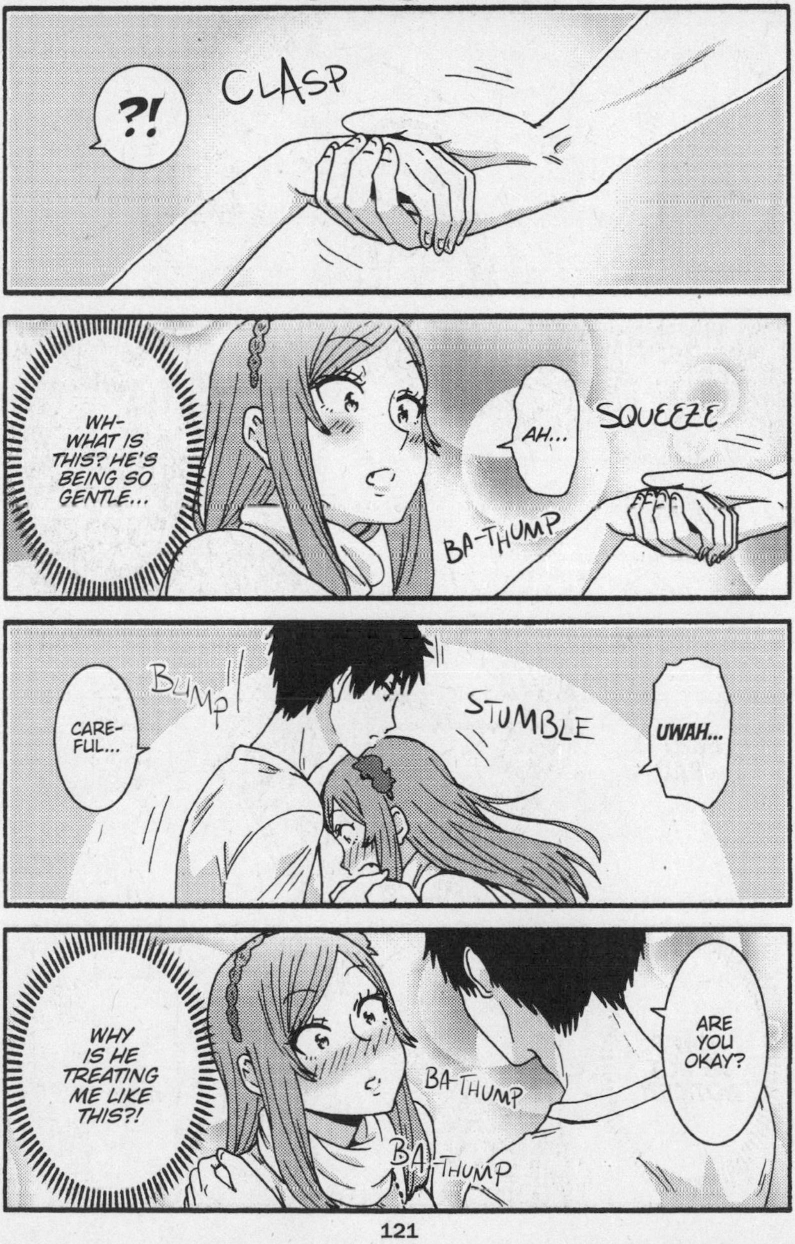
CLASP
?!
SQUEEZE
AH...
WH- WHAT IS THIS? HE'S BEING SO GENTLE...
BA-THUMP
UWAH...
STUMBLE
BUMP
CARE-FUL...
ARE YOU OKAY?
BA-THUMP
WHY IS HE TREATING ME LIKE THIS?!
BA-THUMP

Gotta Milk It

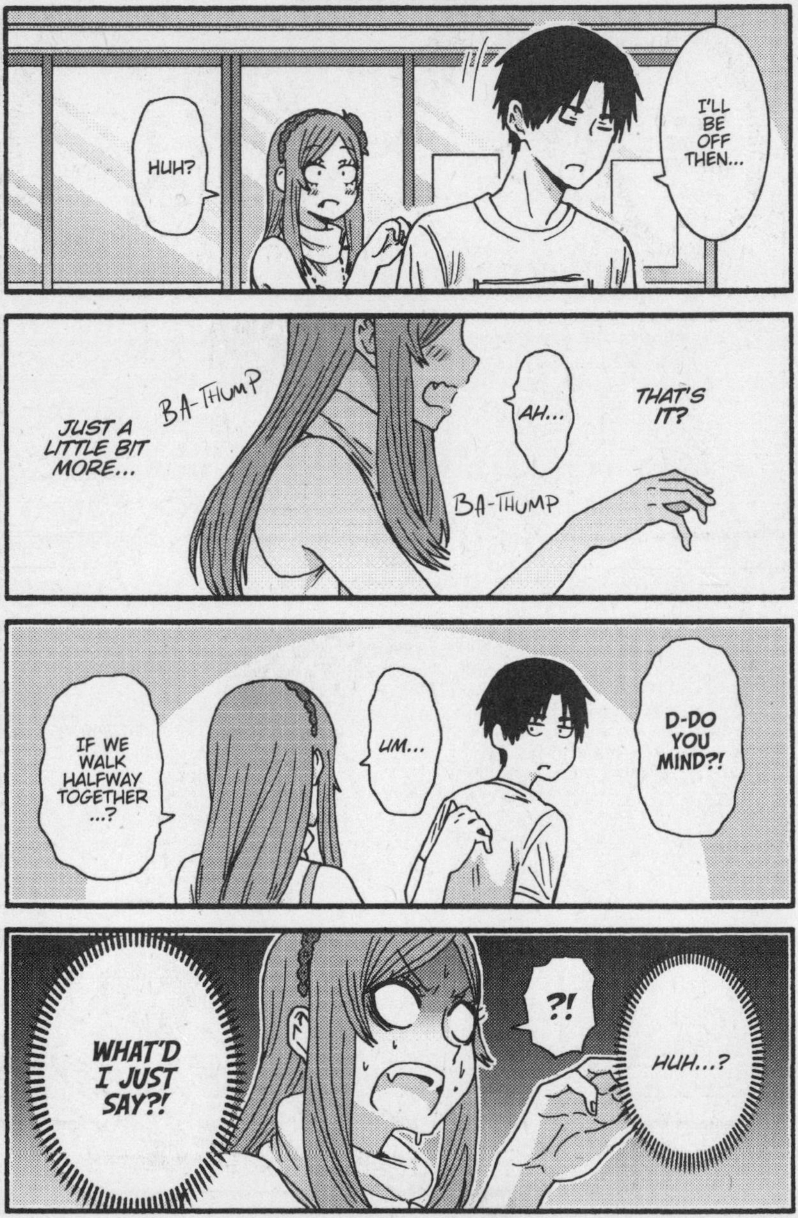

I'LL BE OFF THEN...
HUH?
THAT'S IT?
AH...
BA-THUMP
BA-THUMP
JUST A LITTLE BIT MORE...
D-DO YOU MIND?!
UM...
IF WE WALK HALFWAY TOGETHER ...?
HUH...?
?!
WHAT'D I JUST SAY?!

Those Shoes Are Good for Something

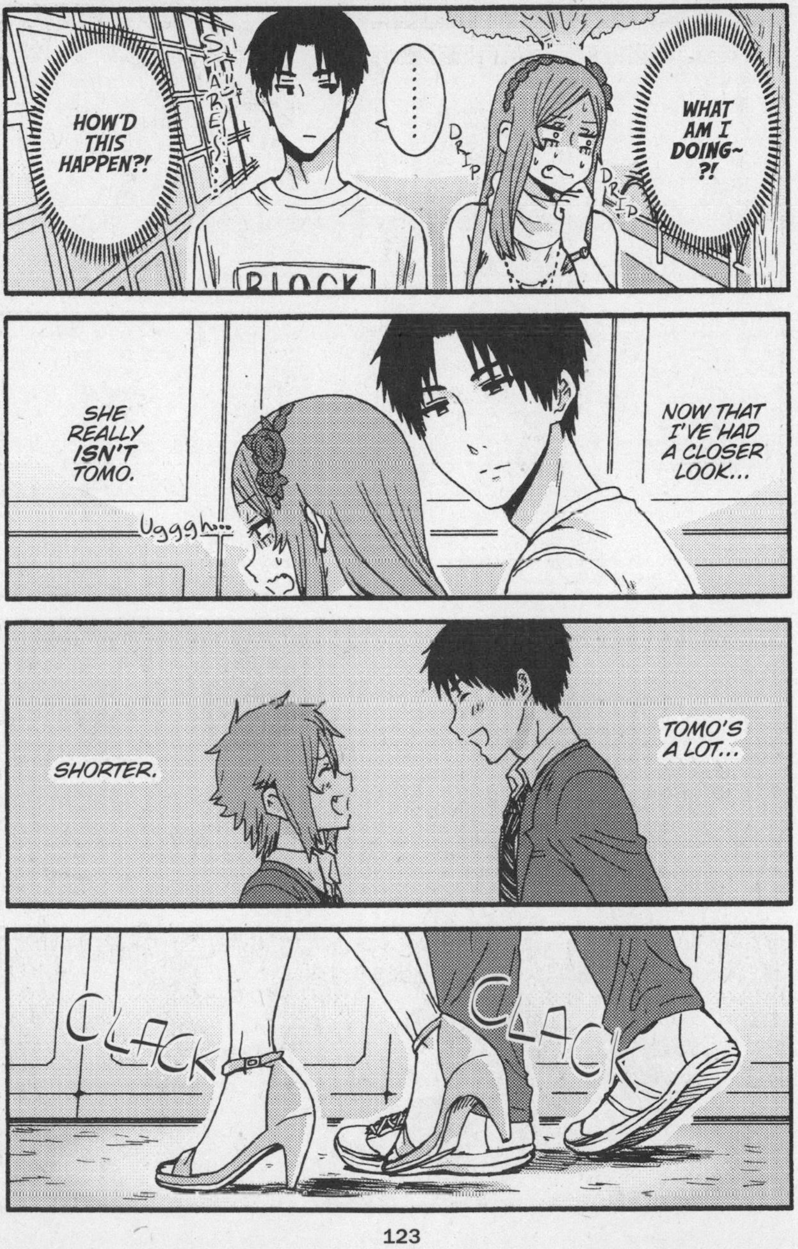
WHAT AM I DOING~?!
DRIP
DRIP
......
STARE...
HOW'D THIS HAPPEN?!
NOW THAT I'VE HAD A CLOSER LOOK...
SHE REALLY ISN'T TOMO.
Ugggh...
TOMO'S A LOT...
SHORTER.
CLACK
CLACK

Fatal Faceplant?

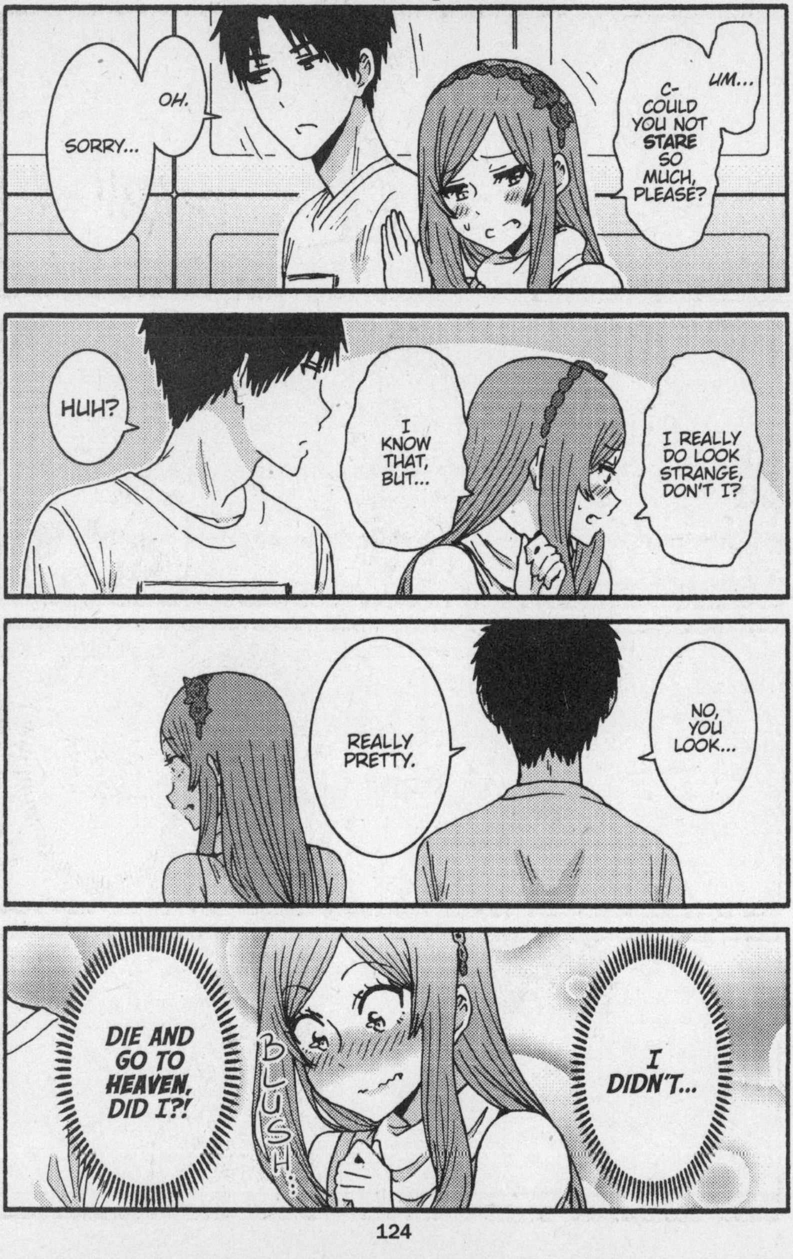
UM... C-COULD YOU NOT STARE SO MUCH, PLEASE?
OH. SORRY...
I REALLY DO LOOK STRANGE, DON'T I?
I KNOW THAT, BUT...
HUH?
NO, YOU LOOK...
REALLY PRETTY.
I DIDN'T...
BLUSH...
DIE AND GO TO HEAVEN, DID I?!

Tomo-chan Slipped Out

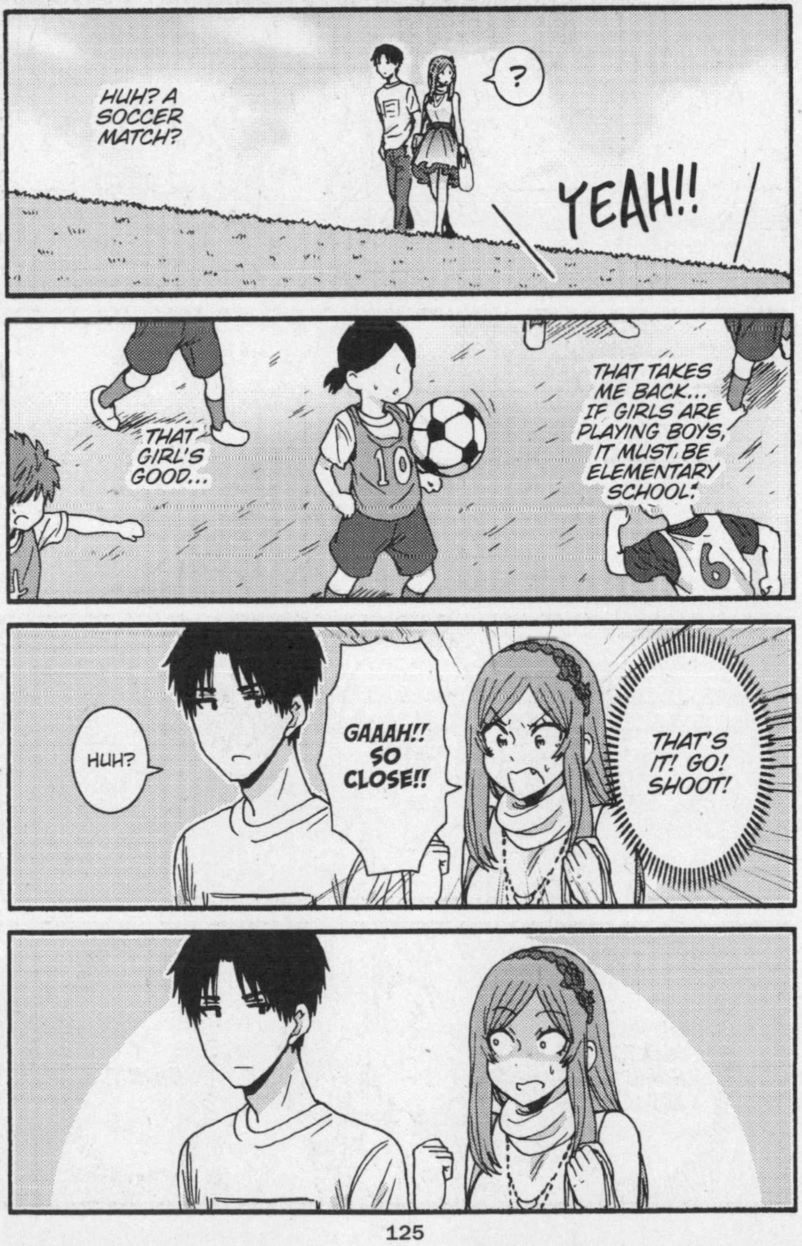
YEAH!!
?
HUH? A SOCCER MATCH?
THAT TAKES ME BACK... IF GIRLS ARE PLAYING BOYS, IT MUST BE ELEMENTARY SCHOOL.
THAT GIRL'S GOOD...
THAT'S IT! GO! SHOOT!
GAAAH!! SO CLOSE!!
HUH?

Feels Overload

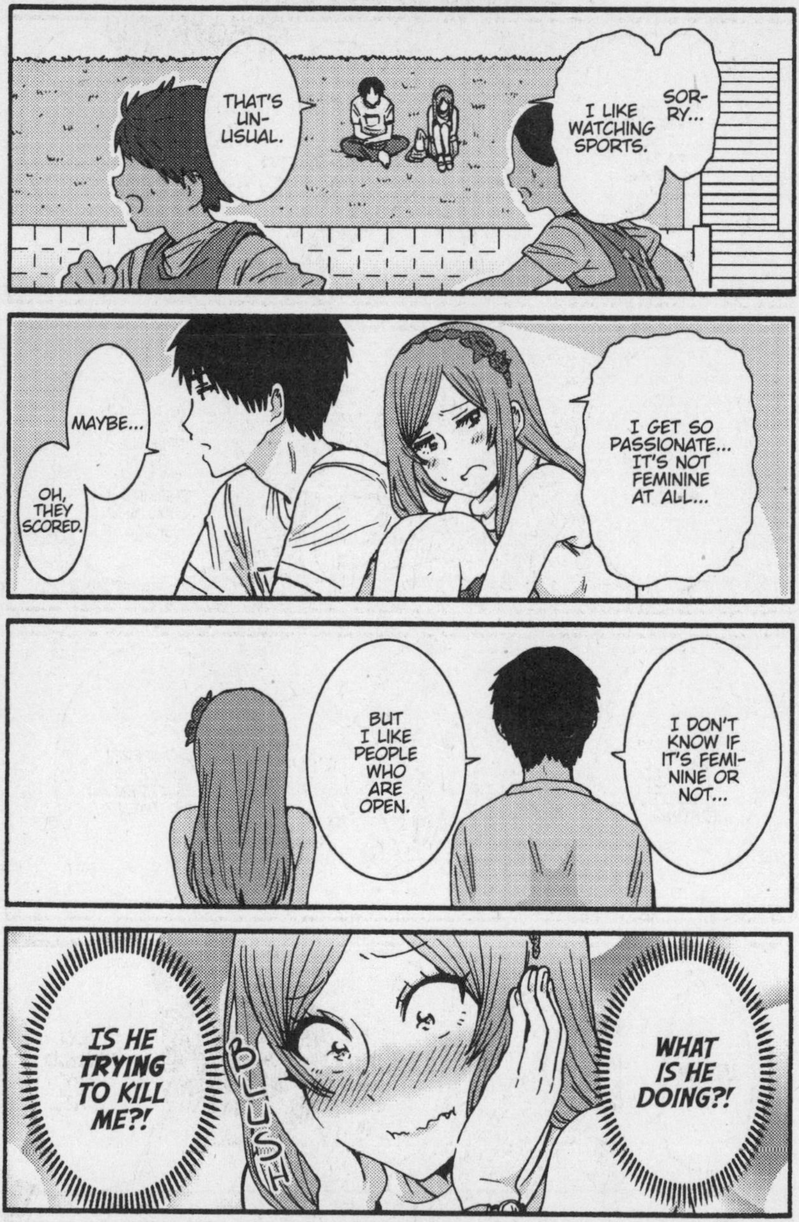
SORRY... I LIKE WATCHING SPORTS.
THAT'S UNUSUAL.
I GET SO PASSIONATE... IT'S NOT FEMININE AT ALL...
MAYBE...
OH, THEY SCORED.
I DON'T KNOW IF IT'S FEMININE OR NOT...
BUT I LIKE PEOPLE WHO ARE OPEN.
WHAT IS HE DOING?!
BLUSH
IS HE TRYING TO KILL ME?!

Echoes of the Past

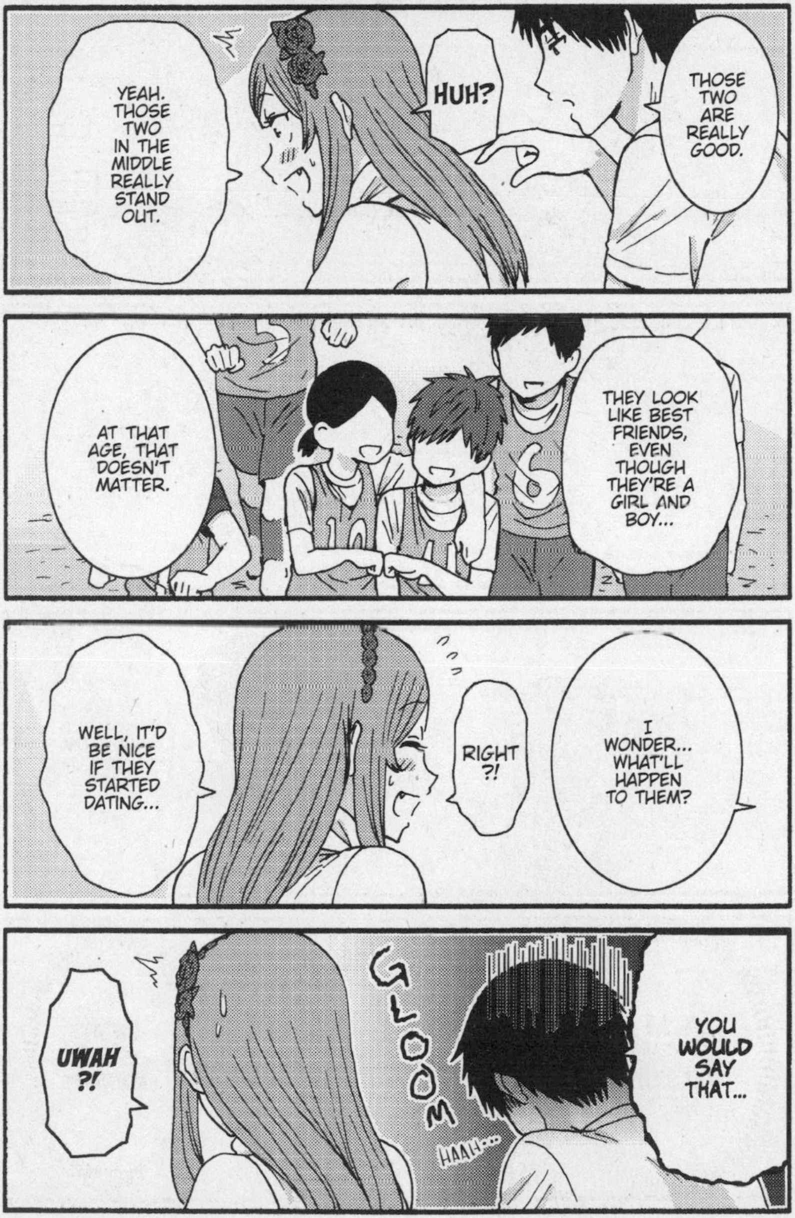
THOSE TWO ARE REALLY GOOD.
HUH?
YEAH. THOSE TWO IN THE MIDDLE REALLY STAND OUT.
THEY LOOK LIKE BEST FRIENDS, EVEN THOUGH THEY'RE A GIRL AND BOY...
AT THAT AGE, THAT DOESN'T MATTER.
I WONDER... WHAT'LL HAPPEN TO THEM?
RIGHT?!
WELL, IT'D BE NICE IF THEY STARTED DATING...
YOU WOULD SAY THAT...
HAAH...
GLOOM
UWAH?!

Goals Shift

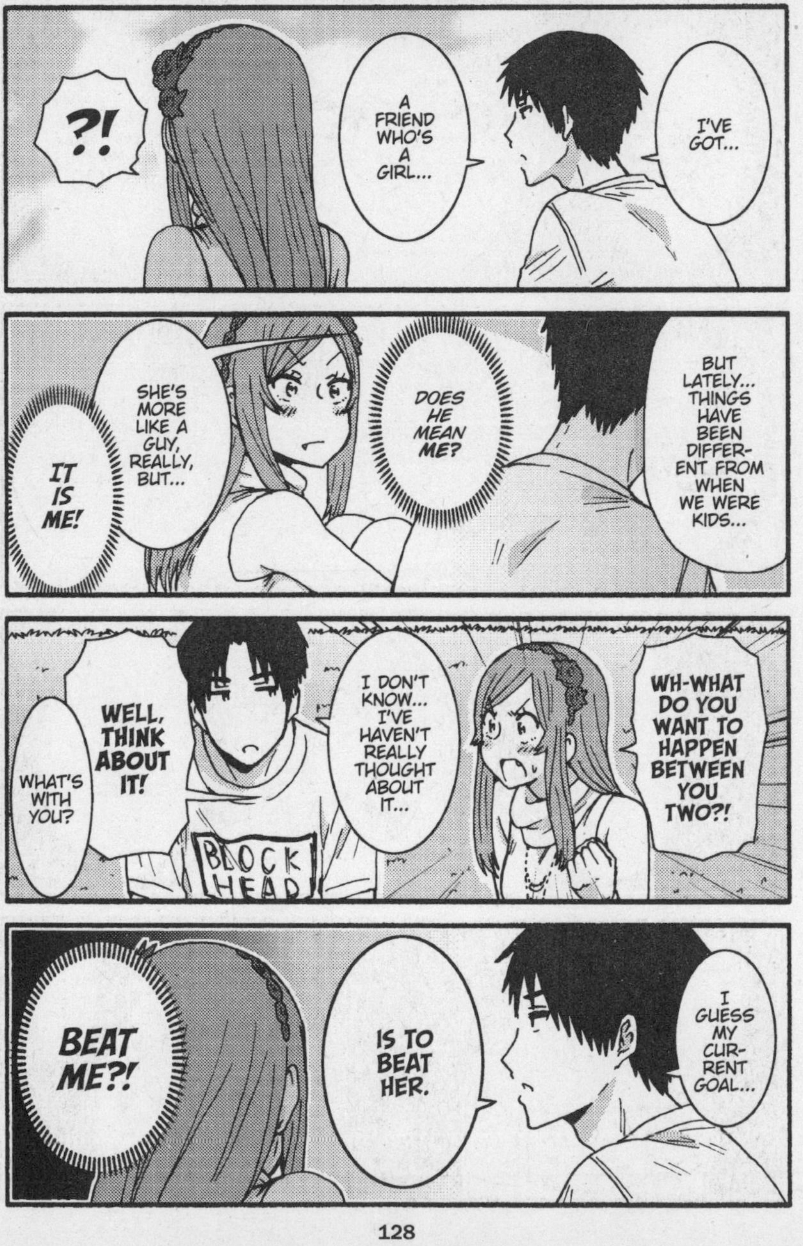
I'VE GOT...
A FRIEND WHO'S A GIRL...
?!
BUT LATELY... THINGS HAVE BEEN DIFFERENT FROM WHEN WE WERE KIDS...
DOES HE MEAN ME?
SHE'S MORE LIKE A GUY, REALLY, BUT...
IT IS ME!
WH-WHAT DO YOU WANT TO HAPPEN BETWEEN YOU TWO?!
I DON'T KNOW... I'VE HAVEN'T REALLY THOUGHT ABOUT IT...
BLOCK HEAD
WELL, THINK ABOUT IT!
WHAT'S WITH YOU?
I GUESS MY CURRENT GOAL...
IS TO BEAT HER.
BEAT ME?!

A Pressing Question

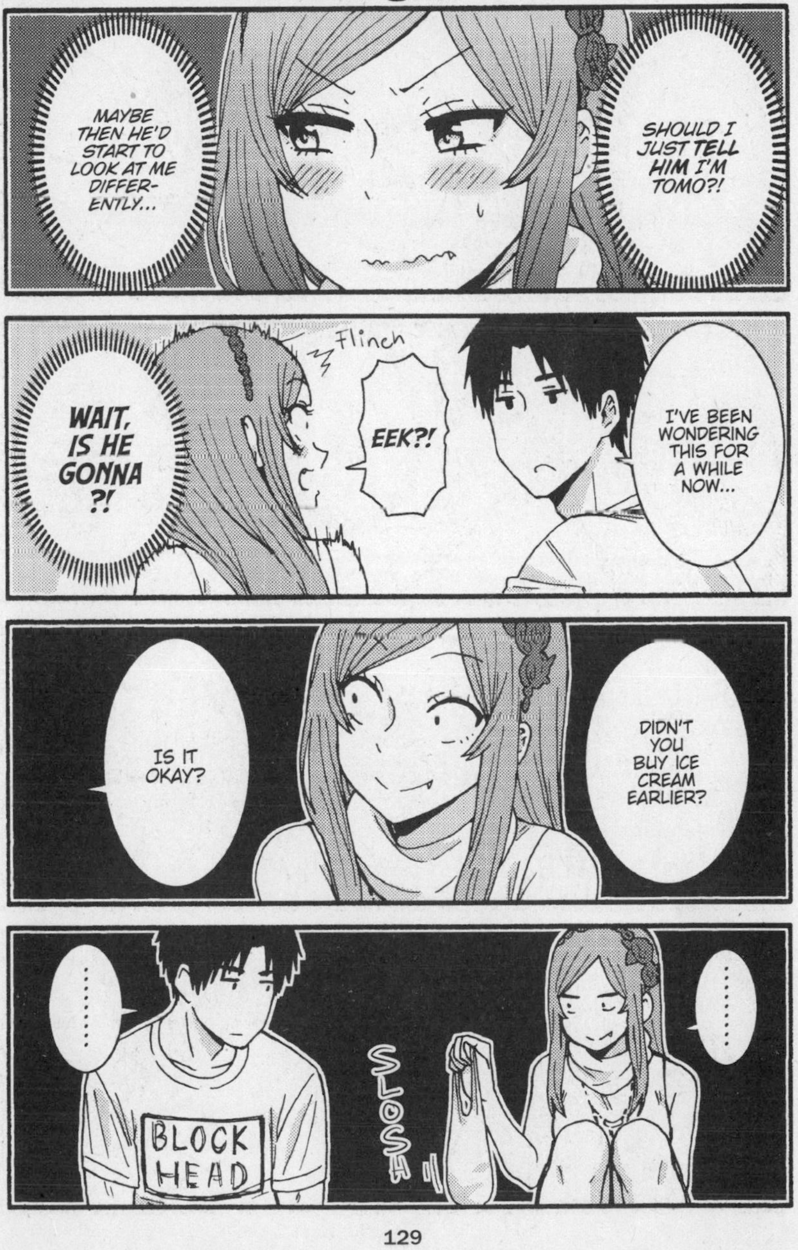

SHOULD I JUST TELL HIM I'M TOMO?!
MAYBE THEN HE'D START TO LOOK AT ME DIFFER-ENTLY...
I'VE BEEN WONDERING THIS FOR A WHILE NOW...
Flinch
EEK?!
WAIT, IS HE GONNA ?!
DIDN'T YOU BUY ICE CREAM EARLIER?
IS IT OKAY?
......
SLOSH
......
BLOCK HEAD

Hundred-Meter Dash in Heels

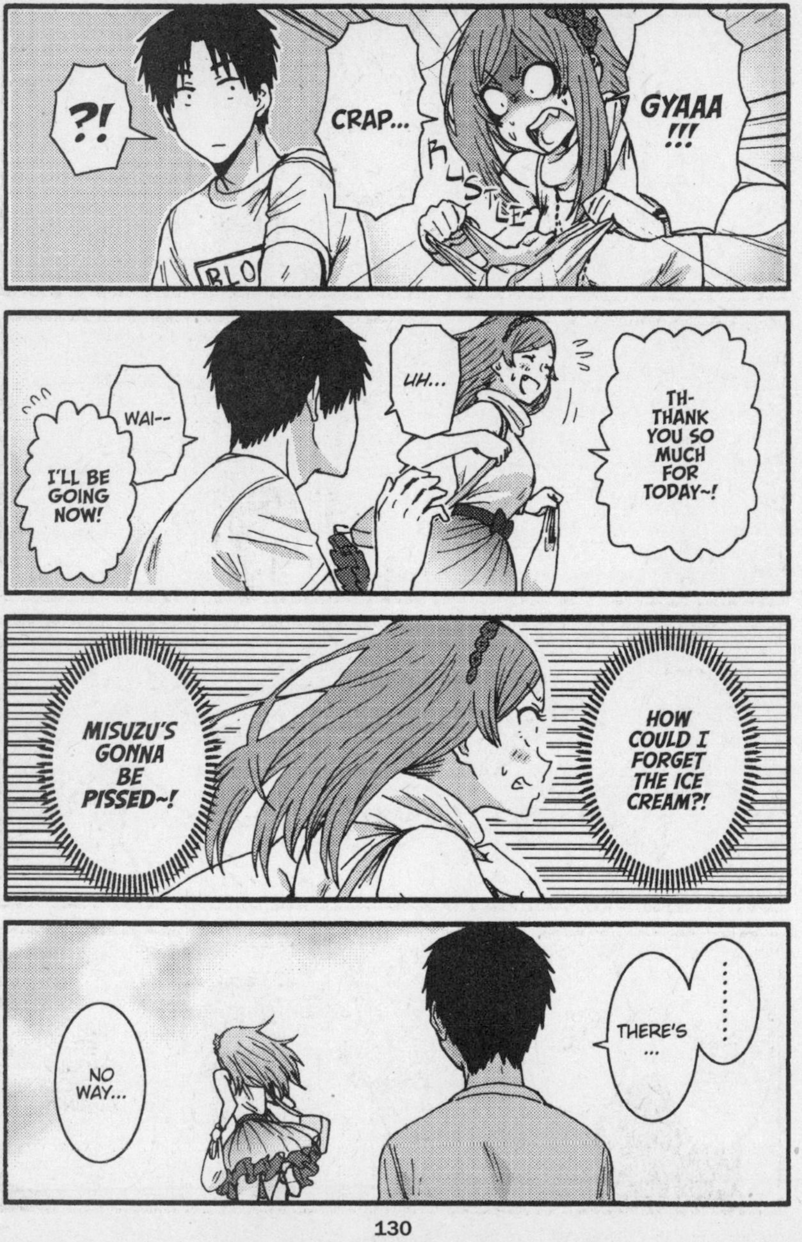

GYAAA !!!
RUSTLE
CRAP...
?!
TH-THANK YOU SO MUCH FOR TODAY~!
UH...
WAI--
I'LL BE GOING NOW!
HOW COULD I FORGET THE ICE CREAM?!
MISUZU'S GONNA BE PISSED~!
......
THERE'S ...
NO WAY...

Ahead of Schedule

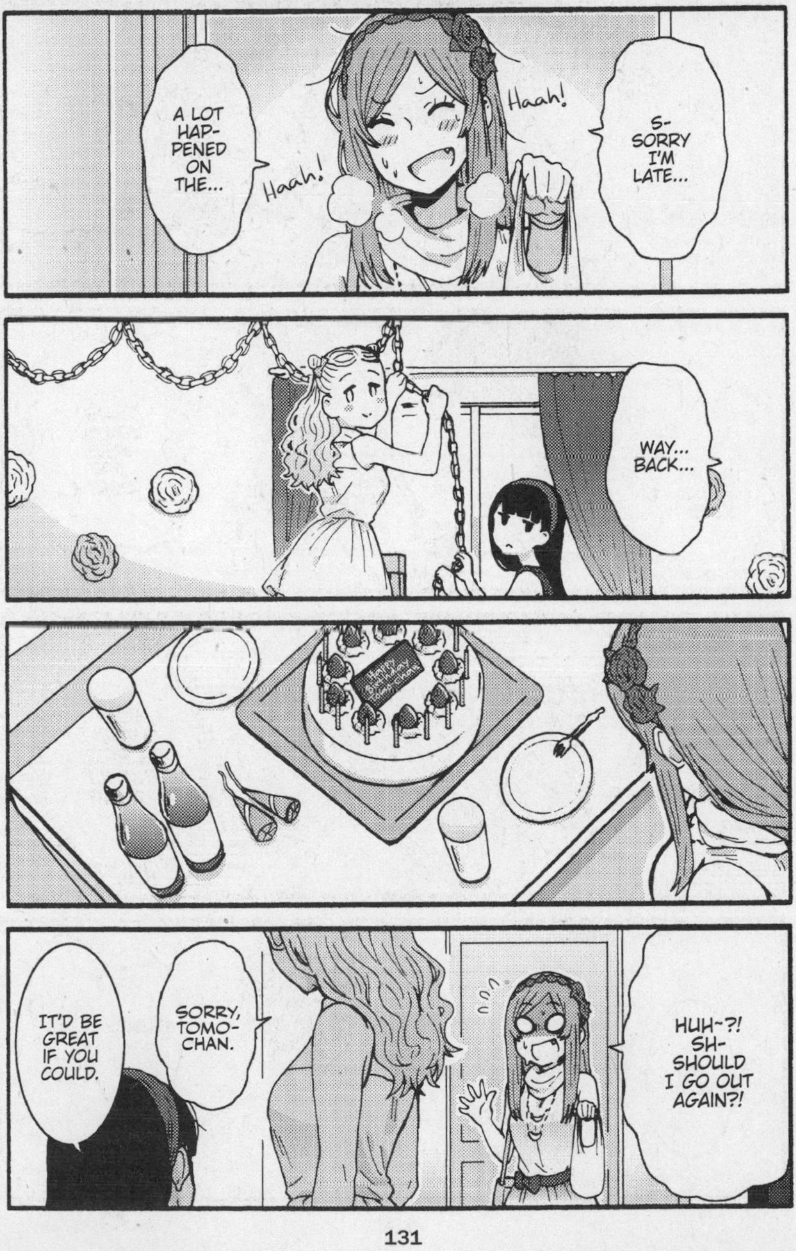
S-SORRY I'M LATE...
Haah!
Haah!
A LOT HAPPENED ON THE...
WAY... BACK...
HUH~?! SH-SHOULD I GO OUT AGAIN?!
SORRY, TOMO-CHAN.
IT'D BE GREAT IF YOU COULD.

Left Wanting More

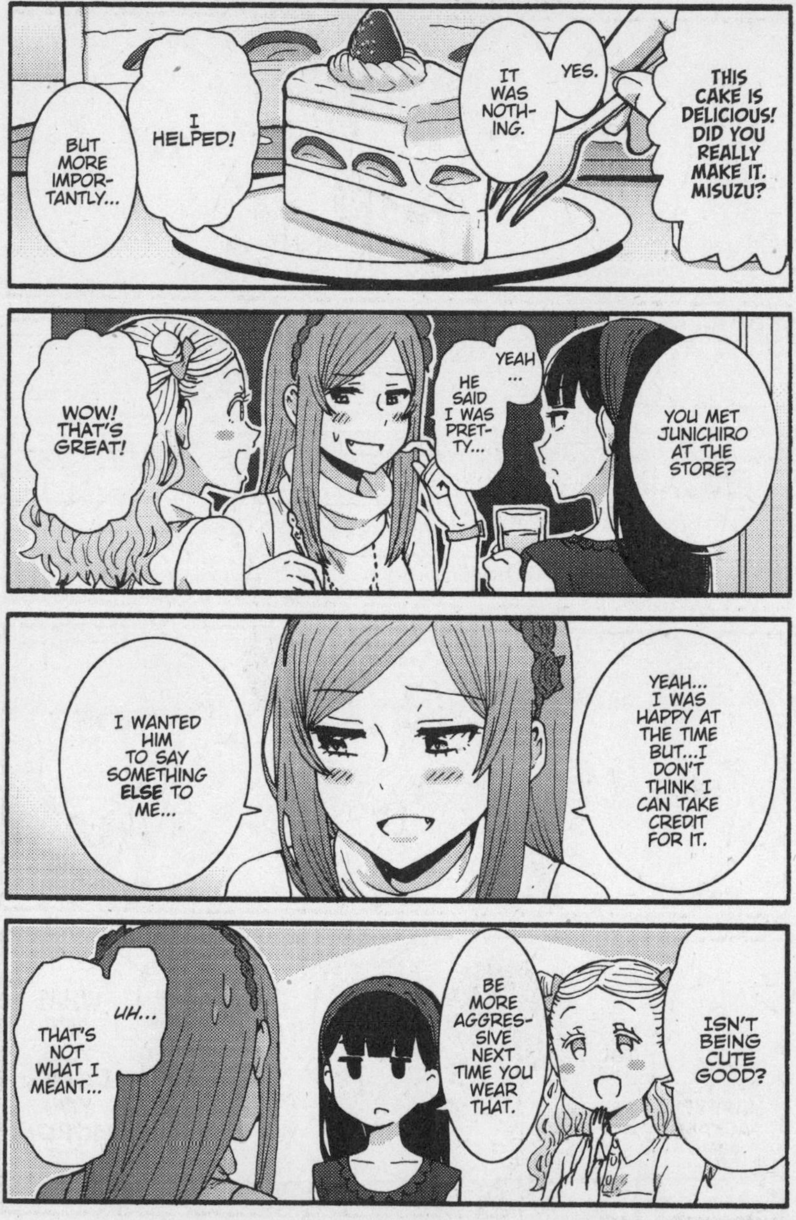

THIS CAKE IS DELICIOUS! DID YOU REALLY MAKE IT. MISUZU?
YES.
IT WAS NOTHING.
I HELPED!
BUT MORE IMPORTANTLY...
YOU MET JUNICHIRO AT THE STORE?
YEAH...
HE SAID I WAS PRETTY...
WOW! THAT'S GREAT!
YEAH... I WAS HAPPY AT THE TIME BUT...I DON'T THINK I CAN TAKE CREDIT FOR IT.
I WANTED HIM TO SAY SOMETHING ELSE TO ME...
ISN'T BEING CUTE GOOD?
BE MORE AGGRESSIVE NEXT TIME YOU WEAR THAT.
UH...
THAT'S NOT WHAT I MEANT...

Just Double-Checking

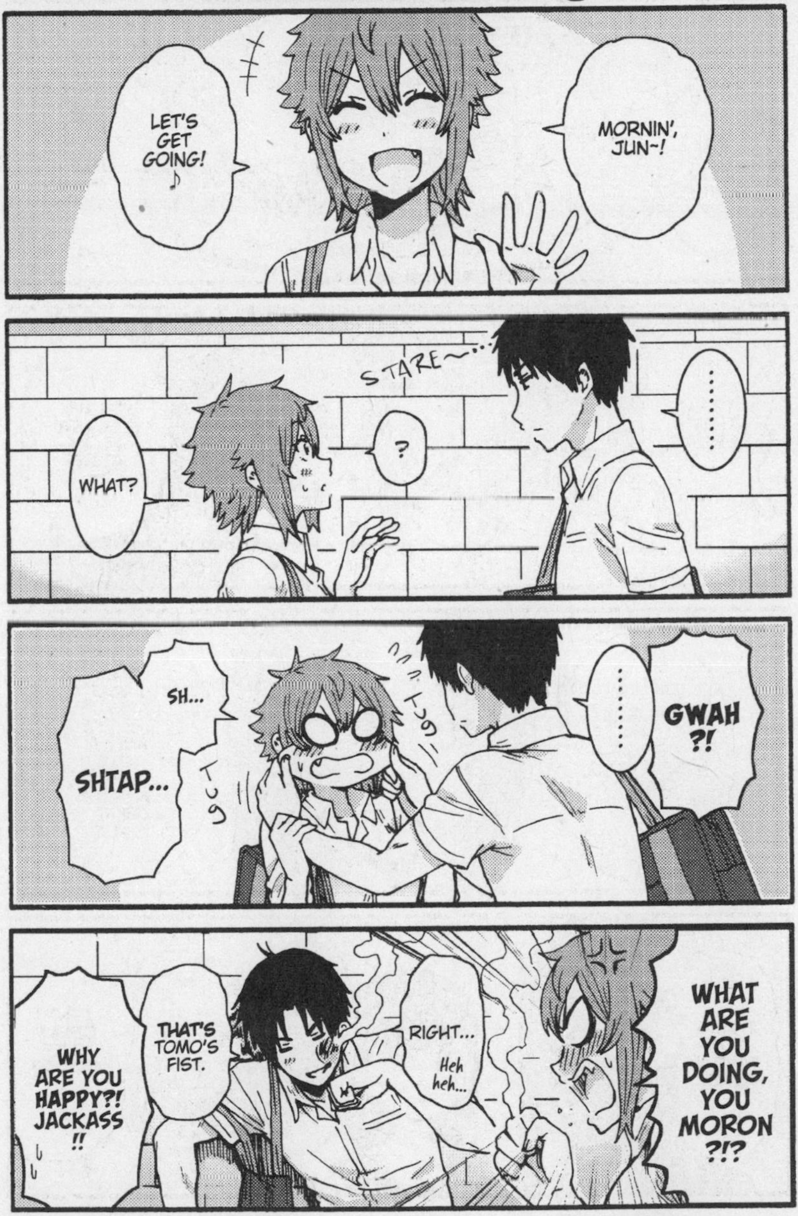
MORNIN', JUN~!
LET'S GET GOING! ♪
STARE~
......
?
WHAT?
GWAH ?!
......
TUG
TUG
SH...
SHTAP...
WHAT ARE YOU DOING, YOU MORON ?!?
RIGHT... Heh heh...
THAT'S TOMO'S FIST.
WHY ARE YOU HAPPY?! JACKASS !!

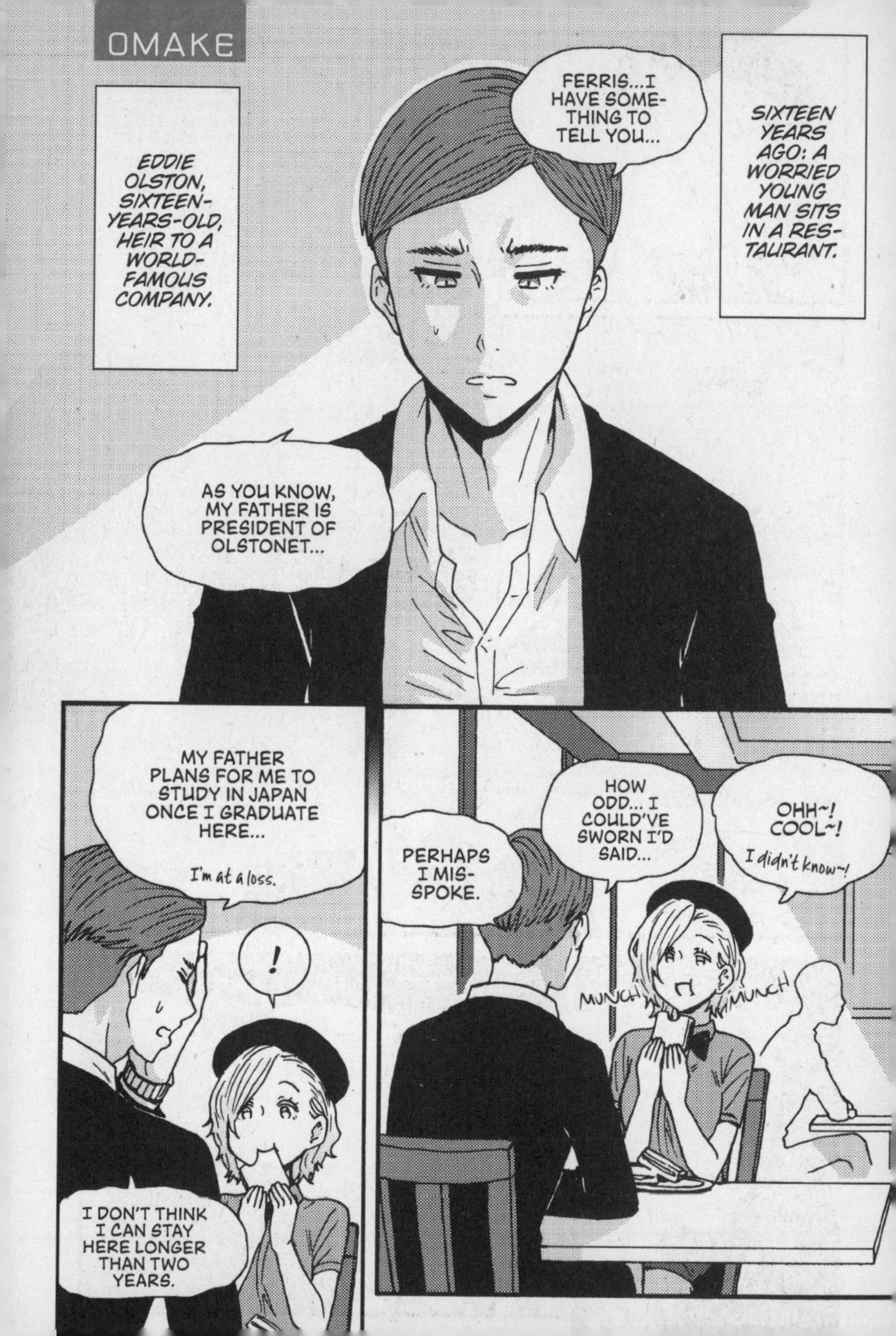
OMAKE
SIXTEEN YEARS AGO: A WORRIED YOUNG MAN SITS IN A RESTAURANT.
FERRIS...I HAVE SOMETHING TO TELL YOU...
EDDIE OLSTON, SIXTEEN-YEARS-OLD, HEIR TO A WORLD-FAMOUS COMPANY.
AS YOU KNOW, MY FATHER IS PRESIDENT OF OLSTONET...
MY FATHER PLANS FOR ME TO STUDY IN JAPAN ONCE I GRADUATE HERE...
I'm at a loss.
!
I DON'T THINK I CAN STAY HERE LONGER THAN TWO YEARS.
OHH~! COOL~!
I didn't know~!
HOW ODD... I COULD'VE SWORN I'D SAID...
PERHAPS I MISSPOKE.
MUNCH
MUNCH

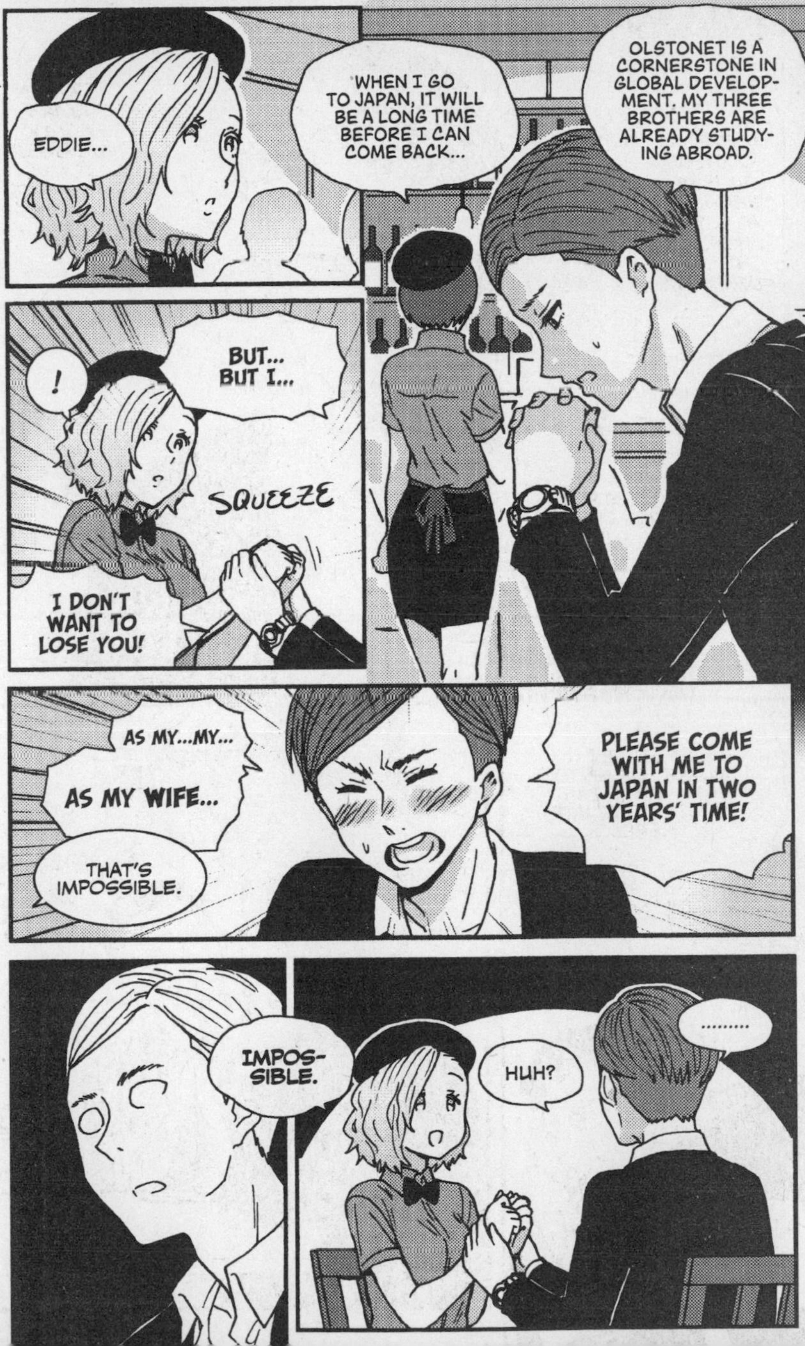
OLSTONET IS A CORNERSTONE IN GLOBAL DEVELOPMENT. MY THREE BROTHERS ARE ALREADY STUDYING ABROAD.
WHEN I GO TO JAPAN, IT WILL BE A LONG TIME BEFORE I CAN COME BACK...
EDDIE...
!
BUT... BUT I...
SQUEEZE
I DON'T WANT TO LOSE YOU!
AS MY...MY...
AS MY WIFE...
PLEASE COME WITH ME TO JAPAN IN TWO YEARS' TIME!
THAT'S IMPOSSIBLE.
....
HUH?
IMPOSSIBLE.

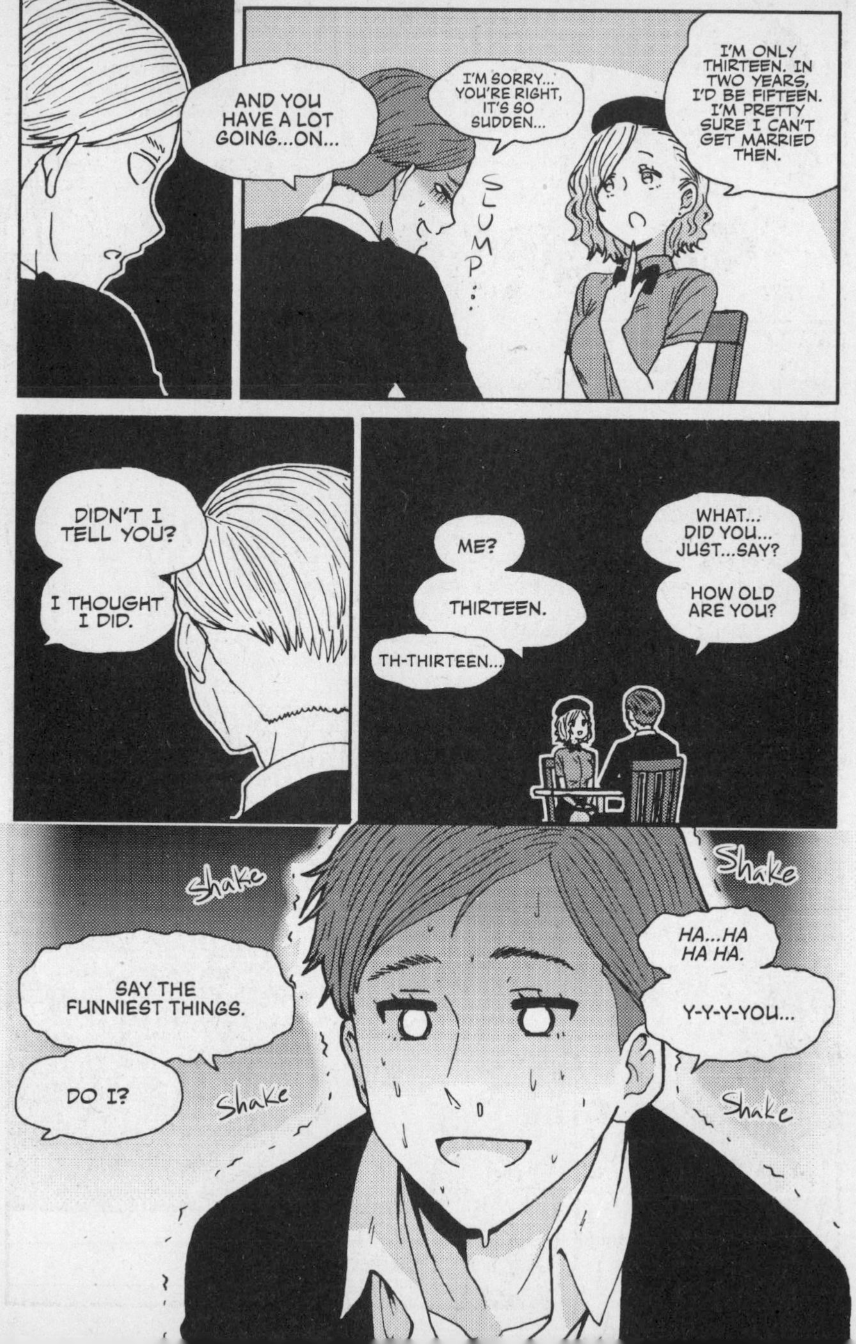
I'M ONLY THIRTEEN. IN TWO YEARS, I'D BE FIFTEEN. I'M PRETTY SURE I CAN'T GET MARRIED THEN.
I'M SORRY... YOU'RE RIGHT, IT'S SO SUDDEN...
SLUMP...
AND YOU HAVE A LOT GOING...ON...
WHAT... DID YOU... JUST...SAY?
HOW OLD ARE YOU?
ME?
THIRTEEN.
TH-THIRTEEN...
DIDN'T I TELL YOU?
I THOUGHT I DID.
Shake
HA...HA HA HA.
Y-Y-Y-YOU...
Shake
Shake
SAY THE FUNNIEST THINGS.
DO I?
Shake

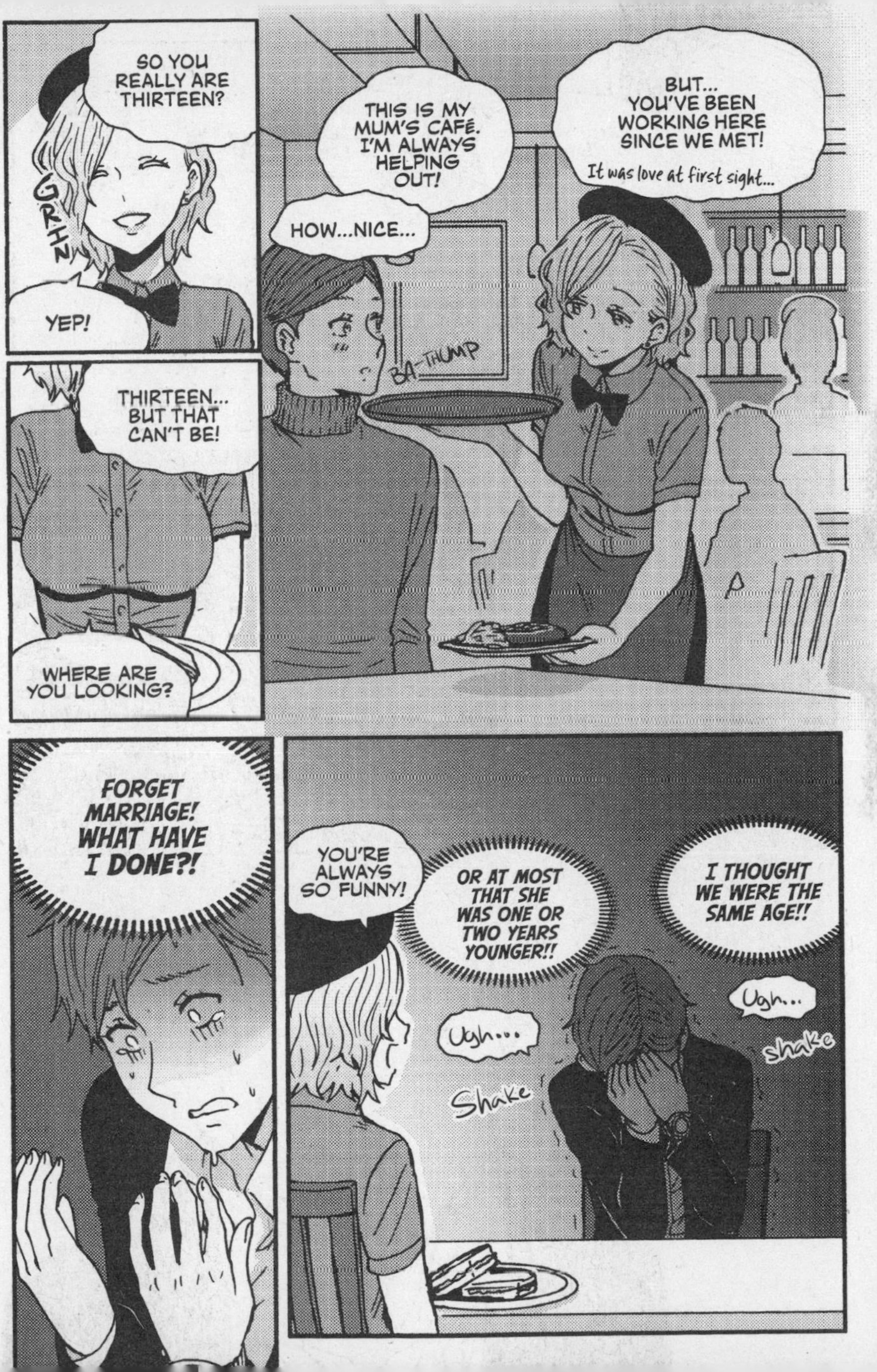
BUT... YOU'VE BEEN WORKING HERE SINCE WE MET!
It was love at first sight...
THIS IS MY MUM'S CAFÉ. I'M ALWAYS HELPING OUT!
HOW...NICE...
BA-THUMP
SO YOU REALLY ARE THIRTEEN?
GRIN
YEP!
THIRTEEN... BUT THAT CAN'T BE!
WHERE ARE YOU LOOKING?
I THOUGHT WE WERE THE SAME AGE!!
OR AT MOST THAT SHE WAS ONE OR TWO YEARS YOUNGER!!
YOU'RE ALWAYS SO FUNNY!
Ugh...
shake
Ugh...
Shake
FORGET MARRIAGE! WHAT HAVE I DONE?!

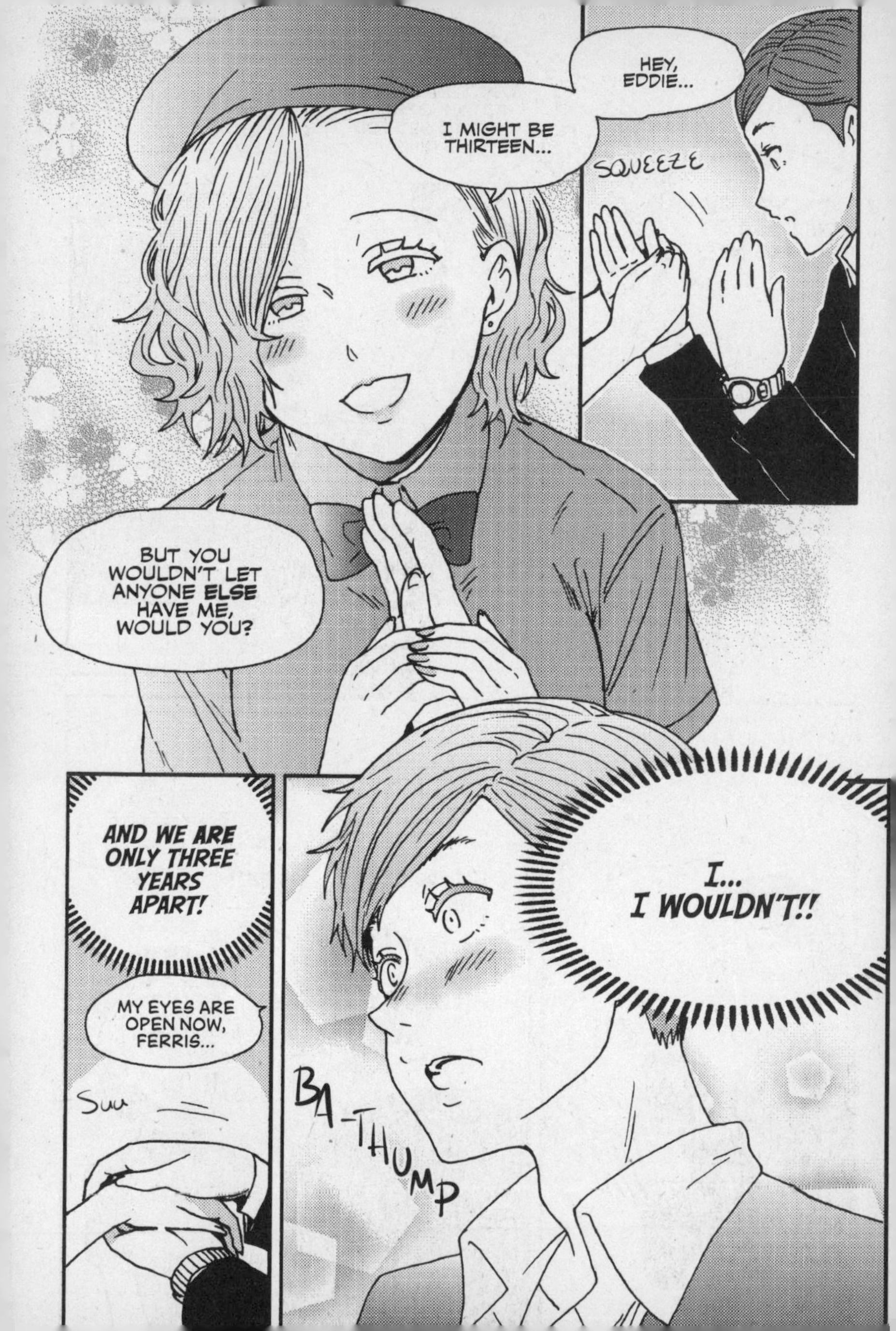
HEY, EDDIE...
I MIGHT BE THIRTEEN...
SQUEEZE
BUT YOU WOULDN'T LET ANYONE **ELSE** HAVE ME, WOULD YOU?
I... I WOULDN'T!!
BA-THUMP
AND WE ARE ONLY THREE YEARS APART!
MY EYES ARE OPEN NOW, FERRIS...
Suu

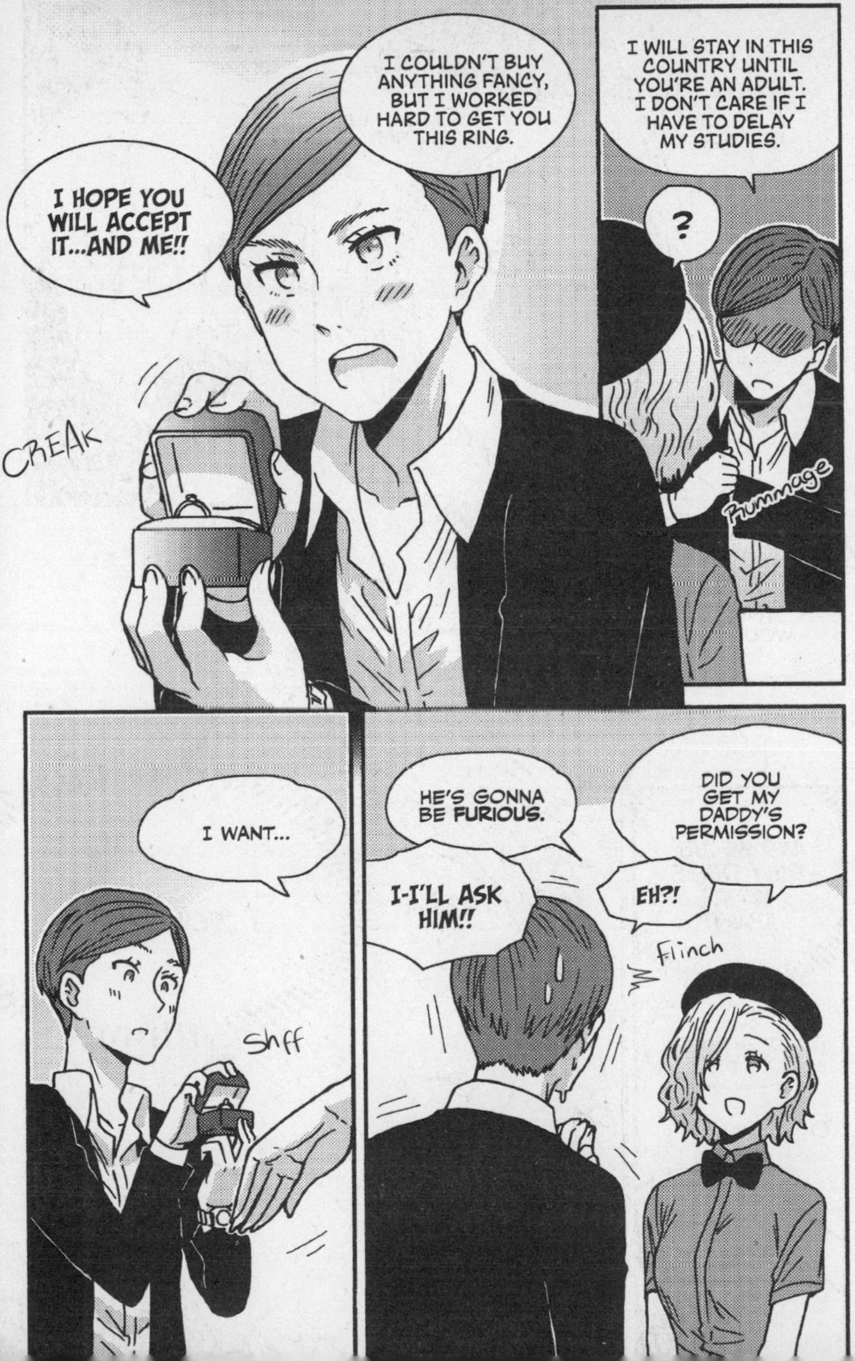
I WILL STAY IN THIS COUNTRY UNTIL YOU'RE AN ADULT. I DON'T CARE IF I HAVE TO DELAY MY STUDIES.
?
Rummage
I COULDN'T BUY ANYTHING FANCY, BUT I WORKED HARD TO GET YOU THIS RING.
I HOPE YOU WILL ACCEPT IT...AND ME!!
CREAK
DID YOU GET MY DADDY'S PERMISSION?
EH?!
HE'S GONNA BE **FURIOUS.**
I-I'LL ASK HIM!!
Flinch
I WANT...
Shff

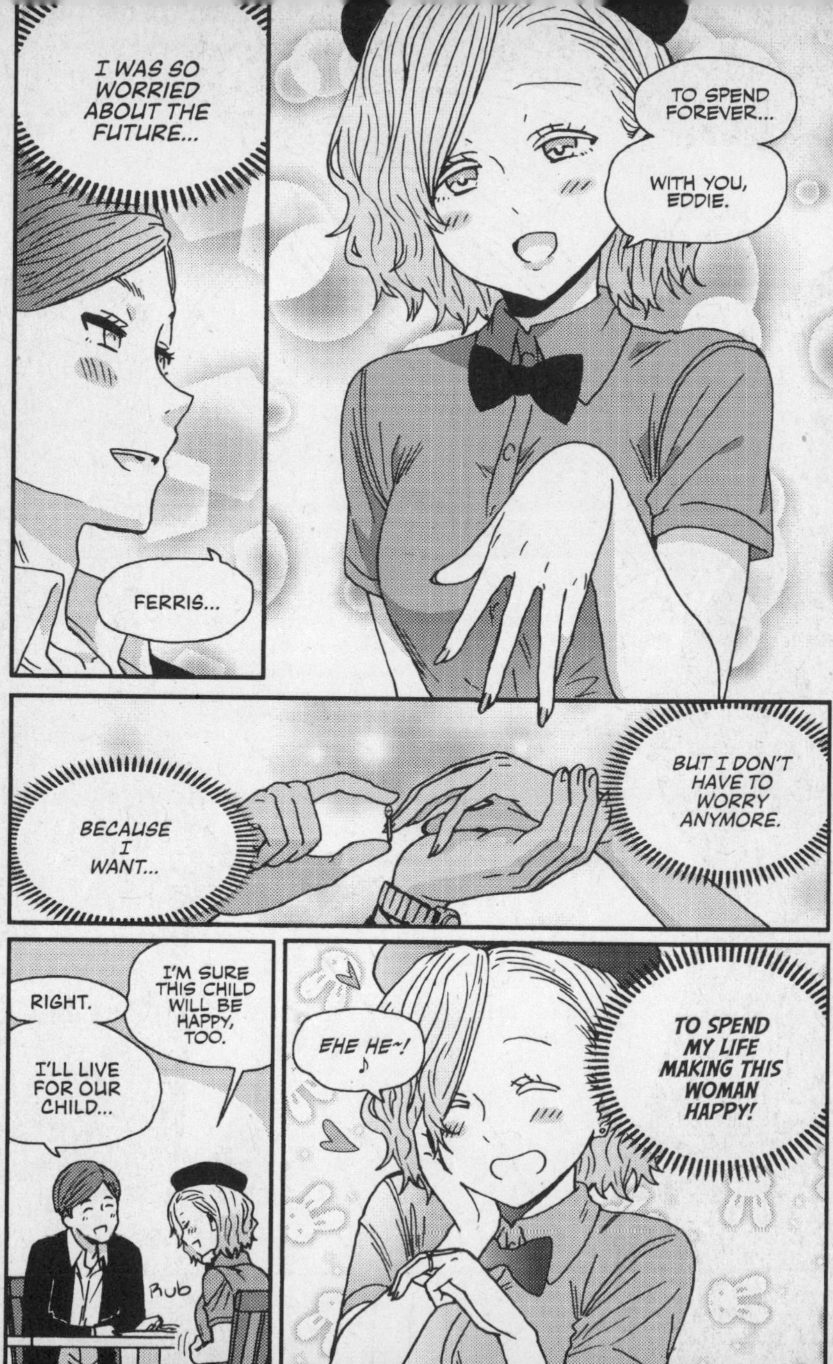
TO SPEND FOREVER...
WITH YOU, EDDIE.
I WAS SO WORRIED ABOUT THE FUTURE...
FERRIS...
BUT I DON'T HAVE TO WORRY ANYMORE.
BECAUSE I WANT...
TO SPEND MY LIFE MAKING THIS WOMAN HAPPY!
EHE HE~! ♪
I'M SURE THIS CHILD WILL BE HAPPY, TOO.
RIGHT.
I'LL LIVE FOR OUR CHILD...
Rub

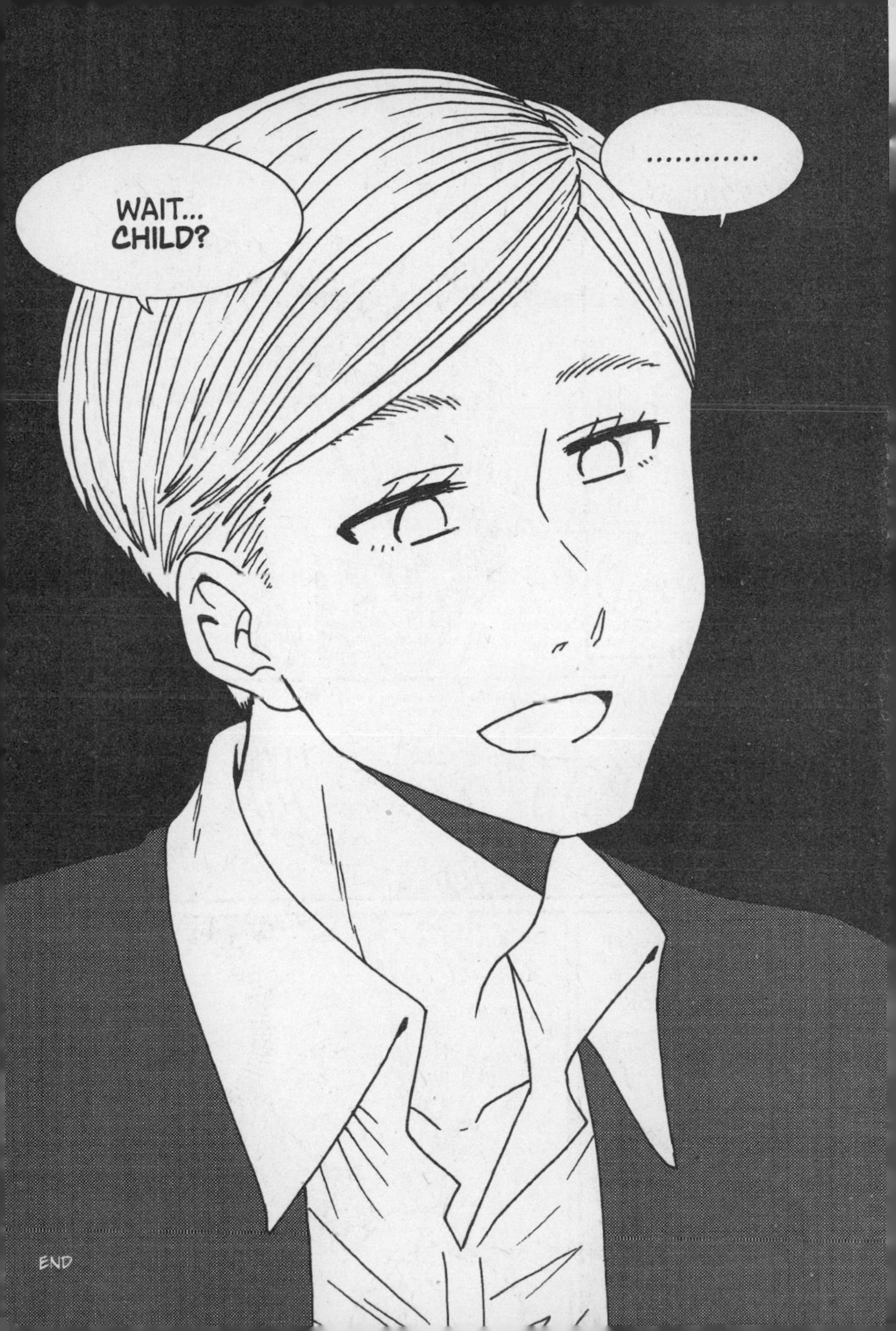
....
WAIT...
CHILD?
END

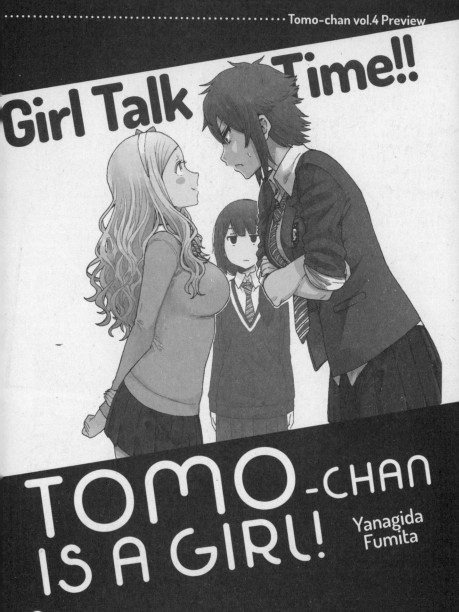

Girl Talk Time!!

TOMO-CHAN IS A GIRL!

Yanagida Fumita

- **Read the original strips on Twitter 4-koma @twi_yon**
- **English Volume 4 coming soon!**

SEVEN SEAS ENTERTAINMENT PRESENTS

TOMO-CHAN IS A GIRL! Volume 3

story and art by FUMITA YANAGIDA

TRANSLATION
Jennifer O'Donnell

ADAPTATION
T Campbell

LETTERING AND RETOUCH
Carolina Hernández Mendoza

COVER DESIGN
KC Fabellon

PROOFREADER
Stephanie Cohen
Danielle King

EDITOR
Shannon Fay

PRODUCTION ASSISTANT
CK Russell

PRODUCTION MANAGER
Lissa Pattillo

EDITOR-IN-CHIEF
Adam Arnold

PUBLISHER
Jason DeAngelis

TOMO-CHAN WA ONNANOKO! VOL. 3

First published in Japan in 2016 by Star Seas Company.
Publication rights for this English edition arranged with Star Seas Company through Kodansha Ltd.,Tokyo.

ISBN: 978-1-642750-15-7

Printed in Canada

First Printing: March 2019

10 9 8 7 6 5 4 3 2 1

FOLLOW US ONLINE: ***www.sevenseasentertainment.com***

READING DIRECTIONS

This book reads from ***right to left***, Japanese style. If this is your first time reading manga, you start reading from the top right panel on each page and take it from there. If you get lost, just follow the numbered diagram here. It may seem backwards at first, but you'll get the hang of it! Have fun!!

1
2
3
4
5
6
7
8
9

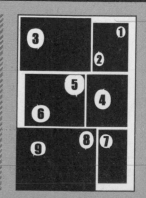